RECYCLING REAL ESTATE: The #1 Way To Make Money In the '80s

Other Books by the Author

George Bockl on Real Estate Investing: How to Build a Big, Growing Income Year after Year, Prentice-Hall, Inc., 1977.
How Real Estate Fortunes Are Made, Prentice-Hall, Inc., 1972.
How to Use Leverage to Make Money in Local Real Estate, Prentice-Hall, Inc., 1965.
Real Estate Investing, Prentice-Hall, Inc., 1979.

RECYCLING REAL ESTATE: The #1 Way To Make Money In the '80s

GEORGE BOCKL

PRENTICE-HALL, INC.
Englewood Ciffs, New Jersey

Prentice-Hall International, Inc., *London*
Prentice-Hall of Australia, Pty. Ltd., *Sydney*
Prentice-Hall Canada, Inc., *Toronto*
Prentice-Hall of India Private Ltd., *New Delhi*
Prentice-Hall of Japan, Inc., *Tokyo*
Prentice-Hall of Southeast Asia Pte. Ltd., *Singapore*
Whitehall Books, Ltd., *Wellington, New Zealand*
Editors Prentice-Hall Do Brasil LTDA., *Rio De Janeiro*

Library of Congress Cataloging in Publication Data

Bockl, George.
Recycling real estate.

Includes index.
1. Real estate investment. 2. Buildings—Remodeling for other use—Economic aspects. I. Title.
HD1382.5.B6 1983 332.63'243 82-12244

ISBN 0-13-768804-0

Printed in the United States of America

To my wife: whose help in researching dozens of recycled projects throughout the country added immeasurably to the insights in this book.

ABOUT THE AUTHOR

George Bockl, President of George Bockl Enterprises, Milwaukee, Wisconsin, has sold more than $350 million in residential and commercial real estate during the past 30-plus years. He has been involved in real estate investments of all types and sizes, including more than 30 conversions of old buildings to new and profitable uses. Mr. Bockl has taught real estate and is the author of three best-selling books, *How to Use Leverage to Make Money in Local Real Estate, How Real Estate Fortunes Are Made,* and *George Bockl on Real Estate Investing,* all published by Prentice-Hall, Inc.

This Book Will Show You How to Create a Substantial Real Estate Annuity Without Leaving Your Job

You're a real estate professional or you're real-estate minded, and whatever you're earning now, you're straining to earn more. You want a tested, proven way to add substantially to your present income, and that's what this book is all about.

Many people may not be aware of it, but there's a recycling revolution going on in the real estate business. It's a quiet revolution, and that's why you may not have heard or read about it. It's gathering momentum fast, and if it hasn't swept into your city yet, it will. The aim of this book is to make you knowledgeable so you can take advantage of it.

Let me dramatize some of the unheard of opportunities: unheard of because they're so new. Do you know, for instance, that the 1981 Tax Law enables you to reduce today's high interest rate by ten percentage points! Sounds incredible, doesn't it? But when you add up its generous 15-year depreciation allowance, which can be accelerated to 175 percent, and its 20 percent investment tax credit when you rehabilitate a 40-year-old building, a 16 percent interest rate reduces itself to 6 percent!

At the end of Chapter 4, I describe how you can borrow $1 million to rehabilitate an old building at 16 percent, and because of the new depreciation allowance and investment tax credit, it becomes, in effect, 6 percent if you or your partners are in a 50 percent tax bracket.

The beauty of rehabilitation is that anyone can profit with this proven investment program. You do not have to be wealthy or quit your present job to profit from this book. I will show you how you can, in your spare time, buy, finance and recycle buildings that can ensure you a $50,000 annuity or a $300,000 profit.

Having triggered your interest, I can anticipate your next logical thought: "Show me." And I will, chapter and verse, with all the details, step by step.

I'll not only show you how I did it, but how others have done it, and with government as well as conventional financing. Further, in order to widen the range of possibilities for those with little money or a lot of it, I'll describe projects varying from the thousands into the millions of dollars.

I'll reveal all I know about how to look for and find old buildings, how to buy them at low prices, and how to plan for their highest and best reuse. The latter is crucial—when to convert an old building to offices, to apartments or stores, and when to recycle in a combination of both or all three. Once you've decided on the new use, cost-cutting becomes of prime importance. In fact, it can make or break your project. You'll learn about many eye-opening, cost-cutting insights to make your rehabilitation feasible, as well as when to retain the old and how to restore and merchandise its nostalgia. For instance, $1,000 of imaginative restoration could add more aesthetics to rehabilitation than $10,000 worth of modern construction.

I'll offer you valuable tips on how to deal with bureaucrats and their myriad regulations. My experience with them may not be the same as what you may encounter in your city, but a common thread runs through all of them, since they all work out of the same Federal manual.

However, we need not limit ourselves to government financing. I cite the example of a $20,000-a-year electrician who bought several blighted buildings from a miltimillion dollar corporation and, using conventional financing and little of his own cash, recycled them into a $75,000-a-year cash flow after all fixed expenses and debt service. And he did it in two years! How does that compare with what you're earning now?

What he did, you can do, if you carefully analyze the steps that brought him success. I describe them in easy-to-follow detail, which will enable you to compare his project with dozens of others, including my own.

You will read how I bought five dilapidated buildings for $150,000 from a multimillion dollar corporation and sold them for $650,000. How did I do it? I recycled a part of one building to show how it was done. This got four buyers so excited that, before a year was up, they bought the remaining four buildings, rejuvinated them, and doubled their money.

You will read the saga of one of the most unique recycling projects in America: the conversion of a 75-year-old furniture warehouse into 109 apartments (Chapter 4). But that's only one facet of the unusual story; the more interesting part is that 50 of the apartments feature shops or services—businesses in living quarters—a nostalgic reversal to bygone days when the corner grocer lived behind his or her store. And what will interest you most is how I bought the 150,000-square-foot building for only $200,000, got a $3 million mortgage to recycle it, and developed a $200,000-a-year depreciation base, all this with very little of my own money.

Like old generals, old buildings need not die. Instead, they can be recycled to gracefully increase in value while you're earning money.

I will revisit with you 16 of my recycled building projects—my successes and my mistakes. I will show you how you can profit from both.

A dust-laden warehouse that I recycled into a medical office building 20 years ago, whose rent was upped from $13,000 to over $200,000 a year, is now yielding the new owner $300,000 a year. You'll learn dozens of lessons from this one.

A building that I saved from the wrecking ball 27 years ago is now the headquarters of some of our leading architects, advertising agencies, and television studios. A hundred years ago, horses were hitched in front of the building and the upper floors were used by a coffee-grinding concern. It is now a charming, Old World asset to Milwaukee's skyline.

Over and over again, you'll learn how you too can remodel, lease, and sell buildings, at a profit, that others have relegated to the scrap heap of neglect. Every city is glutted with recycling opportunities. The revolution is on. Join it!

I've devoted the last chapter to problems and solutions as to whether to buy a good building in a poor neighborhood or vice versa, how to protect yourself from cost overruns, how to find hidden defects, when to sign a mortgage personally and when corporately, how to shelter a $300,000-a-year ordinary income, what types of projects fit certain towns, how to size up tenants, when to keep and when to sell your recycled project, and many, many more insights dredged out of my experience and the experiences of others.

Read the Table of Contents. It'll show you the panoramic view of dozens of practical aids that I and others have used to add millions of dollars worth of value to old buildings. That's where today's profitable real estate action is, and this book leads you directly to it.

It has been said that one of the distinctive marks of a civilization is how its people preserve what they have. Switzerland is a good case in point. I have travelled over its length and breadth, and one of its outstanding features (besides its beautiful mountains and valleys), is its charming old buildings, many 200 to 300 years old, which are aesthetic, functional, and good investments even today. The Swiss reflect the distinctive characteristics of their buildings—they renew and preserve with charming care what other, less civilized societies throw away.

Without a doubt, this book will open your eyes to money-making opportunities and inspire you to arrest blight in your community while reaping extraordinary financial rewards. Isn't the combination of earning money and making a contribution to your country what Enlightened Capitalism is all about? This book will help you play a vital, creative, and *profitable* role in this especially rewarding facet of real estate.

George Bockl

CONTENTS

This Book Will Show You How to Create a Substantial Real Estate Annuity Without Leaving Your Job 7

1. THE RECYCLING REVOLUTION: HOW TO JOIN IT AND MAKE A FORTUNE 17

Why the Recycling Revolution Is Spreading All Over America (18) How to Recognize the Recycling Revolution in Your Own City (20) How to Choose the Most Viable Option in Recycling a Building to Its Maximum Profitable Potential (22) Prospect Building: Warehouse to Medical Center (24) Prospect Mall: Auto Garage to Mini-Mall (25) The Marshall Building: Warehouse to Low-Priced Office Space (27)

2. SPECIFIC DO'S AND DON'TS IN THE RECYCLING PROCESS 29

Capitalizing on the Attractions of Older Property (29) Utilizing the Interior Craftsmanship of Yesterday (29) Concrete Versus Mill Construction (30) Importance of Floor Load (30) Check Soil and Footings (31) Differentiating Between Old Cracks and New (31) Floor Configuration (32) Column Spacing (32) Windows (32) Water Lateral (33) Electric Power (33) Roof (33) Exits and Elevator Shafts (33) Sprinklers (34) Location (34) Recycle in Tandem with City Planning (34) Parking (35) Watching for Old Fire Damage (35) Cosmetic Versus Total Rehabilitation (35) Zoning (36) How to Cut Recycling Costs (36) Begin with a Small Dream (37) A Financial Review of a Recycling Project (37) Deciding Between Selling and Managing Your Recycled Project (39)

3. HOW I SAVED FIVE DYING BUILDINGS AND EARNED $250,000 41

The Anatomy of a Lucrative Investment (41) Horizontal Versus Vertical Revitalization (49)

4. HOW BOLDNESS AND CREATIVITY EARNED ME $600,000 **52**

How I Explored the Building's Highest and Best Use **(54)** How I Found an Unusual Answer **(55)** How to Make a Preliminary Analysis **(56)** How I Financed the Project **(57)** Cutting Costs Creatively **(58)** How I Battled H.U.D. Bureaucracy **(60)** How I Was Led into a Surprise Bombshell—Look Out for It **(64)** The Art of Leasing a Unique Real Estate Shelter **(64)** Why an "Amateur" Sales Expert Is Sometimes More Effective than a Professional **(67)** How to Get Newspaper Features to Promote a Pioneer Project **(69)** How to Get an Interesting Mix of Imaginative Tenants **(72)** How to Provide Creative Management **(73)** A Few Words of Praise in Behalf of Bureaucrats **(74)** How the 1981 Tax Law Can Reduce a 16-Percent Interest Rate to 6 Percent on a Recycling Project **(76)**

5. TEN INNOVATIVE WAYS TO FINANCE A RECYCLING PROJECT **79**

1. Subordinate Seller's Equity **(80)** 2. Offer Seller Equity Position for His Building **(82)** 3. If Owner Refuses Plans No. 1 and No. 2, Buy His Building on a Land Contract **(83)** 4. Convert Your Recycling Project to Condominiums **(84)** 5. Turn a Conglomerate of Retired Artisans into Financiers **(86)** 6. Syndicate Your Need for Equity Capital and Retain Part Ownership **(87)** 7. Finance Your Rehabilitation by Giving Up Half Your Equity to the Lender **(88)** 8. Get an "Angel" to Back You **(89)** 9. Check into City, State, or Private Revenue Bond Financing **(90)** 10. Use H.U.D. Title 221-D4 with a Lower Percentage Loan and Current Conventional Interest Rate **(91)**

6. HOW RECYCLINGS CAN CREATE MILLIONS IN ANNUITIES AND PROFITS **94**

How an Electrician Turned "Junk" into a $150,000-a-Year Annuity **(94)** How an Astute Recycler Earned $5,000,000 with Cosmetic Changes and Innovative Selling **(97)** How a Recycling Project That Could Have Earned $750,000 Slipped Through My Fingers **(98)** How Converting an Old, 40-Unit Apartment to an 18-Family Earned $100,000—A Perceptive Analysis of the Neighborhood Did It **(101)** How an Abandoned Funeral Home Converted into a Rehabilitation Center Earned the Owner an Annuity of $40,000 **(103)** A Tale of Two Hotel

Rehabilitations That Made Millions for the Owner and Revitalized Milwaukee's Downtown **(104)** Recycling Existing Hotels Is Spreading in America and Europe **(108)**

7. CASE STUDIES OF OUTSTANDING RECYCLING PROJECTS IN THE COUNTRY—LARGE AND SMALL 109

Ghirardelli Square **(109)** The Cannery **(111)** Pioneer Square **(112)** Manpower International Inc. Turns a Warehouse Building into Modern Offices **(114)** A Block of Connected Old Buildings in Calgary, Canada, Becomes a Beautiful, Three-Story Mall of Shops and Offices **(115)** Splitting an Old Theater Creates a $75,000-a-Year Income **(116)** Derelict Chicago Buildings Recycled into Apartments and Condominiums **(117)** Stores Without Walls **(119)** Spensor's Corner in Hot Springs, Arkansas **(120)** SoHo—Recycling an Entire Area of Warehouses and Factory Buildings into Living Quarters **(121)** The Canneries of Monterey on the Pacific Ocean **(122)** Trolley Square in Salt Lake City **(123)** How a High School Building in Decatur, Alabama, Was Recycled into Apartments for the Elderly **(124)** Quaker Square, Akron, Ohio—A Modern Shopping Center in an Old Building **(125)** Other Recycling Projects Worth Noting and Comparing Before You Plunge into Your Own **(126)**

8. HOW NONPROFIT ORGANIZATIONS AND GOVERNMENT AGENCIES CAN SAVE MONEY IN RECYCLING OBSOLETE BUILDINGS TO FUNCTIONAL USES 128

How a Montessori School Saved $600,000 **(128)** How an Army Base Became a Community Cultural Center **(130)** How an Old Vaudeville House Became an Elegant Center for Performing Arts **(131)** How a Carriage House Was Converted into the Newark Community Center of the Arts **(132)** How Government Can Save Money by Recycling Obsolete Buildings **(133)** How Government Wasted $29 Million of Our Tax Dollars **(134)** Who Will Lead the Recycling Revolution? **(137)**

9. TECHNIQUES FOR MATCHING REHABILITATION TO THE CHARACTERISTICS OF YOUR CITY 139

Knowing the Type of Tenant in Your Town Is a Vital Prerequisite for Recycling **(139)** Why Rehabilitation Is Advantageously Different in a Tourist Town **(142)** The Future of Small-Town Rehabilitation **(148)** How to Size Up Tenants for Recycled Buildings **(152)** The Difference Between Hunch and Objective Analysis—How to Use Each in a Recycling Project **(157)**

10. MY EARLY RECYCLING PROJECTS REVISITED—TECHNIQUES OF YESTERDAY ARE STILL SUCCESSFUL TODAY 161

I Remodeled Empty Space Above a Garage into a Two-Room Flat—38 Years Ago **(161)** I Changed a Rooming House into 11 Apartments—37 Years Ago **(162)** I Learned Something of Great Value When I Recycled 8 Apartments into 16 Units—35 Years Ago **(163)** Reviving a Dying Downtown Office Building—34 Years Ago **(164)** When I Was Baffled on How to Buy a 100,000 Square-Foot Storage Building, I Hit on Something New—33 Years Ago **(166)** How I Lost $2 Million Through Lack of Boldness—32 Years Ago **(171)** How I Recycled a Warehouse to Manufacturing Space with Deft Leasing and Financing—26 Years Ago **(172)** I Started a Renaissance of Nostalgia When I Saved a 75-Year-Old Building from the Wrecking Ball—27 Years Ago **(175)** Why My Recycling Efforts Didn't Catch on Six Blocks from the Steinmeyer—25 Years Ago **(178)** How I Learned to Merchandise Old Charm—24 Years Ago **(181)** Because I Didn't Know How to Recycle Foul Air, I Muffed a Big Deal—24 Years Ago **(184)**

11. MY MORE RECENT RECYCLING PROJECTS REVISITED—HOW I COPED WITH NEW PROBLEMS IN MORE AMBITIOUS VENTURES 188

My First Big-Time Recycling Venture: Converting a Warehouse into a Modern Medical Office Building—22 Years Ago **(188)** Why I Paid $1.7 Million for a Half-Empty Apartment Hotel That Was Losing $100,000 a Year—15 Years Ago **(193)** How Communal Living for Mobile 80-Year-Olds and Over Stirred My Imagination and Saved My Project **(195)** Home Away From Home—A Dynamic Idea That Boosted My Income **(198)** A Local Yokel Taught Me a Lesson—It's More Hazardous to Recycle in a Town Other than Your Own—Ten Years Ago **(202)** When Recycling Becomes Emotional, Watch Out: A Sad Financial Saga That Ended in a Happy Neighborhood Result—Five Years Ago **(204)** Chalet At The River—A One-Year Retrospect **(207)**

12. KEY PROBLEMS AND SOLUTIONS IN THE RECYCLING BUSINESS **209**

The Agonies and Ecstasies of Recycling Old Buildings to New Uses **(225)**

Index **229**

THE RECYCLING REVOLUTION: HOW TO JOIN IT AND MAKE A FORTUNE

This book will deal primarily with making money through recycling old buildings to new uses, and secondarily with revitalizing the neighborhoods of America, especially its downtowns.

I felt the feeble fluttering of the recycling revolution about 38 years ago (Chapter 10—Recyclings Revisited), but I felt its hard impact about 27 years ago when I heard that one of Milwaukee's oldest and most charming buildings was about to be demolished. I was struck by its irrationality and decided to do something about it. I bought it for $125,000, spent $35,000 refurbishing it (more about that in a later chapter), and sold it within a half year for $210,000. I saved a building, earned $50,000, and spurred the owners of the adjoining buildings to do the same. Today, two square blocks on the opposite side of Third Street have been brought back to its Old World charm. An enclave of old buildings has been spruced up to create a "Gay Nineties" atmosphere to replace a sordid area of dilapidated neglect.

This incident triggered a buzzing of ideas in my mind. Here was a chance not only to make money, but also to make a contribution to my city. There were opportunities galore because people who owned old buildings didn't know what to do with them, and since they were losing money, the buildings could be bought at very low prices.

During the next 25 years, I became involved in recycling projects totaling about $12 million. I didn't have much competition converting the old into born-again buildings because it was a new phase of real estate, and developers didn't think there was enough money in it. But, in other parts of the country, innovative real estate men began looking into the recycling potential, and now it has blown into a full-scale revolution. No question about it, it's the real estate wave of the future. During the next 25 years, hundreds of millions, perhaps billions of dollars will be made by entrepreneurs who will study the potential of rehabilitation and do something innovating about it. It's the most exciting and lucrative aspect of real estate that has hit America in a long time, even more exciting and lucrative than the present condominium pandemonium that has made so many developers wealthy.

WHY THE RECYCLING REVOLUTION IS SPREADING ALL OVER AMERICA

We are entering an age of austerity. It will be marked by a renewal culture for twofold reasons—conversion of energy and economics. Constructing just the skeleton of a high rise building today costs about $40 a square foot plus land. Because so many of the old buildings are losers, it is possible to buy them at extremely low prices—from $2 to $5 a square foot, including land. This should open our eyes to the immense possibilities of recycling at a profit. A word of caution: a bargain is a bargain only if the entrepreneur has the imagination to change a loser into a winner. This is what this book is all about—an attempt to show how a building that's losing money can be converted into a building that makes money and revitalizes a neighborhood at the same time. The time is ripe for recycling opportunities, but only for those who know how to overcome the obstacles in the way. The heartening thing is that the opportunities are far more numerous than the obstacles.

Besides the economic advantages (which I will point out in great detail as I go along), there is developing a general preference for the nostalgic old as against the ostentatious new. This is of tremendous economic importance. For example, collecting antiques has become big business. This turning to the past is what makes recycling advantageously unique.

With a swing to the old and nostalgic, with austerity in the air, and with conservation becoming woven into our culture, it's logical to assume that recycling buildings will play a big role in the renewal ethic. America is coming to its senses. It can no longer afford the throw-away syndrome. The recycling revolution is here to stay for a long, long time.

It has already hit with bursts of activity in the big cities—Boston, Chicago, San Francisco; and medium-sized towns like Akron, Ohio, and Salt Lake City, Utah; as well as small tourist towns like Carmel and LaJolla, California. It's even come to a neighboring village of Milwaukee—Cedarburg; population 8,000. It's going to spread far and wide across the length and breadth of America, providing there will be enough pioneering people to learn the aesthetic, functional and economic intricacies of converting an old dilapidated building into a new architectural gem—the way it was 50, 75 or 100 years ago.

Because America has been prosperous, it negligently allowed hundreds of thousands of old buildings to be relegated on the scrap heap of neglect—but no more. We can't afford that wanton luxury. We'll be taking a leaf from the history of Switzerland. A 200-year-old building in that beautiful country is considered a youngster. Several years ago, I stayed in the Hotel Beau Rivage in Lausanne, Switzerland, built in 1861, yet it's stately elegance was still there. And because the owners were wise enough to retain its grandeur, it still catered to European royalty and its room rates were higher than those in the newer hotels. Switzerland had learned the renewal ethic a long time ago, and it's reaping the harvest of preservation. One of the Swiss people told me, when I was there, that the art of preservation was a mark of civilization. There is a lot of wisdom in that, and it's not surprising that Switzerland is one of the most stable and wisest countries in the world.

Several years ago, E.F. Schumacher, one of the most innovative economists of Great Britain, wrote a book entitled, *Small Is Beautiful*. In it he makes a very persuasive plea for a renewable world. Gigantism, he says, has had its day. It has ravaged the earth with its intense technology. The time has come for more small entrepreneurs to take charge of the earth because their work is more personalized and more caring than that of people who push buttons by remote control. It's one of the wisest books I've ever read, and the reason I mention it is because it applies to recycling. Recycling a building is an individualized venture. It's a work that involves personal caring. It cannot be done by some executive on the 50th floor of a New York skyscraper issuing orders. It lends itself to a small-scale operation where the entrepreneur puts his heart and soul into it because so much of his financial success depends on it. Also, he knows his community; he knows its potential tenants, and therefore, has a far better chance to make it a successful project than one who has only an impersonalized interest.

My appeal, therefore, is to the professionals of the real estate business: the broker, appraiser, mortgage banker, manager, or anyone who is directly or indirectly involved in providing functional shelter to the people in his or her community. I would much rather see 10,000 entrepreneurs get behind this recycling revolution than allow it to be concentrated and controlled by a few corporate giants. So far, small individual entrepreneurs have been involved in it, and I hope it stays that way.

That's enough of generalizations. Now let's zero in on the nuts and bolts of recycling—learning more about it specifically and cashing in on its opportunities.

HOW TO RECOGNIZE THE RECYCLING REVOLUTION IN YOUR OWN CITY

As a starter, study several rehabilitation projects in your city. If there are none, I suggest you take a trip to a city that has them and interview the following people: the owner, the architect, the lender, and the manager of the project. Some don't care to share information, but most are willing.

From the owner, try to get the following facts: what he paid for the building, the cost of the rehabilitation, how he financed it, and what were some of the problems he had to overcome. The architect could give you valuable information about what to renovate, what to restore, and perhaps give a clue to the cost-cutting methods that were employed. Lenders are not the talkative kind, so you might have some problem extracting financial information. However, I would give it a good try, since what you learn from a lender could be the financial key to your project. You can gather a great deal of information from the manager. This person is easy to talk to. Sitting astride the project, the manager is in the best position to tell you what things were done right, what things were done wrong, and the kind of tenants that add or subtract, from the managerial point of view.

After these preliminary steps have been taken, begin studying the various old buildings in your city, not only those that are for sale, but also those that are not. When you have chosen several buildings that appeal to you, begin negotiating with the brokers who have them for sale, and with the owners who don't have them listed. You never know—a building that is not for sale could still have an owner who might be interested in selling it if approached. Investigating several buildings will get you a feel for the market. It's a necessary preliminary educational process.

Keep in mind that most of the old buildings are losers and, therefore, you, rather than the seller, are dealing from a position of strength. Use this advantage to get the building at the lowest possible price, because you'll need a cushion in the event you run into rehabilitation problems, about which you will learn as you continue reading these chapters.

I want to dwell a little longer on the art of buying an old building. It's an important element in structuring a recycling project. Here are several important insights that have helped me and should help you.

The ideal situation is finding a good, under-used building in a good neighborhood. To start your recycling career with a good building in a poor neighborhood is too risky, unless you do it in tandem with a city redevelopment plan or other recycling entrepreneurs. Don't be the sole pioneer in a poor location, no matter how excellent the building is.

It's more difficult to buy an old building from a user—unless the user is going out of business. Look for buildings where the owner is a non-user. The chances are it's a loser, and can therefore be bought at a low price.

Don't rely on yourself to look for buildings. Work with several brokers to increase your chances of finding the building you want.

The most telling argument you can use to persuade an owner to sell an old building at a low price is that he is losing money, and that as soon as he sells it, he begins making money by investing the proceeds at a high rate of interest. If he's the envious kind who's apt to begrudge you the money you might make recycling his old building, your logical response should be that there are only a few willing to take the high risks of recycling; that he may have to wait several years before another bid comes in; that in the meantime he's continuing to lose money; that he can have an immediate reversal from loss to gain by selling.

In all my recycling projects, the owners were losing money on the buildings I bought. And this is the reason why I was able to buy them at bargain prices. Actually, I made the owners happy because they were glad to get rid of losers.

I suggest that you get into the recycling revolution early because as more and more older buildings are recycled—and it's a certainty that they will be—prices will begin to go up. I would even suggest that you buy one or two old buildings on hold for future recycling while bargains are still available. Warehousing old buildings for future use is probably one of the best real estate investments you can make at this time. As an aid to the warehousing idea, I suggest that you rent the buildings on a temporary basis for storage or other low use to tide you over during the holding period. Should you, for some reason, not be able to do the recycling yourself, the chances are that you'll be able to resell the buildings at a profit later—providing you bought them right.

HOW TO CHOOSE THE MOST VIABLE OPTION IN RECYCLING A BUILDING TO ITS MAXIMUM PROFITABLE POTENTIAL

Now that you've bought an old building, the key decision is what is its best and most profitable use. It takes a great deal of native astuteness to make the decision. It's a crucial one. Some of the obvious choices are apartments, offices, and stores. But there are others: nursing homes, mama-papa motels, factory outlets, showrooms for contract furnishings, and others.

Let me offer a few words of caution against getting involved in recycling for uses other than apartments, offices, or stores.

For instance, let's assume that you can buy an excellent building in an excellent location, and you want to convert it into a showroom for contract furnishings. The chances are that you may have to pay a high price for the building. That's obstacle number one. Uprooting companies from their established locations is most difficult. And the odds are that the few who may be willing to make a change have leases that expire two, three, or more years away from the time your space may become available. Then there's also the problem of matching businesses that reinforce each other, like carpeting, lamp, furniture, drape, and other such stores, rather than mixing them with refrigerator, T.V. set, washing machine, and record shops. In Milwaukee, for instance, several people have tried to develop a small showroom complex, but because of Milwaukee's proximity to Chicago, which has the huge Merchandise Mart, all of them failed. I made an attempt to develop a small merchandise mart and failed also; but I protected myself by taking an option on the building, rather than buying it first and developing it later.

What about converting an old building into a factory outlet? That's fine, but the concept is still too new for a beginner. However, if you have your mind set on it, at least be sure you have the following advantages. The building must be bought at a veritable bargain, it should be located about 20 to 30 miles from a large metropolitan area so that the factory-manufactured goods sold at the outlets do not compete with the retail stores that carry the same goods at a higher price. And of course, the outlet must have a blend of tenants that draw customers from each other, it should be accessible to the population center by a modern freeway, and have ample adjacent free parking. I will deal with the factory outlet concept in greater detail in a later chapter.

Converting a loft building or large mansion into a mama-papa motel is a little-used new concept that has great potential, especially for a retired couple who is bored with too much leisure time. However, here too, it's important to note a few precautionary measures. The mama-papa motel in a large city should be located near a huge commercial hotel to take advantage of its overflow or, if it's in a small town, it should be astride a well-traveled highway. More about that later.

Now let's get into the meat and potatoes of the recycling business—apartments, offices, and stores.

If you spot a loft building that has architectural character a block or two off main street, is used for storage or light manufacturing, and can be bought for between \$2 to \$5 a square foot including land, then consider it seriously for apartments, especially if the building is a rectangle of let's say 60 feet by 120 feet. The reason this is the recommended size is because the ideal space between a hallway and a window is 27 feet. It is also the ideal distance from a hallway to a window for office space. Another must to look for is adjacent parking, or a lot that can be bought from the adjoining owner. No matter how desirable an apartment may be, if a tenant has to walk two or three blocks back and forth from his parking space, you have an obstacle that would be almost impossible to overcome. If the recycling project is going to have 100 or more apartments, it would be wise to have a commissary in the building because of the scarcity of food stores in a typical downtown area.

Of course, it's very important to study the earning profile of prospective residential tenants and price the units accordingly. The rental must be below the market compared to similar space in a new building. And it's very important to size apartments to anticipated demand. In a 100-unit or larger complex, the recycler would be safest with a one-third ratio of 500-square-foot studios, one-third of 750-square-foot one-bedrooms, and one-third 1,000-square-foot two-bedroom units. Don't make the mistake of providing all small or all large apartments. It's best to have a mix. It's an obvious sugggestion, but one that's often overlooked.

Let me cite several examples of how I arrived at choosing options for recycling old buildings to new uses.

PROSPECT BUILDING: WAREHOUSE TO MEDICAL CENTER

About 20 years ago, I bought a 100,000-square-foot, 50-year-old steel and concrete building, built to last another 200 years. Its exterior walls were 18 inches thick, and its floors about 8 inches thick. It was used as a furniture warehouse business. The owner was losing $30,000 a year and didn't know what to do with the building, which meant it was ripe for a bargain. After asking $600,000, then $400,000, then $300,000 with no takers, he decided to take my $200,000 offer and run. He ran with it happily to the bank because, instead of losing money, he now had $200,000 to invest.

What to do with the building was now my problem, not his. After contemplating several options (I will discuss them later in greater detail), I finally decided to convert it into a modern medical office building for the following reasons. My building was located within two blocks of one of Milwaukee's large hospitals. There were no doctors' offices within 30 blocks. Adjoining the building was its own parking lot that could be expanded to handle about 100 cars. This was a tough pioneering decision to go from a dust-laden warehouse to a modern medical office building appealing to the crème de la crème of professionals.

I structured a pro forma statement with the following key information: gross rent, $200,000; fixed expenses, $50,000; debt service, $75,000. Armed with these figures, I began searching for a mortgage. I was turned down by half a dozen lenders who smiled benignly at my naiveté for asking for an $850,000 loan on a dingy warehouse. But I didn't give up. I finally met a loan officer who had some of my pioneering spirit. A representative of the John Hancock Insurance Company, he flew in from the east, studied the building, my pro forma, my pictorial renderings and other information for a week before he O.K.'d an $850,000 loan at 6¼ percent with a 28-year amortization. When Jim Gibson, the pioneering loan officer was leaving, he turned to me and said:

"George, you better make a go of it, or I'm going to be in the dog house. My reputation as a creative loan officer rests on how well you do."

I assured him I would do my best, and I did. I successfully leased about 60 percent of the space to the leading doctors of the two nearby hospitals, and the other 40 percent to commercial tenants who did not detract from the tone of the building.

I spent about $300,000 beyond the $850,000 mortgage, which included the $200,000 I paid for the building. I came close to my projections as far as income and fixed yearly expenses.

The recycling project was located about two miles from downtown, surrounded by high-density high-rise apartment buildings and homes. I probably would have done well turning it into apartments, but there were too many of them nearby, and there was no competition for medical office space. But again, I could not have done either without the pioneering lending spirit of the John Hancock Insurance Company, which risked creatively in an untrodden mortgage field. Whenever I look at their 90-story John Hancock Office Building in Chicago, I think of my Prospect Building and Jim Gibson who approved the loan. (More about this recycling in Chapter 11.)

PROSPECT MALL: AUTO GARAGE TO MINI-MALL

Five years ago, I bought a two-story auto showroom, a used automobile car lot across the street, and another auto storage building nearby for $350,000. The owner had been trying to sell them for two years, first at $800,000, then $600,000, then $500,000, but still no takers. The reason? Prospective buyers simply didn't know what to do with them. I confess I didn't know either when I became their owner, but I had a gut feeling it was a tremendous bargain. My main reason for buying the properties was that they were only half a block from my recycled Prospect Building which I have just described. I had a feeling that I would come up with something but, before I made my final decision, I was offered several tempting propositions. One was from a fast-food hamburger restaurant for a 20-year lease at $17,500 a year net for the used car lot of 20,000 square feet of land; the other offer was from a boat company to lease the 35,000-square-foot auto garage for $20,000 a year. I sold the auto storage building for $125,000 within a few months, so that I was left with the two main parcels for $225,000.

I was tempted to take the $37,500-a-year net return on my $225,000 investment. However, I felt that I would not be doing much for the neighborhood going this route, and so I began to think of something unusual.

I decided to convert the building into a three-story mini-mall and maintain the used car lot across the street for parking.

The small shopping center, I figured, would upgrade the neighborhood much more than a fast-food restaurant and storing boats across the street. Also, in all honesty, I thought I could do better economically with the mall idea than taking the fast-food and storage deals.

And what about the fun of pioneering something new? This intrigued me more than the economics.

I recycled the building at a cost of $800,000 and again I found a pioneering lender in The Crown Life Insurance Company of Toronto, Canada, which authorized a $750,000 mortgage at 9¾ percent, 20-year amortization, through its Milwaukee loan correspondent, the Richter-Schroeder Company, Inc. I leased it 100 percent to owners of about 25 shops, restaurants, and a twin theater, bringing a total rental of approximately $180,000 a year.

The activity in the mall added to the activity of the Prospect Building, half a block away. Both projects helped blot out the shadows of neighborhood blight, and catapulted the area into the sunlight of buzzing activity. The Prospect Mall became a conversation piece for people miles around. (More about this recycling project in Chapter 11).

THE MARSHALL BUILDING: WAREHOUSE TO LOW-PRICED OFFICE SPACE

Five years ago, I was given a 100,000-square-foot old building for nothing. Yes, for nothing! Unbelievable? Let me make it even more dramatic. The owner is a nationally-known lecturer in commercial real estate. He owned the corporation that held the building on a 99-year lease at $15,000 a year, and the lease still had 70 years left before its termination.

What would you do if you had a vacant building losing $50,000 a year that had been turned down again and again by several light manufacturing and storage tenants? The owner enjoyed his teaching more than scouting for tenants and losing a thousand dollars a week. He is a good friend of mine and a brilliant lecturer, often getting as much as $500 a day.

"George," he said one day, "I've had it. You can have the building for nothing."

It was a good move. Why lose all the money he could be earning in lecturing by spending time trying to rent an old empty building? I bought it, or rather, stepped into his shoes that were mired in red ink.

But one man's plight can be another man's profit. If you're a recycler at heart, you'll be on the lookout for such opportunities.

The building was four blocks south of one of Milwaukee's busiest intersections. Its seven floors of steel and concrete were built as sturdily as those of the Prospect Building. Its eight-inch floors carried a 300-pound floor load. It was built better than most of Milwaukee's downtown buildings, but it was surrounded by blight on all sides—dilapidated mill-constructed buildings that were half empty, with unwashed windows and dirty cracked walls. At night it was a no man's land. Few people walked its sidewalks.

After ten weeks and a $10,000 loss, I was up against the same problem my friend had faced—there was too much vacant loft space available in the city and no demand for it, even though my building was of superior construction.

I explored the idea of turning it into apartments. It would have been a daring move and that's what excited me. The building lent itself perfectly to this use, but not the neighborhood—not unless five or six other buildings would be recycled into apartments at the same time.

I even went so far as asking the city to rezone the building for residential, which it did, and then I backed down—much to the chagrin of City Hall. Economic prudence took precedence over my daring excitement. It would have been a $2,000,000 gamble and I didn't think I could get the financing for it. Had the building been two blocks closer to downtown, where the adjoining buildings were not as seedy, I might have dared to do it and probably could have gotten the financing.

I always try to put myself in the shoes of the financier. If it doesn't look good to me, I can't mount an enthusiastic campaign to sell it. By the way, that's a good tack to follow: *don't try to sell what you're not sold on yourself.*

After six months of exploring the apartment option, showroom possibilities, and making another unsuccessful try to obtain light manufacturing or warehousing tenants, I hit upon a new idea—converting the building to low-priced office space—not a particularly innovative move, but a practical one.

I launched a newspaper and direct mail advertising campaign featuring office space at one-third what tenants were paying just four blocks away. I was successful to a point. I tried to get $2 a square foot, but I had to settle for $1.50, renting to such tenants as struggling advertising agencies, an art school, printers, social agencies, manufacturers representatives, and others whose pinched budgets called for low-priced space. I leased 80 percent of the building for a gross rental of $120,000 a year, which left a cash flow of $30,000. I spent $100,000 for cosmetic remodeling. (More about this deal in Chapter 11.)

This should give you a bird's-eye view of what goes on in a recycler's mind when confronted with various options. As you read on, this view will be expanded, and you'll be able to see more of the problems and opportunities to be found in the unfolding recycling revolution in real estate.

2

SPECIFIC DO'S AND DON'TS IN THE RECYCLING PROCESS

Now we come to the nitty-gritty of the recycling analysis. If a grand recycling concept is to be realized, it must be underpinned by well thought-out detail. A sound evaluation of the pluses and minuses of an old building and its immediate surroundings is an essential prerequisite to comprehensive planning.

CAPITALIZING ON THE ATTRACTIONS OF OLDER PROPERTY

The exterior character of a building is the first thing that strikes the eye. We can no longer afford meticulous Old World craftsmanship. It is difficult to find the craftsmen to reproduce the architectural charm of bygone days, even if we can afford it. Therefore, a building that has 50- to 100-year-old decorative terra cotta, hand-crafted brick configurations, copper domes, sculptured figurines, and bronze trim has distinctly unique assets. They are valued pluses that add immeasurably to the first-glance appeal of a restored building.

UTILIZING THE INTERIOR CRAFTSMANSHIP OF YESTERDAY

The interior assets of a building are equally as important as the exterior pluses. If you're a recycler at heart, you should be quickened by artistic window trim, ornamental plaster on wall and ceiling, old marble fireplaces, Florentine floor tile, and especially colorful stained glass. The interiors of many old buildings feature beautiful wrought iron balustrades, hand-crafted light fixtures, old-fashioned hardware, hardwood floors—all these should be saved, restored, and polished up to their original splendor. High ceilings laced with concrete beams are valuable features that modern construction cannot afford, and should be made into focal points. In one of my recycling projects, I found a grime-covered oak floor. I sanded and varnished it, and it became the talking point of a restaurant that moved into the space. The old has a nostalgic appeal, now more than ever before. Capitalize on it.

CONCRETE VERSUS MILL CONSTRUCTION

In almost all cases, a concrete building is preferred over a mill-constructed one—for durability, fire protection, and longevity. The codes bear down more strictly on mill buildings than on concrete ones and, therefore, it costs more to recycle the former than the latter. There are exceptions to this rule, and you should be on the lookout for them. I describe the exception in Chapter 10, which describes a building I recycled 27 years ago.

IMPORTANCE OF FLOOR LOAD

Amateurs don't pay any attention to floor load, yet it's a very important consideration, especially if you are to remodel a loft building into apartments. The structural engineer for many of my projects has informed me, in preparation for this book, that a residential building should have a minimum 50-pound floor load (that is, fifty pounds per square foot) in the living area, and an 80-pound floor load in the corridors. I suggest you check those figures with your local code and local engineering firms. Ignoring this important fact could cause a lot of trouble and unforseen expense.

Wood-constructed buildings usually have a low floor load and that presents a major cost hurdle for remodeling. The fireproofing of floors in a wood constructed building is usually required for residential use. Pouring a light layer of concrete is sometimes the answer, but this adds to the floor load, and if the original columns cannot hold the extra weight, you're in for a lot of expense. That's why it is imperative that you have sound engineering advice before you pour a lot of money into a building that may need thousands of additional dollars in structural support before it can be used for your purposes.

CHECK SOIL AND FOOTINGS

After 60 or 70 years, the footings of a building could begin to deteriorate, especially if the building is on wood piling. Should the water level sink, the part of the piles above water become weakened by dry rot. The cost to cap these with concrete or artificially raise the water level is staggering. Checking a building's supporting structure is expensive but imperative. I spent $10,000 in my Chalet At The River recycling project (described in Chapter 4), even though my structural engineer advised me that there were no signs of any structural defects. However, before I was able to get a preliminary commitment for my $3.1 million Housing and Urban Development (H.U.D.) insured mortgage, the government agency demanded a report from a structural engineer showing the condition of the underpinning. It cost $10,000 to test the soil and footings in several places, but I was glad I'd had it done, because when the underpinning was found sound, I was rewarded with $10,000 worth of peace of mind.

To illustrate the importance of testing the soil under a building, I can cite an experience that saved me a lot of money. I took an option from the city of Milwaukee on a half-acre parcel of land, upon which I planned to build an office building overlooking Lake Michigan. I spent about $10,000 on plans to build and promote what I aimed to call Seaway Towers, without giving a thought to the condition of the soil. That was 25 years ago when I didn't know any better. During the course of my planning, someone suggested that, to play it safe, I ought to check the soil. I had already spent $10,000 and was reluctant to spend more, but prudence took over and I hired a soil specialist. His report made me scrap all my plans. The lot turned out to be a swampy rice patch that would have required piling 80 feet deep, at a cost of hundreds of thousands of dollars. Based upon this information, the city returned my option money.

DIFFERENTIATING BETWEEN OLD CRACKS AND NEW

Cracks in a wall are an indication of unsound footings or pilings. However, it is important to ascertain whether the cracks on the exterior of the building are old or new. If they are old, then the building has settled and the cracks are not serious. However, if the cracks are new and an engineer is able to ascertain the difference, this is much more serious. It often pays to reconsider a building if the underpinning slippage is new, since it could mean new trouble ahead. Plan from the bottom up (no pun intended) before seriously considering a recycling project.

FLOOR CONFIGURATION

Don't overlook the importance of a building's floor configuration. A building that's 60 feet wide and 150 feet long lends itself far better for remodeling than a square building 100 feet by 100 feet. A rectangular building costs less to remodel because there's less wasted space. The ratio of net rentable space to the gross area is an important one. If a square building, because of less usable interior space, leaves you with 75 percent net rentable, as against a rectangular building that makes it possible for you to get as much as 85 percent net rentable, the income projection makes the rectangular building far more economically feasible. It's an important point that is often overlooked.

The ideal distance between a corridor and a window for residential or office use is 27 feet. That's why a rectangular building 60 feet by 150 feet lends itself to a long hallway with a minimum waste of space. After allowing for wall thickness, it leaves an eight-foot-wide passageway. It's the ideal configuration.

COLUMN SPACING

It is far easier to arrange space modules when the columns are 20 feet apart rather than, let's say, 10 feet apart. A forest of closely-spaced interior columns can wreak havoc with either office or residential layouts. In most older buildings, the column distance is usually about 15 feet apart. Whenever they are wider, it's a definite plus; when they are narrower, it's a definite minus.

WINDOWS

Windows are exceedingly expensive. In a 150,000 square foot building that's ten stories high, there could be as many as 1,000 windows. If they are well preserved and can be reused with a minimum cost, the savings are considerable. It costs about $200 to replace an old window with a new one. If a building does not have enough windows and you must cut new openings to add them, then the total could be as high as $300 per window. Savings in six figures can be realized if a building has sound windows. Paying attention to them may sound prosaic, but very often it could mean the difference between a project being feasible or not. My advice is to look at, not through, the windows. They involve a lot of money.

WATER LATERAL

If you plan to recycle a loft building into, let's say, a hundred units, you should look into the water lateral from the building into the street. A loft building does not require much water, and the lateral could be too narrow to furnish enough water for 100 apartments. Widening the lateral could cost thousands of dollars and, very often, the city may prohibit you from breaking up the street leading into the main lateral. The same applies for sewer connections. These are unseen items, but they must be looked into carefully. A trip to City Hall and the building inspector will give you the information you need to ascertain the cost of these important additional utilities.

ELECTRIC POWER

A loft building will seldom have enough electric power to light up a hundred or more apartments. Therefore, it is important to check the building's main power lines for the additional load. If it has enough, it's a big plus; if it doesn't, it could cost as much as $25,000, to $50,000.

ROOF

You may not find it pleasant to climb on the roof to check its condition, but it's a must to be sure you won't be surprised with a $30,000 to $40,000 expenditure. I made that mistake in one of my projects and was penalized with a hidden defect of $30,000.

EXITS AND ELEVATOR SHAFTS

Plan your floor layout around the existing elevator shafts and exits. Exits are expensive. I have spent $75,000 building an inside stairwell for a ten-story building in order to provide new exits when I was unable to use the old ones. I also saved $40,000 on elevator shafts in the same building when I rearranged my floor layout to keep the existing shafts, rather than build two new ones.

SPRINKLERS

When you're dealing with a building that's already sprinklered, you have a big plus. It's an asset worth about $100,000 in a 100,000-square-foot building. There are few cities in the country today where either new or rehabilitated buildings, used residentially, are not required to be sprinklered, and you should allow for it in the cost of rehabilitation.

LOCATION

The location of a to-be-recycled building is as important as the building itself—often more important. If it's to be residential in a downtown area, it should not be in the heart of main street congestion, yet not too far away from it. It should be somewhere in the middle, preferable near a small park or, if not a park, near several well-kept buildings. Two blocks away from a busy street is a good distance. Four or five blocks away is too far, especially if that area is seedy and neglected.

In general, the building should not be more than several blocks from a bus line, and not more than a mile from a freeway, if one is available. Being no more than two or three blocks from city hall, the court house, a prominent bank, a department store, or a modern office building is a distinct asset if an old building is to be converted into either offices or apartments.

RECYCLE IN TANDEM WITH CITY PLANNING

It is very important to know that your rehabilitation will be encompassed within an area of city-planned revitalization. Don't try to be a hero by creating an oasis of restoration in a desert of blight. With few exceptions, it's a prescription for failure. But with city planning, rejuvenated buildings reinforce each other's environment and boost reciprocal values. All prosper—the recycling entrepreneurs, the designated community, and the city.

Pioneer Square in Seattle, Washington, which I will describe in a later chapter, is an excellent example of how the city designated a ten-square-block area for revitalization and spent about two million dollars in seed money to get it started. Private entrepreneurs joined the parade, and Pioneer Square is now a shining American example where some 30 old buildings have been revitalized, changing an area from sheer neglect into a community of landscaped mini-parks, and red-bricked, carless streets for promenading. It's now attracting thousands of people daily, served by the small shops, boutiques, and restaurants, housed in old buildings that have been vacant for years. It's now attracting renters of office space for the upper floors.

Recyclers have earned millions of dollars in Pioneer Square because the city fathers had a vision that its entrepreneurs made into a reality.

PARKING

Of course, parking is a necessity. If your rehabilitated building does not have parking and you cannot afford to buy a parking lot nearby, or if none is for sale, you should provide parking for your tenants in adjoining lots. In Chapter 4, I give the reasons why I would not have gone ahead with my Chalet At The River residential project had it not been for the fact that a half block away was a public parking structure with 700 stalls. The safest precaution is to own an adjoining parking lot, providing the cost is such that it would still make the recycling project feasible.

WATCHING FOR OLD FIRE DAMAGE

Even if an old mill-constructed building has all the charm of the Old World, if you find that it at one time had a fire, negotiate with caution, or stay away from it altogether. It may have walls that had buckled in invisible areas. Even if a building next door had a fire, you should check if it damaged the building you're interested in, because you may have buckling walls as the result of an adjoining fire.

COSMETIC VERSUS TOTAL REHABILITATION

If you can buy a shabby, mill-constructed building at a bargain price in an excellent location, you can make more money rehabilitating it cosmetically rather than totally. Feather touch it with a few embellishments like painting, and repairing old plumbing, heating, and electrical systems—at minimum expense. Powder its face; don't perform radical surgery. Let's say you have a 50,000-square-foot building with 10,000 feet on each of the five floors. If you have the persuasiveness to lease one floor to a discount jeweler at $2 a square foot, another at the same price to a carpet company that needs a lot of display space; a third floor to a tile company; a fourth floor to a wholesale lamp outlet, and a fifth floor to a toy assembly company, it is conceivable that you could build your income to $100,000 a year. If you paid $100,000 for the building, spent $50,000 for cosmetic repairs, and your operating costs are $35,000 per year, including taxes and heat, you will then have a net return of $65,000 a year on a $150,000 investment—not a bad deal, even if you can't depend on this stream of income for more than five to ten years. However, if you don't have the ability to do what I've just described, then stay away from such a building. You'd only be stepping into the shoes of the previous owner, who was losing money.

However, if you can buy a soundly-constructed concrete building that's architecturally embellished with unique, nostalgic touches, in a good location, at a bargain price, then, by all means, consider total rehabilitation. Whether your plans call for commercial or residential use, it becomes a project of a magnitude that will require all the insights you'll be reading about in the ensuing chapters. It becomes a serious operation, and you must give it all the care and take all the precautions necessary to insure success.

ZONING

In many cities, rezoning a commercial building to residential use is not an easy task. Don't conclude too hastily that, just because you have a wonderful recycling idea, rezoning will come automatically. I had a wonderful plan to convert a downtown furniture warehouse into 109 apartments (Chapter 4), and it took six months to convince the city fathers to rezone the building from commercial to residential. I was fortunate in having the rezoning considered at a time when the city was in a mood to encourage people to live downtown. If no such encouragement exists in your city, check carefully before you overcommit yourself to residential rehabilitation in a commercial zone.

If you're planning to rezone a residential building to commercial use, then be doubly careful. It's much more difficult to change from residential to commercial than the other way around. Not only will City Hall fight you, but the neighbors will as well. Where the zoning is strict, only in rare occasions will you be able to effect a change. When zoning is loose or nonexistent, the problem dissolves itself.

HOW TO CUT RECYCLING COSTS

Don't use a general contractor for your recycling project—unless he can beat the total cost of the lowest bids of all the subcontractors. Only rarely will a general contractor be lower than the sum total of all the subcontractors. In my Chalet At The River project, a reputable general contractor bid $400,000 more than I was able to negotiate with about 20 subs. It was the difference that made the rehabilitation feasible. Sure, it was a lot more work bargaining with each of the subs, but it was worth it.

The art of restoring the old, instead of ripping it out and replacing it with the new, has two important advantages—it saves money and lends old time character to the project. New is no longer better. Restoration is "in," and knowing how to capitalize on it is an economic advantage that only a few recognize and develop. But this knowledge is bound to spread. The object of this book is to make you aware of it—to put you at the forefront of the recycling revolution.

Spotting hidden defects and controlling cost overruns is part of the cost-cutting process, and these will be detailed in due course. This chapter is aimed at making you see the peaks. We'll get down the slopes and into the valleys as you read on. You'll also get the full panoramic view of successful recyclings—dozens of them—all the way back to 38 years ago, and how they are still being done today.

BEGIN WITH A SMALL DREAM

Start out cautiously on a small scale, using the green-light suggestions and avoiding the red ones. In recycling, as in carpentry, you have to go through the apprenticeship and journeyman stages before you become a master craftsman. What you learn in a $100,000 rehabilitation will prove invaluable in a $1 million project, where the stakes are steeper and experience becomes priceless.

A FINANCIAL OVERVIEW OF A RECYCLING PROJECT

Developing a Pro Forma Operating Statement

When you've chosen the re-use plan for an old building, and arrived at the cost of the project, the next step is to develop a pro forma statement that is a resonable projection of income, expenses, and cash flow after debt service. I want to stress that this pro forma must be prepared with the utmost honesty for two reasons: it will be used by the lender as a basis of his or her loan commitment, and also by you as a test of the project's feasibility. If you tamper with its integrity, you'll be defrauding the lender and kidding yourself. All your work and research will be reflected in the pro forma and it had better be as close to reality as possible.

For instance, don't peg rentals too high to fool the lender, or too low to short-change the project. A balanced judgment, undergirded by sincerity, will go a long way in getting a favorable reaction from the lender. Remember, the lender can make or break your dream. If anything, understate; don't overstate.

Projecting the fixed expenses as accurately as possible is as important as projecting the gross income. Actually, it's even more difficult. It's not easy to guess how the tax assessor will react, what the repairs will be, and how to ascertain the cost of heat, light, and air-conditioning power, especially with today's rising energy costs. Janitorial and management fees are fairly constant, but all the others have great variability, which is why developing a pro forma that can realistically nail down all the mercurial variables into a well-thought-out sum is of utmost importance. It can be crucial. The rule of thumb in my city is that all expenses, including management, should not be more than 40 percent of gross rent in residential, and 50 percent in commercial. If the ratio of expense to income is higher, you'll have less room for debt service, and no room for cash flow. If the ratio is lower, let's say 30 and 40 percent respectively, then you and your lender will see more go-green than stop-red when you negotiate for a loan.

Again, referring to Chapter 4, the H.U.D. officials, with all their expertise, miscalculated the fixed expenses on my project by $40,000, and the rent by $60,000. This is not said to blame, but to stress the fact that gauging the rent and fixed expenses requires fine tuning, and quick moves to bring the ratio in line as the project progresses and conditions keep changing.

In view of these facts, it is imperative that you prepare a pro forma that has integrity and resiliency. You should also be able to explain this many-faceted presentation to the lender with conviction and the utmost candor.

Keeping the Horse in Front of the Cart

Don't start rehabilitation before you have your financing and whatever other legal permissions that are necessary—in writing. I've seen professionals, in their eagerness, jump the gun and start remodeling on a promise. A friend of mine, at this writing, has gutted a floor of 25 old apartments, following a plan to modernize and then condominiumize an eight-story building consisting of 200 units. He's losing $6,000 a month in rents, while waiting to get legal permission to sell his units against mounting opposition. In the meantime, after already losing $75,000, tenants from other floors are beginning to move out. He's in a recycling bind because, while his overall plans are ready, his legal problems are in disarray. My friend is a professional who should have known better, but eagerness often smothers rationality. A legal and financial land-mine can explode right under you if you run ahead without watching your legal and financial steps.

An Experienced Expeditor Can Save Money

It's wise to have an experienced expeditor on the job, even weeks before the recycling actually begins. Pre-planning saves money. I can best illustrate it by pointing out that on a $3 million project, every month that you reduce the time from start to completion, you save about $50,000—in interim interest, real estate taxes, heat, expeditor salary, earlier rent up, etc. It is no exaggeration that a poor expeditor could add $100,000 to a $3 million project, and a good one could save $100,000. It's extremely important to have someone who not only understands construction, but also knows how to dovetail the subcontractors' work so that each flows and follows the other with the least amount of time lost.

DECIDING BETWEEN SELLING AND MANAGING YOUR RECYCLED PROJECT

Your choice should take into account the following factors: if you're in a low-income bracket and you don't like management, sell it—but keep it long enough to realize a long-term gain.

If you're getting started and don't have much of an income against which to offset the 15, 20, or 25 percent investment tax credit that the 1981 tax bill allows, then sell your recycling project for a combination of cash profit and a retention of part of the equity. In that way, you shelter your profit with part of the investment tax credit.

However, make sure that the buyer gets into the deal at its inception, so that he or she qualifies for the tax bonanza. This can get complicated, so I suggest that you and the buyer employ attorneys to protect your respective interests clearly enough so that the Internal Revenue Service approves all your moves.

How much is a $1 million recycling project worth to a buyer in a 50 percent tax bracket? If you buy the building at a bargain and plan and execute its completion from A to Z, you ought to get about 30 percent of the money spent on rehabilitation, or $300,000; you'll get proportionately less if you retain part of the equity. There are many variables in such a deal, and your negotiating posture should vary accordingly. This suggestion is merely a general guideline.

If you're between the ages of 35 to 55, keep your recycled project—even if you're not in a high tax bracket. If you're successful in your first rehabilitation project, you'll try others: then, you can sell one of them and shelter the profit with the high depreciation from your remaining ones. Again, I advise the use of a tax attorney.

I want you to consider another important factor. You may get to like management and quit your job to devote all your time to managing your projects. I can tell you from personal experience that it's pleasant and interesting work, and it's especially comfortable if you don't like a 9-to-5 job. The time is your own, to plan as you please. But you must like to care for other people's needs to enjoy the role of employer better than the role of employee.

3

HOW I SAVED FIVE DYING BUILDINGS AND EARNED $250,000

You can transform a blighted old building into a charming edifice, the same way a cracked, 100-year-old artifact can be restored into a valuable antique. The financial reward of this philosophical observation is as exciting as the aesthetic change. And, what's more, the sociological result of reviving buildings and making money is the revitalization of communities and the renewing of cities.

There's an altruistic and creative ring in the recycling revolution that is absent from manufacturing bubble gum or playing the stock market.

We should regard bringing dying buildings back to life as a noble enterprise—a healthy attitude that enhances the creators and their creations.

But enough philosophy. In the next two chapters, I'm going to show, in great detail, how I actually used the recycling tools I described in the first two chapters: how I fashioned two small fortunes out of dilapidated buildings that others threw on the scrap heap of neglect.

THE ANATOMY OF A LUCRATIVE INVESTMENT

Please follow the step-by-step development of this investment carefully, from the standpoint of buying, financing, merchandising nostalgic charm, leasing, selling, and, above all, changing attitudes.

When the Parker Pen Company bought Manpower International, the largest temporary help agency in the world, they acquired five vacant buildings which were formerly Manpower's headquarters in Milwaukee. Well, they were almost vacant, because one corner of the buildings was rented to a business school at the nominal rental of $500 a month. The buildings were located a block from Milwaukee's main downtown street—Wisconsin Avenue. As in the case in many cities, a block away can make a big difference in value, especially if the buildings are seedy and the immediate surroundings are blighted. Their closest neighbors were a vacant furniture warehouse across the street—the subject of the next chapter—and an 80-year-old neglected office building that was renting space at a quarter of the going rate of Class A offices.

To darken the blight, the former owners of the Manpower buildings had painted them black. The grimy, somber paint was peeling, and since each building had its own original, distinctly-colored brick, the patches that showed through were a mismash of colors resembling a rescue-mission. And if that were not enough, the backs of the five structures faced the muddy Milwaukee River where, alongside a dilapidated wooden retaining wall, grew tall, unsightly weeds. Winos used the indentations of the buildings to warm themselves in winter and sprawled there to sun themselves in summer.

But the buildings were sound. Four had concrete bodies, and the fifth was mill costructed. Building Number One had 30,000 square feet; Number Two, 20,000 square feet; Number Three, 10,000 square feet; Number Four, 10,000 square feet; and Number Five, 40,000 square feet. I number them so you can follow the sequence of the investment more easily.

How I Bought the Five Buildings for $150,000

The Parker Pen Company made several attempts to sell the buildings at $500,000, then $400,000; but, after two years, they still remained unsold. I became interested in them in 1977, when I learned that a downtown owner of a nearby office building had offered $100,000 for them, and planned to spend another $100,000 to raze the buildings for parking. I do not know whether the owners would have accepted such a low offer, but when I submitted my proposal for $150,000, they quickly accepted.

A word must be added about why I was able to buy this real

estate at the exceedingly low price of less than $1.50 per square foot, including land, at a time when it cost $60 a square foot to build a new office building, including land. The Parker Pen people are not exactly neophytes at making money. I certainly did not take advantage of them. But I want the reader to note that some of the biggest bargains in real estate can be gotten from big corporations who often look upon some of their residual real estate as a nuisance. Indeed, the Manpower buildings were a nuisance. Parker Pen was losing $30,000 a year heating the empty buildings, paying real estate taxes, insurance, etc., and losing the interest on what they could sell them for. So, when they got my $150,000 cash offer, they grabbed it and probably said to themselves,"Good riddance."

To support the above reasoning, I would like to cite another instance involving a student of mine who bought an old, unused 2,500-seat theater, eight stores, a free-standing, 12,000-square-foot building, and a parking lot nearby from a multimillion dollar corporation for $350,000. At the time of purchase in 1971, the neglected real estate was grossing $50,000 rent against $55,000 a year for fixed expenses. They were glad to get rid of it for $50,000 down and $300,000 due and payable in three years. Within one year, my protégé raised the rent to $105,000 per year, with just a few imaginative, cosmetic recycling changes, and cut the expenses to $45,000. With that kind of income, he was able to refinance the project and pay off the balance of $300,000 when it became due. Now, his net income is $125,000. Not bad for a thirty-nine-year-old neophyte who masterminded close to three-fourths of a million dollars in assets by recycling old buildings to new uses—real estate that a corporation full of experts, with assets of millions of dollars, did not know how to use. (More about this example in Chapter 6).

The point to note carefully is that local people familiar with local real estate conditions will invariably outsmart outside experts when it comes to buying, selling, or putting a property to its highest and best use. I can point to a dozen examples in which local yokels outmaneuvered some of the most sophisticated experts from other cities.

How I Sold the First Four Buildings

Now, back to the story of the five buildings. In order not to tie up my own money, I went to my bank and borrowed the entire

$150,000 after I explained my plan and convinced the lender how I was going to get a half million dollars out of the Manpower property.

Since the visibility aspect of recycling old buildings to new uses is of prime importance, I sandblasted the seventy-five-year accumulation of paint, grime and dirt off the 40,000-square-foot Number Five building. What leaped out from beneath the ugly black paint and dirt was a revelation—an architectural gem! The original beautiful beige brick, the gray ornamental terra cotta, and the bay windows brought back the nostalgic charm of bygone years. And when I replaced the broken green glass on the first floor front with barn wood and satined it to match the new-found beige brick, several neighbors told me that I had, indeed, found an architectural pearl—and all for only $10,000 of sandblasting and barn wood. With these cosmetic changes as a sales stimulant, I was now ready to start selling the remaining four buildings.

I started with buildings Number One and Two. The proprietor of a secretarial school was using part of building Number One for classrooms and a floor of building Number Two for administrative offices. I learned that, while his rent was nominal and his lease was expiring in a few months, his school was doing exceptionally well.

"Mike," I said, when I met the forty-year-old successful school owner, "you ought to buy the two buildings you're occupying, and let me tell you why. It's very costly to convert a building to qualify as a school. You've got it, and you've got room to expand both the school and your administrative quarters. You're young, ambitious, and successful. You've got 15 years of growth in these buildings. Interested?"

"Maybe, if the price is right," he said, trying to play it cagey.

I watched his face blanch as I said, "$165,000."

"I'm not interested," he said tartly.

"I don't blame you," I said. "But do this, please. I'll give you a month to look around and see if you can find a building for slightly more than $3 a square foot, including land, that will qualify as a school. Remember," I said in parting, "it would cost $1.5 million to replace the buildings you're in. Think about it."

A month later, he was on the phone.

"Can I make an appointment to see you?"

The next day, we sat down and agreed to the $165,000 price on the following terms: $50,000 in cash and $115,000 payable within a year. As a bonus, I told him I would give him a $5,000 discount if he paid the $115,000 on time. He earned the bonus.

With $10,000 profit and three buildings free and clear, I proceeded to sell the others. I sold the 10,000-square-foot Number Three building for $30,000 to an architect who fell in love with the fifth floor skylight. He remodeled the upper floor into one of the most beautiful architectural offices I've ever seen, and leased the balance of the space to several other tenants. I sold building Number Four to a bookseller for $30,000; he used it to store used books.

I was now left with the corner building, Number Five, free and clear, along with $70,000 in profit. I advertised it for half a year for $150,000, with no takers. It was too small for a big user, and too big for a small one. I decided to recycle and lease the first floor, *then* try to sell it.

How I Recycled Building Number Five

The first floor had four empty stores that were in shambles. The corner store consisted of 4,000 square feet and the three around the corner had 1,000 square feet each. It's not easy to rent slovenly-looking space. Most lessees do not have lively imaginations, and are quickly turned off by blight. Yet it is often folly for the owner to remodel without a specific tenant in mind, since the prospective lessee might have different ideas and needs. The way to overcome these difficulties is to paint a clear word picture, and support it with a rendering of how the space would look. But even more important is the financial structure of the lease under these elusively difficult circumstances. There are risks involved, and rewards too, if a deal can be negotiated on assumptions that stand the test of reasonability. The key is making reasonable assumptions.

This challenge was facing me in full measure when I leased the 4,000-square-foot corner store. A seventy-year-old man and his wife, who had been successfully operating a steak house for forty-five years, were being forced to move because the building they were renting was being torn down for parking.

"George," the elderly owner was saying, "I've tried to relocate but it'll take about $50,000 to move and I don't have it. I have a following, though, and I know I can do a $1,000,000 volume in your vacant corner store if you finance the construction changes."

"What if it takes $100,000?" I asked.

"It may," he conceded. "But I'd like to say something beyond money. If I don't relocate and have something to do, I'll go crazy. I must continue. I'll die without it."

He was desperate. I felt sorry for him. From what I had learned about him, he was an outstanding restaurateur, with one weakness. He was prone to gambling. I supposed that was why he had not saved any money. Delicately, I raised the question of gambling.

"Oh," he said, "that's behind me. All I want now, at my age, is work. I'm no longer interested in trying to get rich. Believe me, if I had been smarter about my weakness, I would have all the money I need. Now I need you. When you get me, you'll have one of the best restaurant operators in the city. I have hundreds of friends and thousands of followers."

What did I do? I did what Benjamin Franklin used to do. I added the pluses and minuses and weighed them against each other. These were the pluses—an eager and experienced couple; their restaurant had a city-wide reputation; they had two sons who were willing to join their parents in the operation. The minuses were obvious—an elderly couple; a gambling weakness; no money. When I put the pros and cons on the scale, they were about even. After wrestling with the problem for a few days, I tipped the scale in the couple's favor.

Here was my reasoning: a name restaurant would cast a favorable aura over the building, and its traffic would help lease the other three stores. It did.

I rented one store to a very exclusive dance master for $500 a month, another to a real estate company for $800 a month, and a third to a hearing-aid shop for $600 a month. I spent $50,000 to convert the three bedraggled stores into beautiful, air-conditioned space.

The restaurant rent was $3,500 a month, after I spent $100,000 for remodeling (The original $50,000 estimate had been too low). I now had a rent roll of about $65,000 a year from the first floor, and 30,000 square feet of 75-year-old empty space on the upper four floors. My total investment in the building was $150,000, less the $70,000 profit I had after selling the other four buildings, or a net investment of $80,000. What was the corner Number Five building worth now?

A Lesson in Innovative Selling

I did some creative thinking and came up with a plan that I believe is unique enough to describe in detail. First, let me give you the answer in advance. I sold the building for $450,000 to a sophisticated syndicator, who had sold over a hundred million dollars of real estate in a short period of seven years. He was not exactly a starry-eyed purchaser. He knew what he was doing, but so did I. It was one of the most mutually satisfactory deals that I had ever structured, and one of the most ingenious, if I may be immodest for a moment. Remember, I had tried to sell it for $150,000 before I leased the first floor and couldn't do it. How then did I sell it for $450,000? Innovative financing, that's how!

Here is the way I structured it. Since my prospect was a syndicator but was purchasing the property for his own real estate investment portfolio, I had to devise a financial plan that did not require an outlay of his own money. The reason is that syndicators are notorious for getting into deals with their elbows instead of their money.

"Joel," I said, "let me justify my $450,000 price after I explain how I plan to finance it for you."

"I'm all ears," he replied.

"Since the building is free and clear, I'll convey it to you simultaneously with your borrowing $100,000 against it in the form of a first mortgage and turning the proceeds over to me as a down payment."

"I like it so far. Go on; what comes next?"

"I'll take a second mortgage of $350,000 behind the $100,000 first mortgage, with 13 percent interest, payable monthly for five years or earlier, until the upper floors are remodeled and leased. You have 25,000 square feet of net rentable area and, at $7 a square foot, you'll have an income of $175,000 a year, plus $65,000 from the first floor, for a total gross rent of $240,000. Since we've both concluded that the upper floors could be renovated for about $400,000, the deal would stack up something like this. Your fixed expenses will be about $70,000 a year, since the first floor pays its own cleaning, heat, light, and power. That will leave you $170,000 a year for debt service and cash flow. If you obtain a $850,000 first mortgage based on the figures I've projected, you'll be able to pay off the $100,000 first mortgage, my $350,000 second mortgage, and the $400,000 for remodeling. Your payments on the $850,000 mortgage, including interest and principal, ought not to be more than about $135,000 a year, leaving you a cash flow of $35,000 a year without a dime of your own money in it. Does all this make sense to you?"

"It does, except for one thing. What if I can't rent the upper floors?

"I've given you five years within which to complete the recycling of the upper floors. That's a lot of time. You should be able to do it in a year or less, because you've got several things going for you—good location, low price and strong demand for office space. But, let's say it takes longer than a year. The $65,000 a year rental from the first floor will more than take care of the interest on your $100,000 first mortgage, the interest on my $350,000 second mortgage, and perhaps $5,000 a year for real estate taxes. Your only risk is your inability to lease the upper floors in five years. If, after all you've done, you're going to be timid about not being able to rent modern, remodeled office space, when lesser space is being sopped up all over downtown, then you're not the gutsy entrepreneur I thought you were. Sure, there is some risk, but it's minimal compared to the rewards should you be successful. Look, it's a deal tailor-made for you, and since I'm willing to subordinate my entire $450,000 to make this deal possible for you, I'm in effect risking more than you. In other words, I've got more confidence in you than you seem to have in yourself."

It must have impressed him because, after thinking about it for a while, he said:

"George, we've got a deal." We shook hands and closed it a month later, in 1978.

As of this writing, this is what has happened to the Manpower recyclings. The owner of buildings Number One and Two has expanded his school and administrative offices and, taking a cue from my sandblasting cosmetics, did the same with his buildings. Out jumped two new facades; one was a beautiful cream city brick, the other a pale pink. The architect and bookseller have done the same, and now, instead of the grimy, black buildings, the five structures have been readorned in the charming, multicolored brick with which they had been meticulously built seventy-five years ago.

In addition to eliminating neglect in our downtown, the recycled Manpower buildings added about $1.5 million of real estate value to the area. The school owner of buildings One and Two would not take $600,000 for his buildings today, even though he paid only $165,000. Both the architect and the bookseller have been offered close to $100,000 each for their buildings. But the syndicator didn't do well. He got caught in the buzzsaw of the 1981-82 Recession and lost the building to me. I resold it for $300,000.

Recycling imagination has given an entire downtown city block a new, 50-year lease on life. Just think—these buildings were a hair's breadth away from being gone forever.

HORIZONTAL VERSUS VERTICAL REVITALIZATION

This rather lengthy story illustrates an important real estate principle to which few are paying attention—*the feasible superiority of rejuvenating our country's downtowns horizontally, rather than vertically*. Having given you a specific example of how it can be done, let me expand from the specific to the general.

We are living in an age of energy and material shortages. The era of throwaway squandering is over. We have to rethink our past, and project new insights for the future. Now we are all beginning to grasp the importance of driving less at lower speeds, insulating our homes, avoiding what we can do without, and concentrating on necessities—in short, we are using the principle of conservation to make the transition from reckless abundance to sensible austerity. And, in our search for the ways to make this crucial transition, we have been overlooking one of the biggest reservoirs of energy—our old, underused buildings—billions of dollars worth of real estate which, if renovated imaginatively, would not only help our much-needed national conservation program but, equally important, would eliminate downtown blight. What I have in mind is creating a new community type downtown—a residential and commercial mix to give it a unique neighborhood cast. This would be in drastic contrast to many of the present downtowns featuring white-collar factory/office workers, in tall glass buildings, which are full in the daytime and empty at night.

The nation's downtown decay will not be reversed by a new, thousand-room hotel, a huge shopping center, or a jumbo apartment complex. Aside from being economically unfeasible, they would actually speed up the decay of the remaining stock of older downtown properties.

We are in a new real estate ballgame. The age of bigness has ended; it has been tried and found wanting. Bigness is not progress; the big cities already know that. The evidence is in: new, multimillion dollar skyscrapers do not eliminate adjacent blight; the blight envelopes the skyscrapers. With some exceptions, this is true in every large American city.

What is the solution?

Let's not fall into our past traps. Instead of relying only on new skyscrapers, why not recycle our stock of old downtown buildings: this is where decay begins and spreads. Horizontal redevelopment, with extensive recycling of buildings, adding small additions where feasible, is far more pervasive in eliminating decay than vertical development that leaves the adjacent blight intact. What good is it to build a multimillion dollar, thirty-story giant on half a square block, then let a dozen adjacent blocks rot and decay? It does not make sense, especially when we see what it has done to dozens of cities across the nation.

If the *Milwaukee Journal* had abandoned its seventy-year-old buildings and built a skyscraper, it would have contributed to Milwaukee's blight. By adding some new to the old, it stopped decay in its tracks and turned Journal Square into an aesthetic showpiece that has more charm than most new glass skyscrapers of other large cities.

Instead of planning new big buildings and neglecting the old, we should develop a master plan to recycle what we have. We can radically change a downtown's landscape by imaginatively converting empty factory buildings into living quarters, garages into mini-malls; loft buildings into comfortable, low-priced office space; and small, old buildings into mama-papa motels that now dot several areas of Los Angeles. Such "horizontal" restoration should be ventilated by small parks and open spaces. This type of pervasive redevelopment would probably cost a third of what it would cost new, and yet has all the functional comforts of the new. Thirty million dollars, spent on recycling forty buildings over a ten-square-block area, would have a far greater impact in eliminating blight and, concomitantly, would improve the sociability of the larger area, than building a $100 million skyscraper on one square block.

It has been said that half of our population is engaged in manufacturing goods and the other half is selling them to each other. Let's not sell them in huge factories, where scanners and mechanical devices depersonalize relationships, but, rather, in small shops of old and new buildings, where there may be less efficiency, but more personal interaction.

A downtown that is alive with hundreds of small merchants in renovated buildings may be less efficient, but it *is* more livable. Furthermore, this arrests downtown blight, the dread disease that debilitates buildings, cities, and people.

4

HOW BOLDNESS AND CREATIVITY EARNED ME $600,000

Of the some 20 major recycling projects that I have done during the last thirty years, the unique one I am about to describe is the largest, and the most pioneering. I am using these superlatives to underscore not only the unusual commercial aspect of the project, but also its "romance," something that causes the creative juices to flow in great abundance.

Real estate, a basic industry, is many-faceted. Some of it is prosaic—like the mass building and selling of homes to the public with the same promotional skill big corporations use to sell refrigerators, cars, or television sets. I am not criticizing this part of the real estate industry. It is as necessary, fundamental, and functional as meat and potatoes are for a balanced meal.

Yet some aspects of providing shelter can be many-splendored, such as in shaping a project no one else is doing, in meeting peoples' new needs, or in providing a new model for others to follow. It is in this spirit of romance that I want to describe the present project. Hopefully, you will be as inspired by what follows as I have been by what others have written. That is what genuine progress is all about—people helping people.

In 1976, one of the oldest leading furniture stores in downtown Milwaukee was going out of business. The reasons were probably these: several shopping centers on our city's outskirts had pulled customers away; it had inadequate parking; and the second generation, who succeeded the founder, perhaps did not have the desire, imagination, or interest to roll with the times. The ten-story, 150,000-square-foot, dust-laden warehouse was peddled by a half dozen brokers for $500,000, then $400,000, then $300,000. When the owners could not find a buyer who would take it off their hands (thereby taking them off the hook of losing $25,000 a year), they got rid of it for $200,000! The buyer was not sure what to do with the building, but he *was* sure he had a bargain. As you may have guessed, I was the buyer.

The building intrigued me for several reasons. Number one, the price was right—15,000 square feet of land and 150,000 square feet of sound concrete and brick structure for only $1.30 a square foot! But it was unbelievably cheap if someone only knew what to do with it. And, I might add, there are hundreds of bargains like this available in decaying downtowns all across the country.

Let me go through the thinking sequences from the beginning, so you can do the same when you come across a similar deal. First, let's list the positive attributes of the building, which induced me to buy it; then we'll view the negative ones that had stopped a dozen others before me.

It was a handsome building, located two blocks north of Wisconsin Avenue's prime location. Within two blocks—walking distance—were three major banks, the largest department store, city hall, the performing arts center and a dozen smaller office buildings. The white collar workers within a four-square-block area probably numbered in excess of 35,000—consisting of stenographers and minor and major executives. A half block away was a 700-stall public parking garage, and several surface parking lots were within a block. Across the street was the Milwaukee River. A block to the north was a small but beautifully landscaped park.

Now for the negative aspects. The building had few windows; its brick was smeared over with huge ugly signs. The inside had decrepit plumbing; cavernous, high ceilings (more about that later); old, unworkable elevators; cracked plaster; uneven floors; and only enough electric power for a few dimly-lit light bulbs. No wonder dozens of buyers had turned it down. The building had no parking of its own and none could be purchased from nearby parking-lot owners who needed it themselves. These were enough negatives to turn off anyone who didn't have an imagination.

HOW I EXPLORED THE BUILDING'S HIGHEST AND BEST USE

After I had purchased the building and obtained a $200,000 interim bank loan (the bank appraised it at $400,000), I began to explore how to put my bargain to its best use. One of my ideas was to convert it to a mini merchandise mart, along the lines of the Chicago Merchandise Mart. After checking with a dozen potential users, I gave up. Most of them wanted to know who would be coming in and what it would look like after I had prepared it for their use. Also, most of them had leases elsewhere. Even if I could have been successful in filling it, it would have taken three or four years and about a million dollars to convert it to its new use before I could make a profit. There were too many if's and too many hidden variables to take a chance on. So, I summarily gave it up.

The next seemingly feasible idea was to convert the building to offices. I had already successfully converted a 75,000-square-foot storage warehouse into an office building twenty years ago; I had a model against which to compare my recycling costs. After exhaustive study, I turned this option down for the following three reasons: (1) the interest rate was nearly double what I had paid twenty years ago, (2) the cost of converting a warehouse into office space had tripled, and (3) while I had been able to provide 120 parking stalls for my 75,000-square-foot warehouse conversion, I had none for the 150,000-square-foot furniture warehouse.

One day I received a call from a client who said, "I can use two floors or 30,000 square feet of your building for storage. Will you lease it to me for a dollar a square foot?"

"Let me think about it," I said.

I gave it a lot of thought, and here's why. The chances of renting the remaining eight floors at a dollar a square foot for storage were excellent. The building had tailgate loading off an alley, with two large freight elevators located a few feet away from the loading area. I quickly calculated the feasibility of spending about $100,000 for cosmetic remodeling and then leasing the building's 150,000 square feet for $150,000 a year. Taxes, heat, insurance, and the minimum repairs required for storage tenants, I figured, would be about $50,000 a year, which would leave me a net of $100,000 per year on a $300,000 investment—an extraordinarily high return. I was tempted to take this route, but something was bothering me. While the bottom line looked good for me personally, what I would be doing to my city, which had done so much for me, would not be quite so good. I would be perpetuating blight in the heart of downtown!

I wrestled with the problem during my quiet time—a daily half-hour retreat from the office—when I try to listen to my noblest instincts, which I know are influenced by God. I find that listening quietly to my higher human nature gives me a more balanced perspective than trying to make decisions on the run. When I weighed the benefit of a high return against what I would be doing to our downtown, I decided against it. What's more, I felt good about rejecting it. Then, my listening paid off—quietly.

But now that I was losing $50,000 a year (including interest on the $200,000 loan), it behooved me to do something in the face of having already turned down three alternatives.

But what?

HOW I FOUND AN UNUSUAL ANSWER

My wife and I had been touring the West Coast during our winter vacations. In our browsings, we had noted hundreds of small boutiques in cities like San Francisco, Monterey, Carmel, Santa Barbara, and Los Angeles. Closer to home, we made a study of the vertical arrangement of Chicago's newest downtown shopping center—Water Tower Place on Michigan Boulevard. There, dozens of small shops on eight floors were connected by elevators and escalators, instead of being horizontally spread in the typical, regional shopping centers.

Our travels, and what we found at Water Tower Place, gave us the seed of an idea for our furniture warehouse—but only the seed: by the time we got through with it, we had a different blossom. We went far beyond what we had seen.

My wife and I decided to try something that had never been done before in America. Now, that is quite a sweeping statement; but, as far as we know, what I am about to describe has not been attempted in any other major downtown area.

We decided to convert the dust-laden warehouse into 109 modern apartments. With this imaginative innovation, each of the apartments was to have a boutique or store area in front and living quarters behind it—a sort of nostalgic return to fifty years ago, when the proprietor of the corner store lived in a few rooms behind his small business establishment. We checked the feasibility of the idea with about fifty people. The response was enthusiastic. We talked with artists, photographers, interior decorators, health food purveyors, jewelers, etc., and the general response was "Shops-in-Apartments is a great idea, very innovative; someone should have thought of it long ago." To create traffic for the upper eight floors of stores with living quarters, we decided to lease the lower level and first floor to traffic-generating restaurants and unusual shops.

Now that we had an unusual idea, we had to develop an unusual way of financing it—the golden key that turns any unique dream into reality. But how?

HOW TO MAKE A PRELIMINARY ANALYSIS

I had enough experience to know that when one tailors a financial plan to a project, it is important to first ascertain the rental market, then zero in on (1) the potential gross rent, (2) the operating expenses, (3) the amount of debt service, and (4) the cost of remodeling. Unless all four elements jibe, leaving a reasonable cash flow on the equity investment, the project is not feasible. However, it is one thing to develop a pro forma projection, but quite another to get it to hit in actuality.

I had no problem projecting the operating expenses: taxes, heat, janitorial service, insurance, etc. Greater care was required in projecting the gross rent, because I had to make sure the rentals for Shops-in-Apartments were so reasonable that even reluctant prospects would react favorably. Since I was pioneering a new type of shelter, I wanted the advantage of low prices and a variety of sizes to assure success. I therefore allocated about half of the 109 apartments to be rented for $265 per month, sizing them to approximately 630 square feet each; $350 a month for the 950 square-foot apartments; and $460 a month for sixteen large, 1250-square-foot apartments. I projected a rental of six dollars per square foot for the lower-level commercial space, and eight dollars for the first-floor area. My total projected rent was $500,000 a year.

With operating expenses of about $200,000 a year, and a rental of $500,000 a year, I now needed a mortgage with an annual debt service of about $250,000 including interest and principal, so that I would be left with about a $50,000 cash flow each year for my $200,000 investment, based on 100 percent occupancy. That meant that I would need about a $3 million mortgage at 7½ percent, amortized over forty years. It also meant that my costs had to be no more than $3.2 million, including my $200,000 equity.

HOW I FINANCED THE PROJECT

I started looking for a loan before spending a lot of money on architectural fees and estimates on recycling. Conventional financing at the then available 11-percent, 25-year-amortization, at 75 percent of appraisal would make the deal unfeasible for two reasons: (1) the debt service would be about $125,000 a year higher than the $250,000 debt service I needed, and (2) I did not want to invest approximately $950,000 of my own money in the deal. I therefore looked into the possibility of obtaining financing from the Federal Housing and Urban Development Agency (H.U.D.). Under Title 221-D4, H.U.D. was insuring 7½ percent rehabilitation mortgages, provided the project contributed significantly to the revitalization of an area.

Since our downtown needed revitalization badly, as do other downtowns throughout the country, my challenge was to convince the local H.U.D. office that my project was not only worthwhile, but also unique. To make the best presentation possible, I hired a bank official who was the former Federal Housing Administrator of Wisconsin to explain the project to H.U.D. Because he specialized in obtaining H.U.D. financing for clients, and because the ramifactions of rehabilitation financing were so complex, I was willing to become his client for a hefty fee. His first reaction to my project was negative: he did not like the Shops-in-Apartments.

"Why don't you take the straight residential route, without the shop gimmick?" he urged. "This deal is complicated enough without adding something that's never been tried before."

"Unless I get the shop/apartment combination," I said with finality, "it's no deal" This was the romantic, artistic part of me talking, not my commercial side.

"All right," he said, "have it your way, but you're reducing your chances of securing the loan."

Fortunately, one of the top H.U.D. officials in charge of approving mortgages was also a romantic. He had been a builder in private enterprise, was intrigued with my unique idea, and encouraged me to make the application. A week later he began processing the loan—a bureaucratic tedium which, I might add, took a full year for final approval. But I am getting ahead of my story.

One of H.U.D.'s conditions was that the loan be in the vicinity of $3 million in order to hold down the rentals, thereby making the project feasible. I readily agreed to the condition because I, like H.U.D., did not want to price the rentals out of the market. Further, the debt service on $3 million was about $250,000 a year: in line with what I had projected.

Now came the most difficult part of all—recycling an old furniture warehouse to 109 modern apartments and two floors of commercial space for about $3 million. It was a much more difficult task than getting bids on a new structure. Thus, I tried a short cut. I hired a general contractor, gave him my architectural plans, and said, "Bring it in for $2.3 million and the job is yours."

I didn't bother him with the $700,000 of "soft" costs: interest-during-construction fees, real estate taxes, points to lender, heat, expediting, promotion, and a host of other costs.

Three months later, he came in with a stack of papers, figures, and a sad face. He couldn't do it for less than $2.7 million. My spirits sank lower than his—I had more to lose. I had already invested $100,000 in interest on the $200,000 mortgage, the real estate taxes, the heat, the insurance, and the preliminary architectural fees. With three of the four elements ascertained, gross rent, operating cost, and debt service, I was not about to give up on the fourth—getting the cost of remodeling down to $3 million. Furthermore, by this time the project was no longer a matter of bottom-line cash flow with me, but instead it was a challenge: like writing a novel, composing a symphony, or painting a masterpiece. I was determined to create something that had never been done before.

CUTTING COSTS CREATIVELY

After I analyzed the $3.4 million cost figures, I called in my architect and said, "I don't think the responsibility of an architect should stop at the drawing board. It should go further. He should be able to cut, substitute, and improvise. And, above all, find small, efficient contractors who don't add 20 percent to their estimates to be on the safe side of their bidding. At $3.4 million, both you and I can stop right here," I said. "The project is dead."

"What do you want us to do?" my architect asked.

"I'll give you three months to rebid the job. You and I are going to meet with the low bidders of some twenty different contractors—the masons, carpenters, plumbers, electricians, tile men, painters, cabinet installers, etc. Should we get to within $200,000 of our $2.3 million goal, we'll tell each one point blank that unless all of them take a cut across the board so we can reach our goal, there's no deal. And remember," I challenged my architect, "I want you to use your architectural ingenuity to find ways of cutting costs without sacrificing quality. Use your improvisations creatively in cooperation with the practical knowledge of the small contractors who, in turn, can use their expertise in helping you with your cost-cutting ideas. I'll not only be the referee, but also, when I see an opening, I'll get into the game with some of my own ideas."

After four months and dozens of meetings with dozens of contractors we did it—the remodeling costs came in within $50,000 of our 2.3 million goal.

Here are some of the cost-cutting ideas—how we turned minuses into pluses. Instead of replacing the old with the new, we embellished the old. We gained in two ways: we saved money and added the charm of the restored look. For instance, instead of covering the sixteen-inch-square raw concrete columns throughout the building (about 1,000 of them) with vinyl ($50 each), we decided to spray them white ($5.00 each) to give the apartments and shops the Old World loft look. We had twelve-foot-high ceilings laced with twelve-inch-square beams every seventeen feet. Instead of lowering the ceilings to the usual eight-foot height, we kept the original height and sprayed the columns to match the beams. We did something else that was unusual. Since we were catering to adult couples or singles, we decided not to partition the apartment areas into the usual living room, bedroom,dining room, etc., but to leave them open, except for the bathroom areas. Since we were looking for imaginative, innovative people, our plan was to suggest to our tenants that they divide the areas with their own fabrics, shutters, Chinese silk, or any other way they liked, arranging their living area as uniquely as they pleased. You can readily see how this idea, if it worked (and it did), would save tens of thousands of dollars. By not lowering the ceilings, some of the plumbing and electrical piping was left visible. We covered most of it, but left some open to add to the loft look—and also save money.

The outside of the building, as I mentioned before, was painted over with huge signs and ugly colors. Scraping off the signs and repainting all the brick would have cost $50,000. I toyed with painting the building brown, blue and white to give it a chalet look since I named my project "Chalet At The River." I came to this decision in spite of my success with sandblasting previous recycling projects.

While I was squirming with indecision, a restorative artist called me one day and eloquently pleaded with me to preserve the old exterior look in spite of my "Chalet At The River" name and my plans to paint it to match that name. "Please," he said, "give the building a chance to show its original grandeur." I could tell that he was sincere and had the genuine instincts of an artist.

I talked it over with my wife, as I do other matters involving aesthetics. She agreed with the artist. After several other problems, revolving around whether to paint or sandblast, I fortunately decided in favor of the latter and saved $25,000—another bonus. When the sandblasting was finished, I had a brand new facade of beautiful, cream-city brick: the elegant look the building had 75 years ago when it was a showplace of Milwaukee.

Using the restoration theme and negotiating face-to-face with several dozen contractors, we huffed and puffed our remodeling costs into the $3 million range, making the project feasible and a reality.

HOW I BATTLED H.U.D. BUREAUCRACY

Now began the tedious tangle with the patience-exhausting H.U.D. bureaucracy. It took six months to process the application and another six months to arrive at what is known as the preliminary closing. Before this initial closing, we had to get approval from the following areas—architecture, cost, legal, project feasibility, minority contractors, affirmative action and several peripheral people who did not have the status of department heads. We won some of the battles and lost others.

Here are some of the obstacles we faced and overcame before we received the preliminary approval.

"Do you have a record of the condition of the footings?" one of the H.U.D. officials asked.

I did not, and neither did City Hall.

"Then get a structural engineer," I was told, "and show us that you have a sound building that will stand up for at least the 40 years of our mortgage."

A month and ten thousand dollars worth of testing by a reputable, structural engineering firm solved that problem. The footings and the building were declared sound.

The architectural chief did not like leaving the ceilings in their original beamed state. He wanted me to drop them to eight feet with acoustical tile. I rebelled; it would take away the charming loft look.

"Be practical," he said. "Don't try to be different."

"That's what this project is all about," I argued. "To do something different. Twelve-foot ceilings," I said, "are a big part of the uniqueness. It's what will give the apartments their loft look."

I had to spend two hours with all the department heads on the premises of the building before they outvoted the architectural head and gave me permission to leave the beamed ceilings exposed and twelve feet high.

The next problem was even more difficult and crucial.

"Who ever heard of not partitioning an apartment into separate rooms?" the head H.U.D. architect stormed. "We've got nothing like that in Milwaukee or anywhere else that I know of."

"But this is downtown living," I said, "and there'll be no more than two people in each apartment. The chances are that half of the living quarters will be occupied by widows, widowers, or young, single artists, hobbyists, boutique owners, etc. Why not let the tenants themselves partition off their rooms imaginatively, with shutters, or Chinese silk—something flimsy—instead of sectioning them with solid walls in ways that may not suit their needs."

I then went into a detailed explanation of a building in Los Angeles that caters to adults, in which the apartments were divided with cloth instead of fixed, Sheetrock walls.

"And those apartments rented for as high as a $1,000 a month," I said, trying to convince H.U.D. that my rentals averaged only one-third of the cost of the partitionless apartments in Los Angeles. After much debate, I finally won that battle, too.

Another problem that started as a battle turned into a skirmish. I won it easily when I laid each floor out in an atrium configuration, so that each of the fourteen apartments faced an indoor garden area of thirty-five by fifty feet, instead of the standard labyrinth of narrow hallways, and from which H.U.D. did not want to deviate. I suggested that my plan was more aesthetic, and provided more window space for the apartments. The mild opposition that apartments are not generally laid out in the atrium manner was quickly overcome by my own architect's argument that our idea was not only different, but also better.

Now for the battles I lost. I do not relate these in a spirit of recrimination, but rather as a warning to would-be rehabilitators that, while the bureaucrats are fair, they are also stubborn. They fight to protect the government, just as hard as the entrepreneur fights against them when hemmed in too tightly by their regulations.

One of the walls of my furniture warehouse faced a surface parking lot. There was no space between the parking lot and my wall—or, zero lot line. H.U.D. ruled that I could not have windows on that wall. That eliminated about eight apartments and threw the financial balance of the project (if you'll forgive the pun) out the window. The owner of this adjoining lot was a savings and loan association, which used the space as an overflow parking lot for its customers when the public parking structure adjoining its offices was filled. I got a letter from the president of the association stating that they had no plans to build on the lot in the foreseeable future, then I presented it to H.U.D.

"That letter means nothing," the head architect of H.U.D. told me. "Their plans can change. I'll allow you to put windows on the zero lot line only if you deposit $95,000 with us. Then, if the savings and loan association decides to build against your wall, we'll have the money to indent your building with a light well which, according to our estimates, will cost about $95,000."

"But, isn't it unreasonable to put aside $95,000 for something that may never happen?"

"And isn't it unreasonable," H.U.D. countered, "for you to ask us to potentially block out eight apartments and weaken the safety of our insurance on the mortgage?"

We wrangled about it for weeks with no resolution. Finally, H.U.D. showed a tiny crack in their opposition.

"Get an agreement from the adjoining lot owner stating that, if they build in the future, they will indent their structure fifteen feet by twenty feet to create a light well that can then be used by both buildings."

It was not a bad idea, and I thanked them for it.

But when I tried it on the savings and loan executive, he said, "Why should we limit the design of our building by giving you this letter? I can understand your wanting this agreement, but I hope you'll also understand why we can't give it to you. We don't want to limit the value of our lot by clouding it with a limitation."

I finally gave up and deposited $95,000 to provide for the unlikely contingency that someone, sometime, might be building flush against my wall. The zero lot line battle was a complete victory for H.U.D.—almost. At the closing they relented, and instead of collecting $95,000 up front, they agreed to collect $4,500 a month to be held in trust by them until the sum reached $95,000.

To compound my problems, I lost another battle—this one to the State of Wisconsin. My architect had prepared a fire-protection plan consisting of smoke detectors and a limited sprinkler system costing a total of $55,000. After a lot of haggling it was approved by H.U.D., but not by the State of Wisconsin. The reason for the refusal was a recently-passed state law requiring a full sprinkler system in each new building. The additional cost to meet the state requirement was $65,000. I cited the following argument to overcome the extra financial burden: it was not a new building, therefore the law did not apply.

"But when you get through remodeling, it'll be like a new building," the state officer countered.

"True," I said, "but the main structure will still be 75 years old."

"Well," he said, "do you want us to get an opinion from the Attorney General? It'll take a long time and, chances are he'll rule against you."

"How long," I asked, "before I can get the Attorney General's opinion?"

"Perhaps half a year."

"I can't hold up construction for that long."

"Then I advise you to put in the full sprinkler system."

And that is exactly what I did, because a construction delay would have cost more. Besides, I rationalized, I now had a more extensively (and expensively) fire-protected building than all the high-rise apartment buildings in Milwaukee. I had mine both fully sprinklered and smoke-detectored. Only buildings built in the future would be as elaborately safe as my "Chalet At The River."

HOW I WAS LED INTO A SURPRISE BOMBSHELL—LOOK OUT FOR IT

During the preliminary closing of the deal, I received a bombshell against which I had not been warned. I had to provide $856,000 worth of bank letters of credit before I could receive H.U.D. permission to begin construction. The expert I had hired to lead me through the maze of H.U.D. bureaucracy either was not clear in communicating this requirement for the closing, or I was not listening when he was explaining it to me. The upshot of the matter was that I had to come up with $856,000 worth of equities and treasury bills as collateral before I received bank letters of credit. These were required to protect H.U.D. in the following contingencies: (1) to insure the completion of the rehabilitation, (2) to make $60,000 available as working capital, (3) to insure against operating losses, and (4) to provide money for latent defects. I might add that, while I considered it a hardship and only reluctantly met this request, I must admit that the bureaucrats were no fools in demanding this insurance. How else could they weed out the irresponsible promoters from the sincere and legitimate entrepreneurs? I therefore caution the would-be rehabilitators, who want to use Title 224-D4, to be ready with about $300,000 of letters of credit for every million dollar's worth of project. Do not be surprised the way I was.

THE ART OF LEASING A UNIQUE REAL ESTATE SHELTER

Now comes the most interesting and vital part of the project: getting the $500,000 worth of annual rent from the remodeled eight floors of Shops-in-Apartments and the two lower floors of commercial space. It takes a lot of ingenuity to lease a new apartment or office building, a shopping center, or an industrial park. But these are traditional projects; the planners who have done their homework will usually lease 90 percent of their space within a year after completion. If it takes two or three years to fill it, the project flounders and usually ends up in the mortgagee's possession.

Mine was an avant-garde effort that had no precedents. In addition to the uncertainties that are always present in even millrun projects, mine had the additional uncertainty of an untried market. This made it more risky, but also more interesting.

"Milwaukee is no San Francisco or Santa Barbara," one of my real estate friends commented, when I described my unique Shops-in-Apartments plan. "You don't have the unusual people here to take you up on your unusual idea. People are moving away from downtown. You're trying to reverse the trend. You're pioneering. That's always dangerous." A dozen knowledgeable people made similar comments.

Against this negativism, at least fifty people I questioned said, in one form or another, "It's a great idea! There ought to be hundreds of people who'd like to have a little shop or studio in their apartment and live downtown, where they could save by using their cars less, maybe giving them up altogether."

I talked to artists, art crafters, hobbyists, and retired couples who were thinking about starting a small business to keep themselves busy and possibly earn enough money to pay the rent for their shop-apartment combination. Some became so interested they were willing to say "yes," even before seeing what we had to offer.

After having completed my investigative research, I remained as uncertain as when I had begun. Opinions were sharply divided. But, when you want to do something unusual, the tendency is to accentuate encouragement and blot out discouragement. That is exactly what happened.

To get started, I poured myself into creating a brochure that combined some of the best selling and educational copy I had ever written. It stretched my mind and, in the process, I planted the seeds of desire in many other minds. It had beautiful renderings of the building's exterior, several shots of the commercial mall, the interior, garden-like atrium, and the various-sized apartments. It contained 100 ideas for combining shops in living quarters with this unusual appeal: "I want unusual people to sell unusual things in an unusual environment."

After having printed 5,000 of these brochures, I was faced with the question of where to send them. The shotgun approach of mailing them to apartment dwellers would be inefficient. To be effective, I had to concentrate on unusual people: people interested in doing or selling unusual things in an unusual downtown environment. Therefore, I sent hundreds of brochures to artists, handicrafters, hobbyists and retired people. The response was cautious and sporadic, but we had planted enough seeds to get people talking about the project. We followed up with more aggressive efforts: we attended arts and crafts fairs, and gave talks to retired groups, explaining the advantages of combining a little shop or studio with living quarters.

These were our salient selling points for the elderly:

"At less rent than what you're probably paying now, you can move into a modern apartment and start a little shop of your own, selling exotic plants, homemade fudge, unusual soaps, candles, lamps, toys, and dozens of other items in which you may have or can develop an interest. You'll become part of a business association, advertising your wares to Milwaukeeans or tourists who come to visit our city. Instead of being lonely in your home or apartment, you will make new friends and get into the mainstream of business activity. Perhaps you'll earn $1,000 a year, or maybe enough to pay your rent. If you hit on something really unusual, who knows, you may even earn as much as $5,000 or $10,000 a year."

To young people in arts and crafts, our message went something like this:

"Downtown is where the action is—theaters, restaurants, shops. At less than what you're paying now, you can have your studio or shop combined with your living quarters. It's a new idea that's never been tried anywhere before, and who else should be the pioneers of an untried idea but adventurous young people! It took an adventurous spirit on my part to create this for you. Why not match my effort with a pioneering spirit of your own?"

Slowly, too slowly, we began to sign up several artists, a photographer, an eighty-year-old woman who was still active in her life-long work of teaching facial make-up, and another seventy-five-year-old woman who had been giving massages to wealthy women for the past forty years. The latter had been renting space in an office building and was delighted to move her health spa in order to continue her business on a semi-retired basis in her large, 1,250-square-foot apartment.

But after half a year of effort, during the time we were under construction, we had leased only fifteen apartments. I was not satisfied. I began looking for unusual personnel to accelerate the marketing of my idea. Finally, I decided to hire a nationally-renowned professional management firm, one of the top five in the country, to give me some new slants on how to reach this elusive market.

A competent-looking official from the prestigious firm drove in from Chicago, listened to my marketing problems and, a week later, sent an elaborate written proposal, stressing the successful history of the company and stating in general terms what he could do for me. I was impressed. I hired the firm at $20,000 a year to do the leasing and, when the building was completed, to take charge of its management. The Chicago account executive assigned one of their experts to do what I could not do—speed up the leasing.

After three months of little movement toward improving the marketing situation, I called in the Chicago official and asked, "What's the trouble? I'm getting little better than zero results."

He looked at me knowingly and said sincerely, "It's a very unique project. Perhaps there's no market for it. But give us a little more time. Perhaps we'll come up with something."

"All right," I said, "but please give it more attention."

A month later there was still no satisfactory action. I called in the local expert and, in his presence, called his Chicago supervisor, and informed him on the phone, "I'm sorry, but I have to terminate your services. I hope you will agree that there's no need for me to tell you why." In this fashion, I severed my association with one of the largest real estate firms in the country.

I now turned inward. If I were going to succeed in my pioneering project, the ideas had to come from the one who had the most to lose or win—myself. I turned also to the one closest to me—my wife.

"Honey," I said, "I want you to furnish two models with your abundant exquisite taste. I'm going to give you a $10,000 budget. I'd like you to decorate the units in such a way that it will take people's breath away. Create a free-flowing environment similar to the apartment layouts we visited in Los Angeles. Can you do it?"

"You know I can," she said, and she did.

WHY AN "AMATEUR" SALES EXPERT IS SOMETIMES MORE EFFECTIVE THAN A PROFESSIONAL

Having beautiful models is one part of selling, but finding someone who can translate their beauty into desire is equally important.

I was playing golf one day, when a real estate friend of mine drove his cart over from an adjoining fairway and said, "I understand you're looking for a salesperson to lease your 'Chalet At The River.' I've got a great woman for you."

What are her credentials?"

"She just finished leasing a project for me and she did a fine job."

I interviewed her and hired her on the spot for $16,000 a year. Why? Because she exuded enthusiasm for the uniqueness of my project, instead of the suave professionalism I had seen in the national expert. What I'm trying to say is that excitement over a specific project is often more effective than mountains of national know-how.

"I'm excited about the challenge," she said in accepting the job, "for many reasons. It's revitalizing our downtown, bringing people back to live in it and, most of all, I can't wait to try out your new and unique concept of combining shops with apartments. I'm completely sold on it, and I'm positive I'll be successful."

Indeed she was. I marveled at the way she turned prospective tenants' reluctance into acceptance. She worked long hours, six days a week, amid the dust and rubble of construction. She educated, she convinced, and she allayed the fears of those who were hesitant to try something so radically new and different. Her sheer confidence in what she was selling turned skeptics into believers.

To bolster her confidence in the uniqueness of my project, I matched it with support that was as unique and imaginative as the project itself.

The support I gave my sales agent came in the form of the second floor atrium, where my wife had furnished the models. This I turned into a veritable garden full of ten-foot rubber plants, benches, hanging flowers and attractive paintings. It was lit with perimeter, wood-covered valence lighting with spotlights over the plants to create an atmosphere of brightness and greenery. When prospective clients walked from this beautiful Garden of Eden into one of the meticulously furnished models, it was like going in from a splendid public area to a cozy, well-cared-for home.

But what good was all this planned beauty unless we devised ways for people to see it? Classified newspaper advertising brought few results. Radio advertising was a complete bust. Direct mail to select groups brought only minimal results. We had to have a dramatic breakthrough before all our preparations could be seen by large numbers of people.

HOW TO GET NEWSPAPER FEATURES TO PROMOTE A PIONEER PROJECT

My first breakthrough came with my first feature article in the *Milwaukee Journal's* Real Estate Section. One line of news is worth ten lines of advertising. The reason is obvious: news is informative and objective—therefore it's more believable than self-serving advertising. But it takes some know-how to get a front-page feature with pictures, describing in a human-interest way what cannot be done as well with paid advertising. The usual objection of the real estate editor to running a feature on a new idea is, "You're maneuvering me for some free advertising."

Your answer should be something like this: "It's a two-way street. You need my news to make your paper interesting, just as much as I need your readers to know what I'm trying to do."

In order to override the editor's resistance, you must do two things: give him or her honest information, and think of a "hook" or interesting angle to the story so he or she can hang a feature on it. The feature article, "Klode Building Gets New Look, New Use," written by William Manly for the April 29, 1979 *Milwaukee Journal,* represents such a cooperative effort. It was a major educational breakthrough for me, a news break for the *Milwaukee Journal* and, best of all, a break for the life of my project.

Tens of thousands of people began discussing the feature story—something I could not have arranged with $10,000 worth of advertising.

After a few months, the interest died down and the project needed another lift. It came unexpectedly. An architectural designer was given a two-column article criticizing my plans in the *Milwaukee Journal.* He was right on some of the flaws, and wrong on others. However, he gave me the opening for a reply because his criticism was based on what he had gleaned from a mere three-minute phone interview, and only on what he had seen from the outside. He had not even asked to see the inside. I was helped tremendously, however, when the real estate editor gave me equal space to defend my plans. My response again shows that opportunities—of whatever origin—are available for creative educational copy.

My answer created a discussion among readers, planners, and architects; this, in turn, stirred up interest beyond the importance of our differences of opinion. The favorable fallout was calling attention to the building; it helped the eduational process immeasurably.

But even this soon died down. I was looking for another lift, another "hook" for a story. It came to me one morning while I was shaving. Wasn't the restoring of old buildings a new art form? I ruminated. Certainly it required a different architectural discipline than building new structures. I had visited Switzerland several times and had been inspired by the way the people preserved their old buildings, many of which are two to three hundred years old. They preserved the charm of the old with elegance. It *was* truly a form of art. This made me think of the art editor of the *Milwaukee Journal*, Jim Auer, whom I had met at a writer's club meeting. Yes, why not call him and suggest that recycling charming old buildings to new, functional uses is a new art form that combines the creative touch of the artist and the commercial pragmatism of the real estate developer?

My subconscious musings were rewarded because the art editor thought it was a superb idea. He wrote a two-column feature with pictures, calling attention to how architects, designers, interior decorators, and entrepreneurial pragmatists can join in combining aesthetics and functionalism that would appeal to art-oriented tenants.

Dozens of calls came in after it appeared, and my enthusiastic sales representative signed up several artists as a result.

The axiom that one idea leads to another is as old as it is true. When I saw that focusing on the art aspect of the project was bringing results, I let several weeks pass and then called the interior decorating editor of the real estate section of the *Milwaukee Journal*.

"You're in charge of reporting the interior design innovations in homes, aren't you?" I asked, "Do you cover anything that deals with new environmental living?"

"Yes," she said. "What do you have in mind?"

"Few apartments today," I said, "have the Old-World charm of the loft look. If you want to see an authentic loft environment, come and see us. But talk to my wife. She can tell it better than I. This is her story. Interested?"

"Yes," she said, and the subsequent feature created another

NEW DOWNTOWN MODEL APARTMENTS

SHOWN FOR THE FIRST TIME!

Chalet at the River

823 N. 2nd St.

(Former Klode Furniture Bldg.)

In the heart of the civic center, convenient to shopping and transportation (you don't need a car)

OPEN TODAY, SUNDAY 1-4

ALSO **MONDAY-FRIDAY 10-4**

and by appointment

YOUR CHOICE

★ Apartment With Room for Shop
(Arts, Crafts, Antiques, etc.)

★ Apartment With Services
(Accountants, Designers, Decorators, etc.)

★ Apartment As Residence Only

SPECIAL AMENITIES:

- Heat
- Carpeting
- Draperies
- Garden Atrium on Each Floor
- Completely Equipped Modern Kitchen
- Ceramic Tiled Combination Powder/Bathroom
- Beautifully Lofted Beamed Ceiling
- Laundry Room
- Recreation Room, Sun Deck
- Shops and Restaurants on Lower and Street Levels
- Security Guard
- Burglar Alarm System
- Smoke Alarm and Sprinkler System in Each Apartment
- Parking Attendant

NOW is the time to reserve your choice apartment for February, March or April, 1980. For further details call

Chalet at the River
277-9898
or
George Bockl
272-0069

EQUAL HOUSING OPPORTUNITY

Chalet at the River

FIGURE I-4

stir among the many prospects who were sitting on the fence, undecided whether or not to move into an old building that, for years, had had the image of a neglected furniture warehouse.

These feature articles brought requests from television stations, the project became news, and my wife and I appeared on a talk show. As a result we rented half a dozen apartments. My expeditor and architect were asked to appear on a televised public panel to explain how remodeling old buildings saves energy and preserves the character of a city. That too brought results.

Of course, we did some advertising. We spent about $25,000 on classified and display advertising. (See Figure 4-1.)

However, I am convinced that, without the feature articles, mere advertising would never have gotten our message across to Milwaukee's population of a million.

HOW TO GET AN INTERESTING MIX OF IMAGINATIVE TENANTS

In order to develop a model for revitalizing a downtown through recycling old buildings, I felt that not only was it necessary that the project be financially successful, but vital people must also be brought into the project. I wanted tenants who met high standards of decency and creativity, and who, above all, appreciated the uniqueness of what we had to offer. It was a reciprocal exchange—I wanted unusual people to match my concept. It was not an easy task to sift and winnow without offending the ordinary, while searching for the extraordinary.

For instance, we turned down prospects who wanted to put a billiard parlor in their apartment. Another received a refusal for a pinball emporium, and still another received a polite "no" when a voice over the telephone asked if we could entertain a business that matched roommates. On the other hand, we were not only interested but proud to sign up the two elderly women mentioned earlier, who wanted to continue their health massage and cosmetology businesses, along with several well-known artists who had their work displayed in museums, a vitamin shop proprietor, a health spa/clinic owner, and a woman who specialized in making and selling unusual quilts and aprons.

There came a time, however, when I realized that some of my critics were right: Milwaukee was not a Santa Barbara or a San Francisco. The West Coast had more of the rolling-stone types of people, without roots, who were more willing to try something new. Milwaukeeans, on the other hand, are more prosaic, more apt to remain rooted where they are—in short, they are a more stable but less imaginative community. I say this because, after seven months of feature articles, television, radio, and newspaper advertising, I had only leased about forty Shops-in-Apartments. The handwriting was on the wall: out of a metropolitan population of a million, I could not find 109 imaginative people who dared to uproot themselves and pioneer a new type of downtown living.

I meditated to plot out my next move. I had been turning down tenants who wanted to rent apartments for residences only. Reluctantly, I had to give up my dream of making "Chalet At The River" a Wisconsin tourist attraction. My dream of a vertical shopping center, featuring over a hundred unusual people, operating unusual shops, could not be realized. I compromised in the following manner. I instructed my sales manager to rent only the apartments on the second, third, and fourth floors to prospective shop owners; open up the fifth and sixth floors to tenants who offered services such as beauty shop owners, interior decorators, accountants, attorneys, etc.; and the upper seventh, eighth, and ninth floors for residential use only. It was a blow to my original idea, but I had to admit that the practical businessman in me overrode the bit of Michelangelo that had stirred beneath.

Within two months, all of the residential apartments were leased. During the same period. most of the apartments with services were signed up. The conclusion I drew from this was that not enough people were willing to live in the heart of downtown with a store in their living quarters. Indeed, Milwaukee was not a La Jolla or a San Francisco. I accepted my partial defeat with the consolation that I had tried my best. I had reached too far into uncertainty, and could realize only half a dream. But, when the eight floors of apartments and the commercial space on the first floor and lower level were leased, I still had one of the most unusual projects in the Midwest.

HOW TO PROVIDE CREATIVE MANAGEMENT

I now devoted myself to giving unusual management to the unique conglomeration of downtown pioneers. Tenants were delighted with arranging the free-flowing, partitionless space into all sorts of imaginative configurations. They were especially grateful for the high and airy, beam-laced ceilings, because these gave their living environment a true loft look. No other apartments in the city had this distinctive feature—except for some very expensive homes.

But it was our security system that pleased our tenants the most. We gave them luxury protection for the lowest comparable per-square-foot rentals in the city. We provided smoke detectors and sprinklers hooked up to a central watch, along with a burglar and fire alarm system that brought response in minutes. In addition, we provided security around the clock, consisting of guards in uniform who patrolled the building around the clock. To add frosting on the cake, we offered free valet parking from eight to eleven in the evening for our tenants. These people, like those in the luxury buildings, dropped their cars off at the entrance of the "Chalet At The River" for the parking attendant to drive to an undercover public parking garage half a block away. In addition, a security guard was stationed at the front of the two automatic passenger elevators, near a two-way loudspeaker system that connected him to each tenant in the building. Anytime after five in the evening, when the stores were closed, visitors had to identify themselves to the guard and the tenant they wanted to visit. Going from a dust-laden warehouse, where strangers stalked the sidewalks and winos slept at its doors at night, to a secure living area was indeed a miracle of change. Gone was the empty, neglected environment. Now, in its place were men and women who had a stake in protecting their turf—emptiness gave way to life.

A FEW WORDS OF PRAISE IN BEHALF OF BUREAUCRATS

Although I was flayed and buffeted by H.U.D.'s rules and regulations, I nevertheless want to praise their efforts to protect their boss—the government. It's their job to see that the government does not insure an ill-conceived project; and that, when they do insure it, the developer lives up to all the prescribed terms and conditions carefully enumerated in the manual. Since there is no personal liability on the part of the developer, and since his or her investment is minimal after the project is completed, he or she can walk away from it and dump it on the government. To protect itself, H.U.D. required that I deposit $165,000 for a year, from which it could draw any operating losses, and an additional $60,000 in the event there were any hidden defects that were not discovered during the sixteen months of construction. That is caution, albeit high-priced for the entrepreneur. Yet I cannot blame H.U.D. Are they not indirectly protecting the people's tax money—your money?

Why did I bear all the bureaucratic burdens? Part of it was to pioneer into the unknown, to reach for the evolving portion of real estate action. It was like writing a book and not knowing if it would be published. But, in addition to the inspirational element, there was low interest and tax goodies that I want to emphasize. They were ample.

Getting a 7½ percent, forty-year mortgage (when the prevailing rate was 11 percent with a twenty-five year amortization) cut my debt service on $3 million by about $150,000 a year. Equally important was the $200,000 of depreciation that can be used as an offset against ordinary income taxes—a big government carrot to entice hardy entrepreneurs to fight it out with H.U.D. And, if that wasn't enough, there was another tax goodie: a 10 percent tax credit for the commercial part of the remodeling costs. Unfortunately, it did not apply on the residential segment of the recycling costs. Since about $2 million was spent on residential and $1 million on the commercial restoration, my tax credit was about $100,000—a bonanza worth fighting for. And, should I want to sell my "Chalet At The River," I could realize a profit of about $600,000. That, too, is worth fighting for.

For the 7½ percent interest, the $200,000 depreciation and the $100,000 tax credit, H.U.D. demanded, in return, that rentals be regulated to a point where, after fixed expenses and debt service, the cash flow was to be no more than $30,000 a year. This is tantamount to roughly 10 percent of what H.U.D. allows for entrepreneurial effort, which, in this case, was $300,000. If expenses go up, they allow the rent to rise; if they go down, they expect rents to decline.

Is it fair to limit cash flow and burden developers with hundreds of thousands of dollars of debt; then, when it it is all done, have them set aside huge amounts of cash against operating losses and hidden defects? And what about the dozens of other regulations? Reluctantly I have to say yes, it is fair, because we have to strike a partnership between private and public enterprise. Between Milton Friedman's no government regulation, and

John Kenneth Galbraith's too much regulation, we must strike a happy medium that creates wealth and jobs through a partnership in which entrepreneurs and government work together, and imaginatively. The bureaucrats are at their best when they use their creativity to stimulate private enterprise, and private enterprise is at its enlightened best when it accepts fair limitations to protect consumers. We need entrepreneurial discipline and governmental controls to discourage wild and irresponsible promotions.

HOW THE 1981 TAX LAW CAN REDUCE A 16-PERCENT INTEREST RATE TO 6 PERCENT ON A RECYCLING PROJECT

After reading about my "Chalet At The River" you may complain that, since President Reagan's administration has eliminated the 7½ percent H.U.D. insured mortgages, you won't be able to do now what I did three years ago. Not true! Stop wringing your hands. The government has imaginatively replaced it with equally lucrative incentives for you to rehabilitate old buildings. In some ways, they're even more enticing.

Out of Washington's political and bureaucratic catacombs came, in 1981, some of the most original real estate thinking in several decades. In the 1981 Tax Bill, they gave us the financial tools with which to overcome the prevailing high interest rates. Unfortunately, they do not apply to new construction, but it is a veritable bonanza for financing commercial recycling projects.

The two main provisions of the new tax law, as they relate to real estate, are as follows: A commercial rehabilitation project can be depreciated in 15 years and, at your option, accelerated to 175 percent to give you to close to a 12 percent write-off of the total cost, exclusive of land. In addition, you will receive a 15 percent investment tax credit if the recycled building is 30 years old, 20 percent if it's 40 years old, and 25 percent if it qualifies for a landmark designation. This applies to commercial buildings, but there's legislation pending in the U.S. Senate to extend the tax incentives to residential rehabilitation as well.

Analyze what follows carefully, because it translates into lowering the prevailing high interest rates by 10 percentage points. That indeed is revolutionary! Open your eyes to its possibilities.

Let's see if you agree with my reasoning. Assume that you can obtain a loan of $1 million on a recycling project at 16 percent interest, which will cost $160,000 a year. Let's further assume that, based on obtainable rentals and prevailing fixed expenses, the project is not feasible—the debt service would be too high, due to the 16 percent interest rate. But against that infeasibility, the government is offering you (if you're in the 50 percent tax bracket) two incentives that shrink the 16 percent rate to 6 percent. Just imagine, 6 percent! Consider what comes next carefully.

The 1981 Tax Bill allows you to depreciate a recycled, 40-year-old building in 15 years and, if you wish, you can take accelerated depreciation at 175 percent, which amounts to about 12 percent of the $1 million, or about $120,000 worth of tax shelter per year. It's even more if you add the original cost of the old building. If you're in a 50 percent tax bracket, you can knock off $60,000; this, in effect, reduces your debt service interest from $160,000 to $100,000. Add to that the investment tax credit of 20 percent on $1 million, or $200,000 which, if you wish to spread it over five years, will reduce the $100,000 remaining debt interest by $40,000; thus, in effect, you lower the interest to $60,000 from the original $160,000. These government incentives to spur the recycling revolution actually reduce the 16 percent interest rate to 6 percent for at least the first five years of the project.

What happens beyond the five years, I must admit, gets into the realm of uncertainty, where new variables come into play. Hopefully any problems can be solved as new conditions arise. I admit this a vague forecast, but five years is a long time in this rapidly changing economic climate. If you can lock your financing in at the equivalent of 6 percent interest, do it. Remember, there's always the option of selling your project at a profit after making a hefty cash flow during the first five years. The project would be saleable because the purchaser would have a new, higher depreciation base which, even without the tax investment credit, could still make the recycled property financially desirable at a higher price.

I've presented a skeleton outline of the tax advantages involved in the new tax law, and obviously there are more variables that will come into play. Give this new tax angle serious consideration. It's important enough to call a meeting between you, your accountant, and a tax attorney to see how you can capitalize on this new tax bonanza.

Don't sell the government short on creating new ideas to stimulate the entrepreneurs. Those who think that most of the smart people are working in the private sector, while the not-so-smart are employed in the public sector are wrong. There are plenty of smart government men and women who are not only imaginative in spurring on developers to get at the tax incentives, but who also protect the consumers (all of us) from giving the developers too much. The government gives and takes, prods and disciplines.

If private and public enterprise understand each other, if we make fair demands of one another, recycling old buildings to new uses can become a multibillion dollar business for many years. The advantages of awakening ourselves to this sleeping giant of an industry are manifold. The most obvious ones are filling empty hands with work, indirectly conserving millions of barrels of oil through saving energy, and revitalizing neighborhoods through revitalizing builidngs, which indirectly revitalizes people. And, of course, recycling enriches us creatively and monetarily.

The overriding thrust of saving old buildings is that it gets us back on the track of a renewable world. It ties in with the wise old saying that more character is built by thoughtful austerity than by throw-away prosperity. Preservation and conservation give a distinctive mark to civilization. Recycling old buildings to new uses will help us earn that distinction.

5

TEN INNOVATIVE WAYS TO FINANCE A RECYCLING PROJECT

In order to present a clear picture of the various methods available to finance a recycling project, I'd like to make the following assumptions that can be used in a general guideline and model:

1. Size of building: five floors, 50,000 square feet.
2. Cost of rehabilitation, including cost of original land and building: $1 million, or $20 a square foot.
3. The assumption that the cost of recycling is approximately the same for residential units, offices, or stores.
4. Fifty thousand square feet will produce about 66 apartments, with an average size of about 650 square feet per apartment.
5. Fifty thousand square feet will produce about 42,500 square feet of net rentable office space, after allowing a 15 percent loss for elevators, shafts, stairways, corridors, etc.
6. The net rentable area for stores can be assumed to be about 40,000 square feet.
7. The gross rent of 66 apartments at $325 per month is $257,400, or $238,382 at 93 percent occupancy.
8. The gross rent for 42,500 square feet of offices at $6 a square foot is $255,000, or $237,150 at 93 percent occupancy.

9. The gross rent for 40,000 square feet of stores, at $6 per square foot, is $240,000, or $223,200 at 93 percent occupancy.
10. The assumption that a 50,000-square-foot old building, including land, can be bought at $4 a square foot, or $200,000.

I've made many rounded assumptions for the sake of clarity. Obviously there are going to be variations in size, cost, and rental income of various parts of the $1 million model, but based on my recent experiences of buying and recycling old buildings into apartments, offices, and stores, the above assumptions can be used as general rules for planning and procuring financing. This mock-up is presented only for the convenience of explaining the various finance plans.

Within these parameters, let's now analyze the practical ways to finance a typical recycling project.

1. SUBORDINATE SELLER'S EQUITY

Suppose you found the building you like. You've decided to use it for a residential conversion, and the owner is asking $200,000. Assuming it would cost $1 million to complete the project (according to the model), how do you go about financing it if you have only $50,000 in cash and a lot of enthusiasm?

My approach would be to meet the owner with the approval of the broker, if there is one, and use this potent argument.

"You're losing about $15,000 a year on your building. How would you like to make $20,000 a year instead?" That should be your opening statement.

"What do you mean?" the owner would probably say.

Give him the following explanation.

"There's no future for your building the way it is. It's outlived its usefulness. I have a plan to turn it into 66 apartments, but I need your help with the financing to do it. If you agree to it, I'll start working on obtaining a $750,000 first mortgage, providing your subordinate your $200,000 and be paid out at the rate of $20,000 a year, including interest and principal."

Don't play cute. Be open. Reveal your plans, even at the risk that the owner might use them. But the chances of that happening are remote. What is sure, however, is that he or she will be impressed with your honesty.

"I'd rather have cash," the owner will probably say, after your long explanation.

"But I can't do it without your secondary financing." Then follow up quickly with another argument. "If you were to get cash, you'd probably have to pay about $50,000 in income tax and have only $150,000 to invest. By being paid on the installment plan, you start getting interest on $200,000 instead of $150,000, and you pay a little each year and in a lower tax bracket." Then, to sweeten your offer, wind up with, "I'm so excited about this project that I'm willing to up the ante and pay $225,000 instead of $200,000 for your willingness to subordinate."

Don't worry about showing your eagerness. Even if he's a devious owner, he will be impressed by your openness.

"How sure are you that you'll have the $20,000 a year to pay me?"

It's a logical question and here's where you can deliver the clincher, if you're prepared with facts and figures based on the model I've outlined at the beginning of this chapter.

Tell him, "I've done a lot of work on your building." "I can get 66 apartments out of it at $325 per unit for a total of about $257,000, and if I allow for 7 percent vacancy, I'll have a net of close to $240,000 a year. My payments on $750,000 will be about $110,000 a year, my fixed expenses about $80,000. That will leave me about $50,000 a year cushion or cash flow, out of which you get the first $20,000, leaving me the rest for management and for all my work. You're safe because I'm willing to sign any instrument your lawyer will prepare that prevents me from drawing a dime for myself before you'repaid $20,000 a year."

"Well, it sounds good. Let me think it over."

Let's assume that, after a few days, the owner agrees to your subordination idea. If you make similar comprehensive presentation to a mortgagee, after showing him your well prepared pro forma statement and colored renderings of a typical apartment, you have a fairly good chance of getting the loan. This is especially true when you point out to the tremendous advantages of the additional cash flow that will come into the project as a result of the accelerated depreciation and investment tax credit as a result of the 1981 Tax Law.

If you're rejected by half a dozen lenders, don't give up until you've tried another six. If necessary, appeal to their community patriotism, in addition to the commercial viability of the loan. One of the 12 lenders is bound to say yes.

What I've just explained is not pie-in-the-sky. It's practical. It's worked. I've done it. In Chapter 3, you've read how I subordinated $350,000 in much the same way you asked the seller to subordinate his $225,000.

Naturally, there are going to be variations, but if you can get close to structuring a $1 million deal with only $50,000 of your own money, and have a potential tax-sheltered annuity of $30,000 a year plus $40,000 a year for five years of investment tax credit, you have performed a three-way service: (1) you've turned the building owner's income from a minus to a plus, (2) you've revitalized part of a neighborhood and, best of all, (3) you've created a lifetime annuity for your family.

2. OFFER SELLER EQUITY POSITION FOR HIS BUILDING

If Finance Plan No. 1 doesn't work because you can't get the owner to subordinate his equity, then offer him one-half interest in the project on the following terms: for and in consideration of conveying the ownership of his building, he is to receive one-half of the cash flow of $50,000 a year and, in case of sale, one-half of the profit. In other words, he owns half the project.

This is a generous offer. Another important advantage you should point out is that the $25,000 cash flow is tax sheltered by depreciation, while the interest payments, part of $20,000 a year in Plan No. 1, would be taxed as ordinary income. Also, be sure to point out that he would receive half the $40,000 a year investment tax credit. Offer this plan only if you are convinced that the owner of the building would make a compatible partner and would let you make the rehabilitation decisions without any interference.

I prefer Finance Plan No. 1. Only when you see that there's no other way do you offer Plan No. 2. When you finalize the deal, remember that your partner is to contribute half the $50,000 you were to invest in Plan No. 1. I would stand pat on this point. If he doesn't agree, you may have a difficult partner, and a difficult partner usually produces a sour deal. Sweet deals, no matter how difficult, are better than easy sour ones.

3. IF OWNER REFUSES PLANS NO. 1 AND No. 2, BUY HIS BUILDING ON A LAND CONTRACT

Buying on a land contract is a colloquial term which, in other parts of the country, is referred to as a conditional sale contract. It is selling property without conveying a warranty deed or title to it. Check with your lawyer for a more detailed explanation. However, that's a small matter compared to financing the balance of $750,000 behind a $200,000 first claim on the property.

It can be done if the old building is to be recycled into office space. Here's how. Make a few dozen telephone calls exploring the possibility of leasing the building to a government agency. If luck strikes your way, you may find one that can use the entire 42,500 square feet of net rentable office space at $6 a square foot, producing a gross rental of about $250,000 a year. If you can get a letter of intent for a ten-year lease, I'd hurry and buy the building with $50,000 down and the balance of $150,000 on a land contract. With this letter of intent, you should have no trouble getting a $950,000 first mortgage at the prevailing high interest rates, subject to the agency's signing a noncancellable ten-year lease. Here again ,you must sell the lender on the advantages of the new tax law as they relate to accelerated depreciation and investment tax credit. It's the key to making the project feasible and the mortgage obtainable.

The more likelihood is that you may find tenant interest for a floor or half a floor at a time. The project can still work if you risk buying the building with $50,000 down and try to lease it to smaller users. As you sign up five- or ten-year leases for parts of the building, use them as collateral and borrow enough to recycle the leased space. For instance, if you lease a floor or 20 percent of the building for $50,000 a year for five years to a triple A tenant, it's possible that a lender will advance $250,000 toward remodeling the floor. After you have the entire building leased for $250,000, by using the leases as collateral, you may be able to obtain a $950,000 first mortgage and pay off the $150,000 balance you owe on the land contract. It's a difficult financial adventure, and a very risky one if you don't know how to lease space, but the result is tremendously rewarding if you fill the building with top-grade tenants. The key is knowing how to persuade tenants to move into your recycled building. That's far more difficult than getting the money after you have the tenants.

This method of financing is *almost* impossible for recycling the same building into 66 apartments if you buy it on a land contract. The reason should be obvious. It's difficult to pre-rent 66 apartments from a floor plan. You'll note that I said *almost* impossible. If the building has unusual charm, the neighborhood unusually desirable, and you put on an ingenious advertizing campaign, it is possible that you may pre-rent most of the apartments. A smart lender will take a long look at the list of your tenants and marvel at your ingenuity before turning you down, especially if he likes the building, location, and your honest enthusiasm. It's a difficult undertaking, but that shouldn't stop you from pioneering this financial route.

Remember, the worst that can happen to you, after you buy the building on a land contract and Plan No. 3 doesn't work, either for offices or apartments, is that you will hold on to it and try one of the other plans described in the ensuing pages.

4. CONVERT YOUR RECYCLING PROJECT TO CONDOMINIUMS

If Plans No. 2 and No. 3 don't work, I still don't want you to give up. Try Plan No. 4: convert your recycling project to condominiums. This is a more sophisticated financing approach than described earlier, but it's also a very profitable one.

Here is the way to go about it. Let's continue to assume that you own the 50,000-square-foot building with a land contract balance of $150,000. The first thing to do is to rearrange your apartment layout from 66 units to 50. Make the apartments larger and more varied in size in preparation for ownership. Price them so they average about $30,000 a unit, which is low for an average-sized apartment of about 750 square feet.

Now, take your architectural plans and specifications to a lender and ask for an interim two-year financing loan of a million dollars, based on a bonafide presale of 50 percent of the apartments. Take two years if you can get it, or at least 18 months, because converting a loft building to condominiums is plowing new real estate territory, and potential buyers may be slow to act. Eventually, if you put on an effective advertising campaign backed by feature newspaper articles (see Chapter 6), you should be successful, because similar new condominiums would probably be selling between $45,000 to $55,000 per apartment. Be sure that in your selling campaign, you provide commitments to qualified buyers from a lender of mortgages averaging about $25,000 a unit at prevailing interest rates. It also might not be a bad idea to provide private mortgage insurance for each loan from Mortgage Guaranty Insurance Corporation, a billion-dollar company whose Chairman of the Board, Max Karl, happens to be my brother-in-law. Of course, other mortgage insurance corporations will also do.

In arranging all this intricate financing and mortgage insurance, it is not wise to have a mill-run attorney, but one experienced in structuring condominium sales. You do the creative planning and selling; let him or her protect you and your buyers' equity in the fine points of ownership.

Let's now take a look at the potential profit. Fifty apartments, averaging $30,000 apiece, will bring $1.5 million. Selling costs and attorney's fees ought not to be more than $100,000. In dealing with 50 potential owners, it's not unlikely that you may run into a buzz saw of unreasonable demands, for which you ought to provide $100,000 in cost overruns beyond your $1.5 million original figure. This will still leave you a substantial profit of $300,000 for two years' work and a lot of risk.

A recycled condominium project has these advantages over a new one, or converting an existing apartment building. You can produce the final product at a lower cost than a new one, and you don't have to disturb tenants who are organizing throughout the country to fight the condominium movement that disrupts their living patterns.

But what should make you most proud is that you've turned corroding blight into 50 ownerships. That's a meaningful contribution to society. And what should make you happiest of all is, that while you were involved in doing good, you've earned $300,000. That should give you a greater inner glow than earning the same amount in the stock market or in manufacturing bubble gum.

Profiteering without making a contribution to society is sterile, parasitic. Combining profit with helping people is when enlightened capitalism is at its finest. That's what recycling old buildings is all about: it reverses a throw-away philosophy into a renewable one—the mark of a caring civilization.

5. TURN A CONGLOMERATE OF RETIRED ARTISANS INTO FINANCIERS

This is an avante-garde suggestion that has worked for a travel guide in Switzerland and, with some modifications, can work in recycling a project in America. The idea is the barter plan, which had been in vogue centuries ago, and which the travel guide used to build a $500,000 resort motel at the foot of one of Switzerland's most beautiful mountains.

Here's how he did it, and here's how you can improvise on this plan and put it to work in America.

I met Paschal, the travel guide, about ten years ago when I toured Switzerland. He had no money, but many friends—retired carpenters, electricians, plumbers, and architects; the most important of whom was a retired man who owned a parcel of land that was ideal for a small resort motel. Paschal made each of his friends the following proposition. He would place a mutually agreed-upon value on the land, and the services of the architect, the carpenter, the plumber, and the electrician, and credit each one with vacation time in proportion to how much he owed each of them. They could either use part of their credit for personal vacations, or sell it to others, which arrangement Paschal agreed to honor.

The travel guide told me, as my wife and I and a group of about 30 vacationers were touring Switzerland with him, that his project was almost completed. He was able to get a first mortgage of about $100,000 for materials, and his secondary obligations of $400,000 were to the owners of the land, the architect, and all the retired and moonlighting artisans who sporadically, week-by-week, built Paschal's dream resort. Between tours, he would work on his project himself, and make suggestions to his artisans as to design and getting more for their time. It was indeed an innovative financial plan and, in the evening when we relaxed after a day's tour, Paschal would tell us that he hoped that, when he opened his resort, we and our friends would come and vacation with him because, as he put it:

"I've poured into my inn all that I learned about what tourists like. The location is ideal, the view breathtaking, and the rooms and intimate restaurant will be a tourist's dream. Managing it in a way I know will please tourists will be the crowning achievement of my career. And I'll owe it all to my friends, who are making this dream possible."

"I agree, it's wonderful to have friends," I said, "but without your innovative financing plan, your dream would only remain a dream. I'm going to use your plan in America."

"Be my guest," he said with a smile.

Can this be duplicated in America? Perhaps not in a $1 million recycling deal, but maybe up to a $500,000 project. I know of an innovative entrepreneur who built a $300,000 theater for $150,000 by buying odd-lot building materials and warehousing them for future use, then hiring retirees and moonlighters to build his project. He leased it for $30,000 a year. With variations on Paschal's experience and the theater-builder's ingenuity, you should be able to recycle a small office building, a 20-apartment project, or a mama-papa motel in the same way.

Sure, it's a lot more difficult than getting a 90-percent loan, but when they're not available, you must grope for new ideas. Assuming that, by borrowing and using your own money, you can put together $100,000 for materials on what you think is a sure-fire $500,000 project, how are you going to pay off $400,000 to retirees and moonlighters for the cost of their labor?

Well, how about creating a multi-mortgage, five-year instrument, payable monthly with interest to each according to their due, with a balloon payment at the end. In effect, each will have a piece of the mortgage, just as limited partners have a piece of the equity. After five years, this multi-owned mortgage can either be renewed or payed off, if the owner can obtain single-mortgage financing.

Some variation of this idea is practical only for someone who is determined, hard working, and innovative. It's not for the dilettante, the one-dimensional thinker. It's for the rare and the few.

6. SYNDICATE YOUR NEED FOR EQUITY CAPITAL AND RETAIN PART OWNERSHIP

Using the $1 million model again, let's assume that the owner of the building wants cash and that you can get a $700,000 first mortgage, but you don't have the $300,000 equity money. Here's what others have done and you can do it, too.

Get three investors with $100,000 each, or six investors with $50,000 apiece, and offer each of the $100,000 investors one-fourth of the equity, or each of the $50,000 investors one-eighth of the equity, keeping one-fourth of the ownership for yourself for putting the deal together. This arrangement is fair on both sides. The investors are giving up a small part of their equity for your work, and you're getting one-fourth of their equity for zero investment and a lot of hard work. With the new accelerated depreciation and investment tax credit incentives, you should have silent investors knocking loudly on your door to get in on the deal, especially if you've picked a good building in a good location.

Many similar deals involving new property have been syndicated with some variations along these lines, and there are far more advantages in syndicating a recycling project. In fact, that's where the syndication action of the future will be. The only red flag you should wave before your investors, if you want to hold on to your integrity, is to warn them that there could be cost overruns. It may be more difficult to sell with this disclosure, but you'll avoid many headaches if the overruns do occur. There are enough economies and tax incentives to a well-conceived recycling project that an acceptable overrun should not materially affect the deal. That's why a warning of its possibility is a wise move in the negotiating process.

7. FINANCE YOUR REHABILITATION BY GIVING UP HALF YOUR EQUITY TO THE LENDER

What if you can't or don't want to syndicate the $300,000 of your project? Or, even if you can, you can't find a lender for the $700,000 first mortgage? Then do what others have done. Offer the lender 75 percent of the project—the same deal you offered the three or six investors in the No. 6 Plan. That is, the lender agrees to putting in the $300,000 of equity money, as well as to providing a $700,000 first mortgage at the prevailing interest rate.

Savings and loans have service corporations that allow them to invest 5 percent of their assets in equity projects. Insurance companies and pension funds can do it also with a certain percentage of their funds. A word of caution, however. Prepare yourself well before offering an equity deal to these lenders. They are sophisticated men and women who might turn off a good deal if you make a bad presentation. Detail the assets of the building and location, with all the salient selling points at your command. Emphasize the low cost of the project compared to a new one, and reflect it in your well-documented pro forma statement in terms of lower rents which, in turn, will stabilize the stream of income.

The reputation you have in your community is one of the

ingredients that can make or break your deal. It's an invisible asset that becomes very visible in the eyes of sophisticated decision-makers. This is no time for preaching but, as a practical proposition, entrepreneurs who are active in their communities, who enjoy a good reputation in dealing with others, are more apt to receive favorable consideration than those who are only interested in a "fast buck," and are not careful about the kind of moral trail they leave behind.

I gave a talk about the economic feasibility of rehabilitating old buildings to new uses before a group of mortgage bankers. I stressed the new opportunities for putting their money to work in old buildings. During the lunch hour and discussion workshops, several of the mortgage bankers declared a keen interest in the recycling revolution, providing they got a piece of the action. They weren't satisfied merely with interest income. They wanted equity participation. But they strongly emphasized that they would only consider providing mortgage as well as equity money to someone who had a track record of successful, honorable dealings.

During the discussion sessions, one of the lenders said:

"There's a common belief that the lenders have the money and the developers have the experience. But when the developers get through with us, they wind up with more experience and more money. We want to change that; we want some of their money."

8. GET AN "ANGEL" TO BACK YOU

If none of the seven finance plans explained thus far work, there are still others. One that is used often is finding an "angel" who likes the role of being an inactive silent investor. When you find one, and they are around if you look, offer him the following tempting proposition.

Assuming that you can obtain a 70 percent fluctuating interest rate mortgage (in vogue today) for your $1 million recycling project, you can offer your angel the following persuasive arguments to induce him to invest $300,000 in your project. Give him one-half ownership and 80 percent of the investment tax credit and depreciation allowances. In return, I would ask that the interest on the $300,000 second mortgage, or your angel's investment, be a nominal 7 percent, with no principal payments for, let's say, ten years.

It's a good deal for you, because you're getting one-half equity in a $1 million project without any money—just hard work. Because of the low interest rate on the $300,000, the half of your share of the $50,000 cash flow, less the some $20,000 interest to the investor on his $300,000 at 7 percent, would be $15,000 a year. After your own management fee of $10,000 that will come out of the $50,000 cash flow, you may wind up with a yearly income of about $21,000 for as long as your own it, or half the profit when the project is sold five or ten years later. The angel will get his $21,000 interest on $300,000, along with a $4,000 cash flow and 80 percent of the investment tax credit and depreciation.

It's an excellent deal for your investor because he's probably in a high tax bracket and can use the investment tax credit and depreciation more advantageously than you. The greatest advantage of all, of course, is that upon sale, he gets his $300,000 back, plus one-half of the profit.

If you've picked a good building in a good location, the financial structure I've just outlined is fairly balanced for you both.

There are many angels "flying" around looking for deals like the one I've just described. All you have to do is find out where they are.

A few suggestions on where to look. Get a list of Rotarians in your city and circularize them with an effective letter. Also, it's not too difficult to get a list of people earning over $100,000 a year. They're good prospects; and every city has a group of well-known millionaires. If you don't know any of them, get someone who does to introduce you to one or two. And I'm sure that, if you give the matter some thought, you'll invent your own ways to find the angel who is, as I've indicated, also looking for you.

But, at the risk of being repetitive, let me state that you don't approach anyone until you have detailed plans, beautiful renderings, a documented pro forma, and a well-rehearsed presentation in your mind. The rest will fall in place by virtue of the deal's logic, undergirded by the lucrative government incentives.

9. CHECK INTO CITY, STATE, OR PRIVATE REVENUE BOND FINANCING

If you have a recycling project that the city thinks is worthy, such as a housing complex to revitalize its downtown, or if the State Housing Authority deems your housing project socially beneficial, then either one could fund tax exempt revenue bonds so as to reduce the interest rate for your rehabilitation. But such funding is done selectively by the city or state if the need is urgent, if the preparation by the developer has been thorough, and if his character is spotless.

There are many advantages for revenue bond financing. Because the bonds—either state or city—are tax exempt, the interest rates are lower, perhaps five points below the prevailing conventional interest rates. Also, the amortization of the bond is a lot longer than in conventional financing and the lower interest rate is constant, whereas conventional interest rates fluctuate and could go higher if they are tied to one of the many indices. Also, the percentage loan of the project's appraisal is higher than that of conventional financing. If you're fortunate to have your project qualify for either city or state funding, you're indirectly adding value to your final product because the debt service will be smaller and, hence, your cash flow larger.

If your project does not qualify for revenue bond financing, or if your city or state do not have such funding vehicles, you might try a private bond issue. The company handling such financing usually has a number of salesmen who have many small investors as clients who buy such bonds in small denominations, from $1,000 and up. The interest rates are the conventional prevailing ones, and usually even higher, and there's often a steep commission to the seller, perhaps $100,000 for a $1 million bond issue. It's not the best way to go unless there's a great deal of cushion in your project and all the other routes are closed.

If you do decide to use the private revenue bond route, be sure you pick a reputable one, and get an attorney who specializes in this type of legal work to represent you.

I've never used private revenue bond financing, but I know others who have. It's one of the ways, and it just might happen that in your city or state it could be the only way. I want you to be as persevering as I am in dredging up every conceivable plan to make your recycling dreams come true.

10. USE H.U.D. TITLE 221-D4 WITH A LOWER PERCENTAGE LOAN AND CURRENT CONVENTIONAL INTEREST RATE

This is somewhat complicated, so please follow carefully. The Carter administration had what was known as a Tandem 221-D4 H.U.D. insured mortgage plan at 7½ percent, 40-year amortization. I used it for my "Chalet At The River" financing, and this is how it worked. The developer payed 7½ percent interest and the Government picked up the difference between this low interest rate and the prevailing one, which was several points higher. The Reagan administration eliminated this program because in 1981, the difference in rates was about 8 percent—too large a subsidy for an administration that was elected to slash the budget to the bare bones.

In preparing for this book, I asked the H.U.D. Deputy Director in Wisconsin how a developer might still use Title 221-D4 without the 7½ percent low interest rate. This was his answer: H.U.D. was still insuring loans under Title 221-D4, not at 7½ percent, but instead at the prevailing high interest rate and with a 40-year amortization. This is more advantageous than conventional financing, because private mortgage bankers and savings and loans will commit only for short terms at fluctuating rates.

However, there's a big disadvantage between the original H.U.D. 7½ percent interest plan and the present one. Instead of qualifying for a 90 percent mortgage and taking 10 percent for acting as your own contractor so that the developer's investment on a $1 million project would be nominal, the present H.U.D. plan calls for high current interest rates and a lower percentage insured mortgage. This could reduce their mortgage commitment to as low as 60 percent. Now you would have to have more equity money in the project—$400,000 more. Under the 7½ percent plan, you not only had less investment, but could also afford to offer space at below the market level. But now that the Reagan Administration has eliminated the huge interest differential subsidy, no matter how worthy your project, you have to use your ingenuity to raise the $400,000 equity money. But that should not be difficult because the present administration's new tax law offers as much inducement as the one it has eliminated.

The disadvantages of the new higher interest rates, the lower percentage mortgage, and the many regulations you have read about in Chapter 4 may discourage you from using the updated H.U.D. plan, but it's worth considering because of the 40-year amortization, which is a big plus compared to the prevailing shorter-term loans.

You now have ten finance plans for your recycling project. Choose the one that fits your needs best, and good luck.

Remember, the harder you work, the luckier you get.

This may be an unusual request, but I'd like to have you write me a note if what you've read here has helped get your project off the ground. This does not bring me extra royalties but will give me a good feeling to know that someone, somewhere, is being helped.

6

HOW RECYCLINGS CAN CREATE MILLIONS IN ANNUITIES AND PROFITS

HOW AN ELECTRICIAN TURNED "JUNK" INTO A $150,000-A-YEAR ANNUITY

Someone's problem is another's opportunity—unfortunately. We should not rub our hands with anticipatory glee to take advantage of someone else's plight, but if he or she can't hack it, we can help the person out and make a profit doing it. This is the way of the world—there are "leaners" and lifters."

One of the world's "lifters," an electrician (not so ordinary, as you'll discover when reading his story), was listening to a real estate lecture I was giving about ten years ago, at the University of Wisconsin, on the subject of "How to Get into a Big Real Estate Deal with Little Money." Among other examples, I described how an owner of a run-down, 20-family apartment building with vacant stores was experiencing a $5,000-a-year negative cash flow that was cutting into the income he needed for living expenses. He owed $120,000 on a first mortgage and his rent was $40,000 a year. His fixed expenses and debt service totaled $45,000 a year. This property, I told my audience, could be bought by someone who had a good enough credit to borrow $40,000 from a bank. With that down payment, I said, I could arrange for a buyer to assume the seller's $120,000 first mortgage and have the seller give a second mortgage of $60,000, to be paid off at the rate of $7,000 a year, including interest and principal. The owner wanted $220,000 for his property, and as I told my students, a buyer had to be ready to reach into his pocket until he turned the negative into a positive cash flow.

"But there's an opportunity here," I said, "for a smart, hard-working handyman to upgrade the neglected apartments and stores into profitability, even after assuming the payments on the two mortgages and interest to the bank on the $40,000 loan."

After my talk, the electrician (let's call him Bob), came up to the podium and quizzed me for more details about the "losing" property. Two months later he bought it. None of the other 50 adults in the audience showed any interest or asked any questions. Bob was the only "lifter" in the room.

After one year of hard work in which his wife and son participated, he restored the neglected fifty-year-old building to its original charm. He water-pressure cleaned the exterior to bring back the brick's original cream color, painted out the graffiti in the dimly-lit hallways, replaced the flickering fluorescent tubes with antique incandescent electric fixtures and modernized the old kitchens and antiquated bathrooms at a fraction of what a plumbing contractor would have charged.

After the recycling job was completed, Bob raised the rents and most of the destructive, slow-paying renters moved out. A more responsible group of tenants moved in, and with the rental of the improved commercial space, the yearly income zoomed to $60,000 within two years. Bob was no longer in the red.

Everyone gained in the transaction: (1) the seller, who was on the verge of losing his property because his losses were cutting into his meager capital at the rate of $5,000 a year, was now on the plus side with $7,000 a year; (2) the first mortgagee was more secure because the property was now held in stronger hands; (3) and the new owner did best of all. Within the first year, he was even, and three years later, due to good management and inflation, he was enjoying a cash flow of $15,000 a year, after all fixed expenses and debt service on the two mortgages and interest to the bank on his $40,000 down payment. Now, ten years later, he owns the property free and clear and nets $75,000 a year in profits.

An unbelievable story? That's not the end of it. What followed was even more incredible.

Next door to the store and apartment building was a 60-year-old, 2,500-seat movie theater with eight dilapidated stores, an adjacent vacant two-story, 12,000 square-foot vacant building and a vacant lot a block away that could accommodate a hundred cars. It was owned by a multimillion dollar corporation that was listed on the New York Stock Exchange. One of its executives probably looked at the bottom line of the property's operating statement for several years and saw only "red"—rent at $50,000 a year, and expenses of $60,000. He must have decided to get rid of the junky property because the corporation listed it for sale. The combined heap of neglect would have cost $3 million to reproduce, but what good was it if it was losing money? The theater was too big to use as a modern movie house, its bowling alley in the basement was gathering dust, the adjacent two-story building had been empty for years, four of the eight stores were occupied by derelict tenants, and there was not enough business to utilize the lot a block away.

The wealthy corporation tried to sell the property to a few wheeler-dealers in our city for $750,000, then $500,000, but there were no takers. It was dubbed a "loser" and the "knowledgeable" buyers weren't interested. But Bob, flushed with recycling confidence, was extremely interested. He called me for advice to support his interest, and I said, "Go ahead, buy it. You'll do well with it."

A month later, Bob bought the "nuisance" real estate for $350,000 with $50,000 down and the balance payable in three years. This time Bob didn't have to borrow the $50,000. He had it!

Bob and his family spent a thousand hours gilding the figurines and the ornate plaster in the theater to bring back its original Oriental motif. He leased it to a company that specialized in old-time movies and special events that required room for large audiences. He refurbished the bedraggled eight stores and rented all of them to more responsible tenants. He hired a manager to operate the eight bowling lanes. He leased the first floor of the adjoining 12,000-square-foot vacant building to the leading beauty salon in the city and obtained an office tenant for the second floor. With the added activity of the theater, stores, and bowling alley, the vacant lot became a valuable parking area.

Today, ten years after I gave my lecture on "How to Get into a Big Real Estate Deal with Little Money," the unassuming electrician became an extraordinary recycler—in his spare time. Starting with practically no money of his own, but using unusual savvy and hard work, he now receives a gross rental of $125,000 a year from his 20-unit apartment building and the enlarged, recycled commercial space. And, if that is not dramatic enough, he receives $175,000 a year from the theater complex he now owns free and clear. He's wealthy, far wealthier than any of the top-salaried executives working for the corporation that sold him the "junky" properties, and probably more financially secure than half of the Harvard graduates in the country.

My lecture changed his life in a way that I hope this book will change yours. Bob's story illustrates the important point that recycling is for the small and intermediate entrepreneur, rather than the big corporations who are too far removed from the personal attention that rehabilitation requires. Bob saw and did what the sophisticated executives didn't see and couldn't do.

Just imagine: Bob now enjoys a net income of over $150,000 a year! It's an astounding success story of an "ordinary" electrician becoming an extraordinary recycler.

HOW AN ASTUTE RECYCLER EARNED $5,000,000 WITH COSMETIC CHANGES AND INNOVATIVE SELLING

Bankers are known for financing big buildings to project big images. Our largest bank in the state was no exception. It discarded a beautiful 50-year-old, ten-story, 350,000-square-foot building and replaced it with a $75 million, forty-two-story skyscraper a few blocks away.

The executives of the bank tried to lease the space they left behind and couldn't. They tried to sell the building for $10 million and couldn't—not with more than half the space vacant and the building losing money. It had been sliding down hill economically and physically for several years until an astute recycler saw the possibility of remodeling the custom-built bank space into smaller office units. He bought it for $6 million with a nominal down payment. Just as astute bankers know how to make money with money, so intelligent recyclers know how to make money out of old buildings.

The recycler carefully examined the custom-built vacant bank space and put on a blitzkrieg campaign for small users who were impressed with the plush accessories the bank left behind. Combining smart rehabilitation with innovative selling, the new owner leased the half-vacant space within 18 months. He increased the rent from about $1 million a year to close to $2.5 million and the value of the building zoomed up to $11 million.

I appeared on a television panel with the recycler of the old bank building where we discussed ways and means of rejuvenating American downtowns. He's a master at it—a gentle, soft-spoken man who sees opportunities that are not obvious to others. In one swift, astute move, he made more money than the bank's entire upper echelon makes in five years. Marshall Field of Chicago was once reputed to have said, "There's no faster way to make money than in real estate." To that, I'd like to add that there's also no faster way to lose it if you don't know what you're doing.

The cosmetic recycling of the old bank building illustrates one of the most important real estate axioms: matching the right tenant with the right space is the fastest way of adding value to a property. For instance, if you raise the occupancy of a building from 80 to 90 percent, and if we assume that the additional rent is $150,000 a year, you've increased the value of the building by $1 million, based on today's expected 15 percent return on invested capital. This assumption is based on obtaining firm leases from substantial tenants.

The recycler of the bank building knew that he didn't have to spend a lot of money to convert the plush bank space to other office users. This was an important key to the recycling process. Remodeling 200,000 square feet of vacant space could cost $4 million and then the deal would not only have been marginal, but it also could have bankrupted an inexperienced recycler. An experienced rehabilitator capitalized on the deluxe space the bank left behind, and did it for less than $1 million. He analyzed its potential and knew what to do with it.

Don't be awed by big corporations; they often present the best opportunities. This is an age of specialization. You may not know what they know, but in recycling, you should know what they *don't* know. That's when opportunities knock the loudest.

HOW A RECYCLING PROJECT THAT COULD HAVE EARNED $750,000 SLIPPED THROUGH MY FINGERS

Rehabilitation has the mystique of uncertainty, and dealing with uncertainties is not for everyone. Some, like myself, are mesmerized by them, while others freeze and avoid their elusive entanglements.

I know a $150,000-a-year executive who has one of the best-informed real estate minds in America, who made millions for others and could have made millions for himself, but he shied away from uncertainties.

"I don't like to take risks," the national expert told me, "it unnerves me. I'd rather advise others and let them make the big money rather than spend sleepless nights worrying about the outcome of a project."

Of course, he could afford to avoid risks because he was smart enough to make big money without taking them.

We need counselors like him, the true professionals in the real estate industry, to advise the restless entrepreneurs who thrive on uncertainty.

I have a good reason for this lengthy philosophical prologue. I once lost $750,000 because, in one of my indecisive moments, I fell prey to the syndrome of too much analyzing. I got what is known as, "The paralysis of analysis."

Let me explain. In late 1980, about a half year before the new favorable tax law relating to rehabilitation came into effect, Milwaukee's most interesting, oldest, and largest of the Gay Nineties office buildings came on the market. Toward the beginning of the 20th century, it housed the world's largest German newspaper. From this stately brick and terra cotta edifice, the owner of the building ran his far-flung publishing empire.

But that was almost a hundred years ago. When I looked at it in 1980, its former elegance of arched windows, colonnaded entrance and copper domes were buried under the grime of insensitive neglect. The interior matched the exterior in squalor. Its dimly lit corridors were a mishmash of imitation wood, drab Sheetrock, and age-stained original marble. Beyond the corridor doors, the offices reflected feeble attempts at makeshift remodeling. The tenants were content to live in slovenliness because of the low rent. The old beauty barely peeked through the years of neglect; an architectural jewel turned into a sow's ear.

Adjacent to the former stately building, which jutted out on a triangular lot with the tip facing a small park, were four smaller buildings equally dilapidated, occupying about 20,000 square feet of land and belonging to the same owner. The centerpiece, the former German newspaper building, had eight stories with approximately 10,000 square feet per floor. The total rent from all the buildings was $300,000 a year and the expenses were about the same.

I studied the buildings for weeks—they fascinated me. They presented a puzzle within an enigma. What compounded my confusion was that I was used to paying $2 to $4 per square foot for old buildings, but this owner stubbornly stuck to a $1 million price for approximately 125,000 square feet covering all buildings. I made what I thought was a stretch offer of $600,000 with a $150,000 cash down payment. It was summarily refused. I upped it to $750,000 based on the following reasoning: My game plan was to sell the four adjacent small buildings for about $400,000, leaving the prime, 80,000-square-foot building at a cost I could live with—$350,000, or about $4 per square foot.

The gross rent of the key building was $200,000 a year, at 80 percent occupancy, with expenses of about $180,000. My plan was to spend about $750,000 for the following improvements: sandblast the exterior brick and terra cotta; restore the lobby to its original, ornately plastered ceiling; remove the dusty suspended ceiling tiles in the corridors; adorn the 12-foot-high coffered ceilings with antique incandescent fixtures; replace the hissing, one-pipe original hot water heating system with a two-pipe plant; replace the myriad unsightly window units with zoned central air conditioning; modernize the antiquated washrooms; and modernize most of the interior offices. I would then set up a new rental schedule of $7 a square foot.

I calculated that, based on 65,000 square feet of net rentable area at $7 a square foot, I would gross about $455,000 a year which, at 93 percent occupancy, would net close to $425,000. I projected the operating expenses at $220,000 a year, therefore the income before any debt service would be slightly over $200,000. A building with that net, uniquely restored and with utilities modernized, would have a value of $1.8 million.

But on with the story! While my $750,000 offer was sitting on the seller's desk and my mind was exploring the various recycling options and financial plans, a $900,000 offer came in and the seller accepted it.

Did I spend several weeks of intensive thinking for naught? I don't think so. Of course, I was disappointed, but I learned a lot as I mentally took the deal through its paces. I also learned something new from the man who bought the buildings.

Because I'm a preserver, I limited my thinking to reselling the four ancillary "baby" buildings to rehabilitators who would restore them and reinforce what I had in mind for the "princess" of the block. But the buyer had a better idea—commercially, that is. Adjacent to the four small buildings were the central administrative offices of the second largest savings and loan association in the state. Next to this office building was a 700-stall public parking garage that they used for their personnel and customers. My competitor, however, convinced the savings and loan executives that they ought to have a private parking lot, and sold them the four buildings for $550,000.

My disappointment was now double-edged: first that I didn't get the deal, and second, that four interesting buildings were soon to feel the crushing blows of the wrecking ball. This is not to blame the buyer—he has a right to get the most profit out of the deal—but I also have a right to be disappointed. I dislike seeing old buildings die, especially when they can be brought back to life. However, the buyer did begin to restore the original beauty of the key building. He sandblasted the exterior, removed the dusty tile from the lobby's eight-foot ceiling and opened it up to its 15-foot height, where the original ornamental plaster was restored to its former elegance. Then, for some reason, he stopped his restorative work.

I can only guess, but my hunch is that, with the new tax law which would qualify the building for a 25 percent investment tax credit because of its landmark possibilities, the owner is taking a longer look at his profit potential. He can syndicate it now for more money than before the new law went into effect. If he plays his financial cards right, as he appears to know how to do, he may wind up with a $1 million profit. And the "princess" that slept through decades of neglect will be awakened by the kiss of a recycling "prince."

HOW CONVERTING AN OLD, 40-UNIT APARTMENT TO AN 18-FAMILY EARNED $100,000—A PERCEPTIVE ANALYSIS OF THE NEIGHBORHOOD DID IT

Several years after World War II, when I was just getting started in the real estate business, there was a great demand for small apartments because returning G.I.'s were getting married and needed inexpensive nests to begin their lives anew. I had an idea of how to meet that demand: I bought an old but magnificent seven-family apartment building for $35,000 and divided it, believe it or not, into forty small apartments, each having a kitchen and bathroom. I was able to get that many units because each apartment consisted of nine huge rooms. At the turn of the century, the area had been about a mile from the central city, and the building had attracted the wealthy folks who didn't want the responsibility of owning a home, and who chose to live in a luxury apartment, just like so many people do today.

When I bought the building in 1947, the neighborhood had changed and so had its occupants. The building was now occupied by large families, or several single people who pooled their assets in order to afford the low rent. The distinctive marks of its former luxury were marred by dirty windows, weeds where flowers used to grow, and trash on the steps that led to a slovenly entrance.

The location was now ripe for small apartments for young married people. When I finished remodeling, I did something that helped me and the returning G.I.'s. I advertised that I would rent only to G.I.'s and give preference to those with a baby, or who had one on the way. The rental market was tight then, and many building owners refused to rent to couples with small children.

Well, grateful returning soldiers swarmed to the building with their brides and babies, and each apartment was filled within days after its completion. It was a small token of showing my gratefulness for their service to our country.

Ten years later, I traded the property for a free-and-clear lot worth $200,000, upon which I built a new $3.5 million office building.

This lengthy introduction dramatizes what another innovative young man did in 1979—in reverse: recycling small apartments into large ones, and earning $100,000 in six months.

Jim bought a century-old, run-down 40-unit apartment building for $165,000. The rent was only $13,000 a year, from occupants who were as derelict as the building: people who had lost their way in drugs and alcohol, some of them squatters who led directionless lives.

For years, the building, its tenants, and the neighborhood were in shambles. But the neighborhood had changed as a result of responsible people who organized to upgrade their community. And it worked. But, before Jim, the owner of the building had let the change pass him by. His building and its tenants remained in utter neglect, and finally he lost the building in foreclosure. Jim perceived the change in the neighborhood, saw an opportunity, and cashed in on it.

He assumed the lender's $165,000 of foreclosed debts and developed a pro forma statement, based on spending $135,000 to change the converted 40 units back to the 18 larger original apartments. These had contained a living room, dining room, sitting room, kitchen, large pantry, and three bedrooms. His rent projections were $275 to $300 a month per apartment, plus rentals from several stores on the first floor, for a total of $65,000 a year. Based on his carefully-prepared operating statement, Jim got a $290,000 mortgage commitment, which was almost enough to pay up the $165,000 of debts against the property and the estimated cost of "decycling" the slovenly 40 units back into the original apartments.

Jim's first move was to clear the building of all tenants. Within a month it was empty, and workmen began building new walls where the old, plastered ones were beyond repair; restoring original moldings and cornices; getting the tile-trimmed fireplaces to work; modernizing the bathrooms and kitchens; and repainting every square foot of the building's interior. In addition, the exterior was sandblasted to its original cream-city brick.

The large, spanking new old apartments attracted teachers, graduate students, and young working couples with children. They must have liked what Jim did, because all the apartments were leased within a few months. With a $65,000-a-year rental, and a cash flow of $20,000 a year after debt service and all fixed expenses, Jim had a choice of keeping or selling the building for $400,000. With practically no money of his own in the project, but a lot of innovative perception and hard work, this was not a bad choice. He sold it for $400,000 and earned $100,000 in six months.

HOW AN ABANDONED FUNERAL HOME CONVERTED INTO A REHABILITATION CENTER EARNED THE OWNER AN ANNUITY OF $40,000

There's no limit to recycling ideas. Jim, the same young man who converted the 40 units to 18 apartments, pulled off a recycling coup ten years ago in which the rewards for imagination went beyond the believable. But it happened, and it can happen to you.

Jim got wind of a state agency's need for a men's rehabilitation center that required a good building in a poor neighborhood, where the neighbors would not offer too much resistance to such a facility. It was not an easy requirement to fill, but while others curiously looked around, Jim searched the city for weeks to find the rare combination that would satisfy the state, the city code, and the neighborhood, and have the functional facilities needed for the inmates. His long and arduous hunt paid off.

He found a large, abandoned funeral home in a seedy location and presented a comprehensive, remodeled layout for 40 inmates, complete with adequate public washrooms, cooking facilities, and an apartment for the caretaker. It also had a good-sized yard—an important requirement.

Jim had no problem buying the sturdily-built, two-story brick building for $15,000. It was in foreclosure and the mortgagee pounced at the offer—he had a loser on his hands and didn't know what to do with it. Over the ten-year period, Jim spent about $200,000 in three stages of upgrading the facility, during which time he collected an average $5,000 a month, or $60,000 a year in rent. His annuity was about $40,000 a year, after subtracting his $200,000 expenditures from the $600,000 he received during the ten-year period.

It sounds like an unbelievably high annual return, and it is if you compare Jim's work of a few months with what a nationally-known history, economics, or sociology professor gets for teaching and writing for an entire year.

In a way it's not fair, but in a capitalistic society, ingenuity often pays off way beyond the work involved. It's what sparks progress. It's especially true in recycling, where few know its secrets and still fewer have the courage and the imagination to succeed.

While the state was saving money compared to what it had been paying to house these inmates in their previous, more expensive quarters, Jim was making it. That's what imaginative recycling does for users and owners.

A TALE OF TWO HOTEL REHABILITATIONS THAT MADE MILLIONS FOR THE OWNER AND REVITALIZED MILWAUKEE'S DOWNTOWN

This is a story of a small-town boy who decided to do big things in a big city. He's a very good friend of mine, so what follows is laced with intimate observations based on shared personal reflections. It's a story of unusual ingenuity, rare courage, and unbelievable success—success beyond my friend's wildest dreams.

Milwaukee has been famous for its beer but not for its hotels. Now it's famous for both, because 18 years ago, an innovative young man from the small town of Appleton, Wisconsin, moved to Milwaukee to flex his commercial muscles. He heard that an old, prestigious family hotel, the Pfister, was for sale. I heard it too, but he listened (and I didn't), and he bought it.

At the beginning of the century, it was Milwaukee's only prestige hotel. Only the traveling elite could afford its luxuries and high rents. The Pfister was to Milwaukee what the Waldorf Astoria was to New York. But after the 1929 Crash, the owners lost it and it kept sliding into neglect as speculator after speculator bought it, milked it, and hung it on the next buyer, who again wrung from it what he could, without putting anything into it. My friend Ben had a different idea. He was going to put a lot into it because he figured he could get a lot out of it. His idea was no less than to make it one of the most prestigious hotels in America.

He bought the 200-room derelict building, most of which was used as a rooming house, along with an adjoining vacant lot, for $900,000 with $100,000 down and the balance on a land contract. That was a good start. The price was right and the location superb: on the main downtown street, three blocks from Lake Michigan.

Ben was not only astute but also a man of vision—a rare combination. The small-town boy from Appleton quickly learned that Milwaukee was a one-hotel city, dominated by the 1,000 room Schroeder Hostelry—owned and operated by an elderly, wealthy bachelor who was more interested in giving away his money to charitable causes than in operating his hotel. That important fact was the key to Ben's planning.

"George," he told me one day, "the Pfister was the Number One hotel 40 years ago, and I intend to make it Number One again." This was no idle boast. He meant it.

"It's David against Goliath—you against the Schroeder," I said with a smile. "You'd better have a faultless slingshot and an accurate aim. The Schroeder has been the only hotel in the city since the Pfister went 'kaput,' and you know its owner is one of the richest men in town."

"I know, and that's why I see a big opening." He saw something I didn't.

Here was no ordinary man, and he went about his task with extraordinary skill. His aim, he told me, was not only to restore the Pfister's 200 rooms to their original splendor, but also make them more spacious by reducing them to 150, adding an adjoining 200 new rooms, designed to meld with the old, rather than have the old conform to the new. He hired a brilliant local architect and an equally brilliant interior decorator from Los Angeles. He instructed them to concentrate on restoring the hotel's nostalgia in architecture, decor, fixtures, and furnishings, to bring back the aura of past prosperity. Ben also planned a 450-stall parking garage on the adjoining vacant land that leads into the hotel.

I would have considered his plans visionary had it not been for his exuding confidence. It made him and his plans believable. He was not a wealthy man then, so I asked the next logical question.

"How are you going to finance it all?"

"I'm going to get a $5 million first mortgage, and syndicate another million in equity money among five of my friends. Want a piece of it?"

"I'll pass," I said, and let several million dollars pass me by.

What follows is the amazing story of how Ben revolutionized the hotel industry in our city. He did everything he set out to do, and more. The Pfister became not only the Number One hotel in Milwaukee; it was also selected by the industry as one of the ten most prestigious hotels in America.

The $6 million that went into the Pfister is now worth about $25 million. It should give you some idea of what I missed when I foolishly refused a piece of the investment.

This recycling phenomenon was only the beginning of Ben's genius. As the Pfister's fortunes waxed, the Schroeder's waned. It was losing money and avalanching into a third-rate hotel until it was stopped by Jim, another friend of mine, who bought it in 1970 for the unbelievably low price of $4 million. But it was not low enough, because Jim was not a Ben. He was an astute multimillionaire who had built tens of thousands of homes, yet he didn't have Ben's hotel touch. He spent $500,000 cleaning up the ragged edges to make the Schroeder more competitive, but to no avail. The Pfister remained *the* hotel in our city.

Jim was too smart to continue losing money at the rate of $500,000 a month. He persuaded an international hotel chain to buy the Schroeder, and in all probability said to them, "Look, I'm not a hotel operator. You are," and offered them $500,000 in cash if they would buy it and assume the Schroeder's $4 million mortgage. That must have been too tempting to refuse. They bought it, spent Jim's $500,000 with another cosmetic fix and promptly began to lose more money than Jim did. The Pfister was still the number one hotel in town, and even the international hotel chain could not buck it. The international Goliath was no match for the local David.

Then a startling thing happened. The international chain owners approached Ben to buy the Schroeder.

Ben's x-ray business vision quickly penetrated the unusual situation and he reacted in a most unusual way. Yes, he would buy their money-losing hotel, provided they payed him $1.5 million in cash to assume the nearly $4 million mortgage. They blanched, and paid it. It was better than losing close to a million dollars a year.

Now Ben's recycling mind went to work once again. He saw what the previous three owners didn't—that the 1,000 small, antiquated rooms were no longer adequate for modern demands. He did what came naturally to him: he followed a successful precedent—in this case, the Pfister. Modern, spacious rooms and ample adjoining parking were the answer.

What a fantastic job he did! Bristling with success and with $1.5 million in his pocket, he arranged for a $9 million loan and another million in equity money to gut the entire interior and enlarge the 1,000 undersized rooms of a former era into 525 fashionable, king-sized rooms to attract conventioneers. He made no attempt to concentrate on nostalgia as he had in the Pfister, but instead emphasized the existing public areas that were not arranged up to their maximum potential use. Ben also did the obvious, which was not so obvious to his predecessors. He built a 500-stall parking structure that was connected to the hotel—a necessity that others had failed to provide.

Ben, the recycler, is now the hotel king of our city; still doing superbly at the Pfister and almost as well at the Schroeder, in spite of a new 485-room Hyatt Regency Hotel that opened in 1980, only two blocks away from the Schroeder, which is now renamed the Marc Plaza.

I want to put the startling economics of recycling in sharp focus. Granted that construction costs have risen since Ben recycled his hotels, when you compare the $15 million cost of rehabilitating the some 900 rooms of the two hotels with the $28 million cost of the 485-room Hyatt Regency, the contrast is dramatically in Ben's favor. Room for room, public area for public area, restaurant for restaurant, there's not much difference between the recycled hotels and the new one. The big difference is the debt service on the $25 million for the new 485 rooms, and the debt service of about $10 million on the recycled Pfister and Marc Plaza. And there's another big difference. Ben has 900 stalls of adjoining undercover parking, and the Hyatt has none.

If you had a choice, where would you invest your money: in the recycled hotels or in the new one? I know your answer. So would I.

Today, Ben Marcus is still Milwaukee's hotel generalissimo.

RECYCLING EXISTING HOTELS IS SPREADING IN AMERICA AND EUROPE

The recycling of existing hotels, or buildings originally designed for other uses into hotels, unquestionably makes good economic sense. It particularly appeals to those who want to create "period" atmosphere anew. Not only independent operators, but large hotel chains as well, are making a play for the highly specialized market, catering to the fashionable and affluent by means of elegantly recycled period buildings.

Holiday Inn, for instance, is converting a group of houses in Bruges, Belgium, into a hotel. Hyatt Regency has incorporated an 18th Century house into its hotel in Charleston, South Carolina. The Sonesta Hotel in Amsterdam is using a 17th Century church as its conference center. (Sonesta Hotels occupy many recycled buildings.)

Hilton International has recently announced the conversion and extension of a monastery and church tower that date from the Middle Ages, into a new hotel in Budapest, Hungary. Howard Johnson has converted a group of warehouses into a hotel facing a major canal in Amsterdam. San Francisco's Stanford Court Hotel has been completely recycled and refurnished. El Convento, in San Juan, Puerto Rico, is another fascinating conversion.

Recycling has become a tested route to "new" hotels. It's a part of the recycling revolution.

So if you're thinking of getting into the hotel business, do what Ben and others are doing—recycle. Don't sleep on the idea, put it to work. It makes a lot of sense and millions of dollars too!

7

CASE STUDIES OF OUTSTANDING RECYCLING PROJECTS IN THE COUNTRY— LARGE AND SMALL

There are hundreds of recycling projects in the country that you can use as guidelines for your own particular project. Ideally, you should visit a few of them to get a visual feel of what others have done. But if time, money, or other reasons prevent you from doing it, you should be able to glean many ideas from the following descriptions of some of the most unusual rehabilitations that run the gamut from an old mill in a small town to Ghirardelli Square in San Francisco. We might as well start with the most famous one—Ghirardelli Square.

GHIRARDELLI SQUARE

Ghirardelli Square, San Francisco's most famous rehabilitation project, is a collection of the early 20th Century buildings of a former chocolate factory. They are located on one block at the waterfront overlooking the Golden Gate, and were generally unnoticed except for the aroma that came from the manufacture of chocolate and candy bars. When the company moved to a new plant in another city, the property was bought by a San Francisco businessman, William M. Roth, with the intent of preserving the old buildings.

He had set the pace and style for the recycling revolution. Ghirardelli's special charm is the subtle mixture of buildings, outdoor spaces, art objects, colorful wares and people. It is above all, a place for a great variety of activity: shopping, eating, strolling, sitting in the sun, or just enjoying the passing scene and the view of San Francisco Bay. My wife and I spent hours walking through its maze of shops, restaurants, and theaters.

The site slopes steeply toward the Bay and Victorian Park, a broad expanse of lawn making possible a parking garage underneath the buildings—a necessity for such a huge tourist attraction.

The buildings enclose two large plazas and many small, intimate open spaces, such as decks, terraces, balconies, and wide landings on stairways. These serve in various ways. Some become part of outdoor restaurants, while others are transition points between levels of the complex. The simple landscaping is used to differentiate levels and spaces as much as to enhance the visual environment, and color is introduced with flower-filled planters.

A festive holiday air pervades Ghirardelli Square, especially in its open spaces. The terraces and landscaped places are scaled in such a way to create a sense of intimacy that quite belies the actual presence of so many people.

Some of the restaurants open directly from plazas, while others are located off landings of broad steps leading into the plaza from the street; the upper-floor restaurants in the taller buildings overflow onto balconies that give superb views of the Bay. Exteriors of the old buildings were cleaned and repaired where necessary, but otherwise, were left unchanged. Interiors were replanned to accommodate dozens of small shops—too many shops.

My personal reaction to Ghirardelli Square is that it's too big, has too many shops and too many people. Those who like big crowds, huge shopping centers, and giant food stores will find excitement in Ghirardelli Square. It's massive, even though the owner has done a magnificent job of creating small, intimate areas that interestingly connect one with the other. It's successful. It's famous. It's big.

Perhaps my personal opinion stems from having been fatigued and surfeited by seeing too much in too short a time. But that's only my reaction. The hundreds of thousands who flock to it every year obviously have different views.

THE CANNERY

A few blocks from Ghirardelli Square in San Francisco is The Cannery, a recycled project on a scale much more to my liking. The Cannery is a complex of shops and restaurants in an old, three-story loft building, originally used as the Del Monte Food Cannery. A survivor of the 1906 earthquake, the building today survives only in its exterior walls. Everything else is new, designed for its new function as a shopping center. What has resulted is a collection of small shops and a variety of restaurants of different sizes, connected by an interesting system of walks, corridors, steps, escalators, balcony decks, and a glass-walled, outside elevator.

The scale is neither grand nor intimate, but something in between. It's right for a public place but, at the same time, conducive for leisurely browsing. The architects chose to work with the same exterior material—brick—to detail the interior partitions.

The Cannery's location is definitely urban, although not in the central business district. It is, however, near many tourist attractions: Fisherman's Wharf, Victorian Park, and the terminus of a cable car line and Ghirardelli Square, all of which are equally popular with San Franciscans and tourists. It is also near a number of new apartment buildings and various offices, small businesses, and many restaurants. Location alone thus assures a steady stream of people to the Cannery.

The Cannery's architecture was more clearly visible just after completion of its restoration, I was told, than it is now that shrubs and trees have matured. With this lush vegetation, however, has come an environment of almost Mediterranean character, particularly in the open spaces on the ground level. The brick detail adopted from the original cannery walls gives the inside and outside of the building a stark and austere look—a strong element of simple elegance.

Somehow I felt more at ease browsing through The Cannery shops than at Ghirardelli Square. I guess I'm the type who finds more interest in one beautiful painting on a wall than in the same wall cluttered with many pictures. A Japanese artist once pointed out to me the aesthetic wisdom of such an attitude, and now I believe in it more than ever.

PIONEER SQUARE

Pioneer Square in Seattle, Washington, is one of America's best examples of the partnership between private enterprise and public responsibility in rejuvenating a large, worn-out area of a city—about 52 acres—into a beautiful, landscaped, cobblestoned promenade. My wife and I had walked its car-free, tree-lined streets and admired the nostalgic treasure of 1890 vintage buildings, each with its architectural uniqueness vying for attention, showing off its restored splendor. We were in a dream world of a hundred years ago.

Pioneer Square is Seattle's most historic area. It's the place from which the modern city of Seattle developed. In 1970, the city established the Pioneer Square Historic District, and a board to oversee its conservation.

The city invested about $2 million vacating streets, paving some of them in red brick, installing new lighting, developing a landscaped, parklike environment consisting of colorful benches, shrubbery, and trees—in short, recreating the Old World atmosphere of a century ago. This spurred entrepreneurs to buy the old buildings in the district and recycle them to economic feasibility. The benefits to the city and investors were far-reaching beyond their expectations. It's an example of an enlightened citizenry, recognizing its own heritage, and an equally enlightened public response to preserve and conserve. It's a shiny example of the restoration of an entire neighborhood that other cities should study and emulate.

Three buildings led the rejuvenation parade, with many smaller buildings following in their footsteps. The Pioneer Building, one of Seattle's most significant buildings architecturally and historically, dates from the period immediately after the 1889 fire, which completely destroyed the city's first business center. For several decades after its completion in 1892, the six-story red brick Pioneer was the city's most desirable office address. It lost its prominence, however, as did other buildings in the Pioneer Square District, when business moved to cheaper land and larger sites to the north. And, like the other buildings in the abandoned financial center, it began to deteriorate. It lost most of its tenants, and for many years was a shelter for derelicts.

But because of the city's foresight in creating the Pioneer Square Historic District ten years ago, a group of investors bought the building, rehabilitated it for office use, and restored its prestige as a business address. The exterior was sandblasted, the decorative terra cotta detail was cleaned and repaired, and the structure was strengthened where necessary. Inside, the sky-lighted courts were fully restored, giving the building its former distinction. The handsome stairway, with its fine wood bannister connecting all floors, had been restored to its early elegance.

The Maynard Building, one block south of the Pioneer Building, was completed in the same year—1892—and it too figured in the city's history, serving as the financial center during the Alaska gold rush of 1897-98, and on its upper floors, provided handsome offices for the city's professional firms. But the Maynard, too, fell into decay. In the various uses to which it had been put, it suffered considerable mutilation of its fine oak paneling and other interior detailing. Finally it succumbed, and for 30 years its only occupants were pigeons.

Two courageous developers bought it, repaired the spalled stone exterior, replaced damaged ornamentation, and brought the building back to its original appearance. The architects painstakingly pieced together parts and details to achieve a sensitive restoration of the original public areas. A new elevator cab that retained the "gold cage" look was designed to fit into the original shaft, and the carved oak banister of the stairway that wraps around the shaft was restored.

The Grand Central Hotel building was a lively landmark in the days of the Alaska gold rush, but, when that was over, it too lost its patronage and gradually decayed physically. Again, because it was a collective effort of the community, two developers purchased and restored the old building, rechristening it "The Grand Central On The Park," and returned it to its original use as an office building. Except for cleaning the exterior and changing the store windows at street level to give consistant scale to the streets facades, little needed to be done on the outside of the building. Major alteration at street level was the creation of an arcade concourse connecting with the new, city-financed Occidental Park, which is a prime attraction for visitors to the area. A restaurant with a glass-enclosed pavilion projects into the park, and stairways complete the alterations, one leading down to the basement shops and cafés, and the other leading to a mezzanine bakery. The upper floors of the building have been converted to office use.

My wife and I visited many of the shops and restaurants in Pioneer Square, especially those below ground level where some of the saloons were restored to the way they were before the great fire of 1889. Waiters in aprons and waitresses in hooped skirts act out their 19th-Century roles against a backdrop of the primitively rugged Gold Rush days.

I have detailed Pioneer Square in the hope that other cities using it as a guideline will concentrate on rehabilitation, rather than putting their money into skyscrapers and letting the old buildings die. This philosophy is not only built on dreamy nostalgia, but on hard, sound, economic feasibility. It pays to preserve—for profit and for people.

MANPOWER INTERNATIONAL INC. TURNS A WAREHOUSE BUILDING INTO MODERN OFFICES

Elmer Winter, former president of Manpower International Inc., whose headquarters are in Milwaukee, is no ordinary man, so it is not surprising that he solved his 65,000-square-foot office space needs in an extraordinary manner. When you can create prize-winning art, as he did, out of chrome from wrecked automobile bumpers, then turning a 20-foot-high, steel-girded, one-floor warehouse into unorthodox office space should be a simple task.

What should arrest our attention, however, is that his unorthodox methods not only saved his firm a lot of money, but also produced a new form of office space that is practical, aesthetic, and should serve as a model for others to imitate.

The cost of an open-area warehouse is about one-fourth the cost of a modern, multi-storied office building. What Elmer did, after buying the warehouse, was to spotlight the steel girders of the 20-foot-high ceiling with powerful light fixtures to produce diffused, 50-candle-power lights to shine down on a veritable forest of 6-foot-high, moveable, multicolored partitions, arranged in various-sized offices. The aisles between the offices are like outdoor streets, with the various departments fanning off from the wide walkways. The traffic pattern is such that people from one department can get to the another much faster than by waiting for elevators to get from one floor to another.

Elmer told me that the company had changed office layouts and department configuration dozens of times, in a matter of hours, at little cost. The same changes in standard partitioned offices would take months and cost plenty. It's an unusually practical and cost-cutting benefit.

In addition to the structural economy and manpower time saved from having the entire work force on one floor, is the health benefit. A 20-foot-high ceiling is like working outdoors. There is more oxygen per person than in offices with standard, 8-foot ceilings.

Soothing color is important for the eye and the psyche. As I walked through the Manpower corridors, the white blending with the subtle pastel colors gave me a feeling of being out in the open rather than inside an office building. There was a quiet industriousness that somehow was not only different, but also much more pleasant than what's found in the enclosed cubicles of the typical office building.

This is not an example of creating nostalgia. The warehouse building was practically new. It's an example of a bold approach to solving the high cost of massive office space needs. If you can combine economy, aesthetics, health, and efficiency by doing the unusual, it merits attention and exploration. It's proof that recycling is a many-faceted idea. Its adaptations are endless.

A BLOCK OF CONNECTED OLD BUILDINGS IN CALGARY, CANADA, BECOMES A BEAUTIFUL, THREE-STORY MALL OF SHOPS AND OFFICES

There are no limits to the use of imagination in recycling old structures to new uses. I found one of the most unusual adaptations on a visit to Calgary, Alberta, Canada, where an entire block of buildings of various heights, with different colors and different architectural exteriors, are all joined together by an interior, three-story mall of shops and offices. To cut down on costs, only the basement, first, and second floors were used. The upper floors were either vacant or used for storage and second-rate office space.

The focal point of the recycling was the three-tiered mall that was 300 feet long, with all types of stores fanning off on either side of a pedestrian walkway. The signs and entrances of the shops were as varied as the merchandise, which included clothing, plants, candies, herbs, health foods, yarns, cheeses, tobaccos, glassware, jewelry, interspersed with services such as an advertising agency, a small printing shop, and an employment office. The service-oriented businesses were in the lower level, the retail shops were on the second and first floors. The highest rent, first-floor shops had entrances off the street as well as from the mall.

The old-look exterior was in sharp contrast to the modernistic interior, where the recycling money was spent. The shops were expensively fixtured, and as my wife and I browsed through them, we noticed that the customers seemed to match the prosperous image of the storekeepers.

The main point of this recycling story is that, if the location is good, as in Calgary's case, old floundering buildings losing money for their owners can begin making money for a new, imaginative owner. Of course, it's not easy to assemble a series of buildings—one unreasonable owner can block the project. But where recalcitrance can be transcended by cooperation, building a new mall in old buildings in a good location can prove to be a bonanza for someone with guts, imagination, and persuasiveness.

SPLITTING AN OLD THEATER CREATES A $75,000-A-YEAR INCOME

The old cliché that we should change with the times makes sense only on a selective basis. Some things, like conservation to insure a renewable world, ought never to change. But preference for small movie theaters over huge, cavernous ones seems to be a sign of the changing times, and perceptive recyclers are taking advantage of it and making money.

Steve was one of them. Sheboygan, Wisconsin, a town of 50,000, had one of those large, 1920-vintage movie houses that was no longer adequate for the 1980s. It was losing money, and the owner was glad to get rid of it for a pittance. Even though the new outdoor movie theater was drawing business away from the old downtown movie house on Sheboygan's main street, Steve saw commercial possibilities in recycling the big theater into a twin—two small theaters.

His commercial instincts proved correct. He bought the "klunker" for less than $50,000. He removed the old fashioned balconies, divided the area in half and, after spending $150,000 for the latest equipment and decor, carved out two modern, 300-seat theaters out of the old, ungainly movie house.

The result was an instantaneous success. Apparently a small, intimate theater, and having the choice of seeing one of two movies at one location, promotes attendance. Steve told me that he's earning $75,000 a year from his twins. Not a bad return from a $200,000 investment. What's more, it's given a boost to Sheboygan's downtown.

Steve took a big gamble; or did he? His risk was reduced by his being aware of a changing trend, that people prefer small modern theaters to big old ones—something the previous owner either didn't know, or didn't have the recycling imagination to try.

When I visited Palm Springs, California, in 1980, I was puzzled by seeing a quartet—four small theaters in one building. It didn't make sense to me, until Steve explained that multitheater complexes are revolutionizing the movie industry. Steve knew when to change with the times.

DERELICT CHICAGO BUILDINGS RECYCLED INTO APARTMENTS AND CONDOMINIUMS

For a change of pace, I'd like to switch from Sheboygan to Chicago: from a small town to a big city. Here are some examples of what's happening in the Windy City, where the recycling revolution is reaching hurricane proportions:

One of Chicago's oldest and biggest ice boxes is becoming one of the city's newest residential addresses. Before the construction crews could begin transforming the 16-story North American Cold Storage Building, a refrigerated warehouse, they had to wait more than four months for it to thaw out. There was concern that, after having been frozen for more than 70 years, the whole thing might just disintegrate when the ice melted. It didn't. Once it thawed, workmen had to punch 500 window openings in the solid red brick facade and peel off layers of interior insulation, including the original horsehair wall covering.

The 73-year-old Fulton House, as it is now called, has been divided into 112 luxury apartments. It's located on the north edge of the Loop business district, and will join a group of other major recycled Chicago buildings, next to the massive Merchandise Mart. The Fulton House looks like a giant outdoor antique, and it will lure unusual tenants who are attracted by uniqueness. Its rare facade may even command higher rents than a new apartment building.

Sears, Roebuck and Company's original Chicago mail-order warehouse, a turn-of-the-century building not far from the cold storage building, is being converted into 80 loft apartments.

A bookbindery and the plant where the Chicago racing form was printed are also being redesigned as loft apartments.

The former American Furniture Mart, a massive block-square building on the shore of Lake Michigan, which, until about 18 months ago, served as a national showroom for some of the top lines of furniture, will be converted into rental units and condominiums. With more than two million square feet of space, it is believed to be the biggest single conversion to residential use ever undertaken in this country.

The former home of Chicago's Columbia College, two blocks south of the Furniture Mart Building, is also being transformed into loft apartments.

A small building, an abandoned rubber refinery, is being converted to 18 loft apartments on the north edge of Chicago's downtown district.

Roughly three square blocks of architecturally historic buildings where Chicago's printing and typesetting industry was once centered, known as Printing House Row, are now being converted into hundreds of modern apartments. The ambitious Printing House Row project will create a new downtown residential neighborhood in an area that for years has been a blighted paradise for "winos," despite its listing on the National Register of Historic Places. Of the several 100-year-old buildings in the district, the biggest and one of the first to emerge fit for habitation is the 22-story Transportation Building, transformed from abandoned railroad and shipping company offices and one-time print shops, into 294 rental apartments. It would have cost more than a million dollars just to level the giant brick building.

Now, instead of becoming another parking lot, it is being rented as one- and two-bedroom apartments. Its rehabilitation cost of about $8 million is less than half what it would have cost to construct a similar building today. The architect in charge of the rehabilitation claims that a new building would not have been as attractive as the rehabilitated one. "Old buildings are more sensitive to people," he said. "They are more glamorous; there is more attention to detail, and there is better craftsmanship."

And all this is only the beginning. In Chicago, there are about six million square feet of vacant space on the fringes of the downtown area that could be converted to residential use—enough space for about 6,000 living units. It is estimated that, if all were converted, housing for 10,000 to 12,000 people could be provided, strengthening the economy of the city's core and putting idle property on the tax rolls.

Every city in the country, with variations, can do what Chicago is doing. There, the recycling is in full bloom.

STORES WITHOUT WALLS

Here is a cost-cutting idea worth exploring in every city of America. I found it on Main Street in Santa Barbara, California, when I visited there in 1978.

A food store chain of about 15,000 square feet apparently didn't do well in its downtown Santa Barbara location, and a recycler bought and converted it into a mall of small shops for less than $4 a square foot. When I converted an automobile agency into shops, I spent $20 a square foot. How did the Santa Barbara owner do it for so much less?

He tried something unusually innovative and it worked. Instead of building partitions and aisles the way I did, he simply white-sprayed the high ceilings and walls of the interior, then leased open space at $8 a square foot. Meandering narrow walkways separated a plant store, a glassware shop, a children's clothing store, a candle boutique, a homemade preserves store, a homemade rug shop—and an array of some 20 small shops that looked like a department store with 20 individual owners. Each shop had to open at the same time in the morning and close at the same time in the evening to avoid leaving any businesses unattended. I presume owners worked out a security system that protected them from each other, from the public, and from intruders when the entire shopping area was closed.

The main thrust of this project is that the department store idea saved the recycler about $250,000 in construction costs by eliminating partitions, lowering ceilings, creating separate heating and air conditioning zones, and providing individual lighting. It looked like a farmers' market, except instead of fruits and vegetables, you saw a collage of gifts, candies, breadspreads, canned foods, and yarns, all merging interestingly into one huge display of merchandise.

I asked a young glassware merchant, "How's business?"

"Great! I wish I had taken more space."

"How about security? I see you have a lot of valuable glassware. Who tends the store if you have to leave for a few minutes or for several hours?"

"My next door neighbor keeps on eye on it, as I do for him."

"Bothered by theft?" I pursued.

"No."

"Do you like the open-store idea?"

"Yeah, it's great. Keeps the rent down."

The cost-saving rehabilitation must have been successful because as I was leaving I noticed construction going on in an adjoining building. Upon inquiring, I found that the food store owner was adding space to his original recycled project.

It's cost-cutting at its finest, providing, however, that you have the right building, in the right location, in the right city, and have the know-how to lease space to unusual merchants, with unusual merchandise, that will attract local and tourist buyers to generate a profit for both lessor and lessees. It's a new idea that will work only in select places. It's one that should be thoroughly explored before being plunged into.

SPENSOR'S CORNER IN HOT SPRINGS, ARKANSAS

Hot Springs, Arkansas, is no Santa Barbara. It's more prosaic and does not have the tourism that Santa Barbara enjoys year round. But there are recycling opportunities in staid towns as well as in glamorous ones.

Spensor's Corner involved two standing old buildings with a parking lot in between where, several years ago, another building had been razed. The developer's key decision was to excavate the parking to create a below-grade, landscaped patio, exposing the basements of the two buildings and opening them as prime rental space. Without this key decision, the project might have flopped.

The buildings are connected to each other at all levels by balconies, ramps, and stairs. Total square footage of both buildings was 26,000 square feet. An open, multilevel court area, opened to streets at both ends, drew attention and traffic.

The major tenant was a 7,000-square-foot seafood restaurant at patio level. This anchor tenant created traffic for 20 small shops so that the two joined buildings not only had the advantage of a good downtown location, but also the bustle of a restaurant as well. The 20 specialty shops ranged in size from 350 to 1,300 square feet, and they've become a beehive of activity.

Before the rehabilitator bought the 94-year-old buildings, they were vacant and deteriorating rapidly—a sorry sight of dilapidation, leaking roof, dry rot, and a home for pigeons.

The developer of Spensor's Corner merchandised the past. He exposed old wood and brick for interior finishes, which proved to be both interesting and cost effective. His major costs were: an elevator, $50,000; heating and air conditioning, $77,000; electrical work, $47,000; plumbing, $22,000; sprinklers, $30,000; roofing, $22,000; awnings, $12,000; and glass and glazing, $30,000. The total cost of renovation was $675,000, which breaks down to about $26 a square foot. The entire project was financed conventionally.

I have no way of comparing the profitability of the Spensor's Corner project with the Santa Barbara partitionless idea, but my instincts tell me that I would rather have my money in Santa Barbara than in Hot Springs. But, in the long run, who knows? There are so many variables and uncertainties playing on each other. That's what makes recycling so interesting and intriguing. A digest of different kinds of recycling ideas can only help to reduce the uncertainties to a manageable level.

SOHO—RECYCLING AN ENTIRE AREA OF WAREHOUSES AND FACTORY BUILDINGS INTO LIVING QUARTERS

Congestion brings out the worst in people and the best in people: cunning and caring. New York is a crucible for both; it's smart without a heart, as well as caring and sharing. Out of the tension of New York's dichotomy flows a steady stream of new ideas. Converting warehouses and factory buildings into living quarters is one of them.

SoHo is a rich amalgam of architecture and people; a mix that seems to work better in New York City than in any other place in the world. *So*uth of *Ho*uston Street, hence the acronym, is in lower Manhattan, the district that contains the nation's most variegated and best preserved collection of cast iron industrial buildings dating from the 19th Century, as well as a liberal sprinkling of handsome brick and limestone facades. The whole area bespeaks the mercantile pride of people who believed that the humblest warehouse was a place of commerce.

Home to generations of small industries, SoHo today is in the process of change and renewal as manufacturers move to the suburbs and active young people take over the lofts and storefronts. The first wave of new residents consisted of artists, attracted by large internal spaces and low rents, followed more recently by stockbrokers, lawyers, doctors, and even a few rich dilettantes—all drawn by the challenge of uniqueness.

Once a wilderness of decaying buildings, it has now become a residential enclave of a new breed of settlers: imaginative, avant-garde people who know how to make the old new again.

Loft living in SoHo has, in the past decade, taken on an elitism in the artistic and creative world that was once associated with neighboring Greenwich Village.

When high rents began to squeeze artists out of Greenwich Village, artists fanned out into the dilapidated factories and warehouses of nearby SoHo. They set up their studios with the help of a New York housing law amendment that permitted artists to live and work in industrial buildings.

The newcomers discovered that for relatively low rent, $300 to $1,200 a month, they could get 1,200 to 4,000 square feet of wide open space. The loft offered high ceilings, skylights, and tall windows from which to take in Lower Manhattan cityscapes. They also have demanded hard labor to make them habitable. However, the work for most of them was a labor of love. The result was intensely personal, as only a work of great love and patience can be, a daring mixture of period and style put together with great skill by imaginative people.

Today, only 15 years after the pioneers began to revive and restore SoHo, some of the residents face the same threat that forced them out of Greenwich Village—soaring rents and eviction notices. The discord of congestion has set in again.

But that's New York—where the worst and best mingle in a profusion of confusion.

THE CANNERIES OF MONTEREY ON THE PACIFIC OCEAN

In contrast to New York's ingenuity of converting loft buildings to living quarters, the much smaller town of Monterey, California, turned blocks of old canneries into a multibuilding shopping center. "Why not another SoHo?" I wondered as my wife and I exhausted ourselves going from building to building, and store to store, marvelling at the imagination with which people converted junk into interesting selling space. The answer came soon enough. Monterey is a tourist town; it is not congested like New York. Hence, the recycling was beamed toward the tourist trade rather than people's living quarters.

In my opinion, however, Monterey missed the boat. The cannery buildings are located within a wedge golf shot to the Pacific Ocean—that's a hundred yards. The view is magnificent and should have been reserved for residential use. But things usually develop according to immediate needs rather than long-range plans. The press of people developed SoHo; the potential tourist trade commercialized the ocean front.

The developers of the vacated canneries used all kinds of recycling devices. One of the rehabilitators extended the first floor of his area with a glass deck over the water and used it as a dance floor to attract visitors who frequented his restaurant. He featured "Dancing on the Water" in his advertising. Another developer told me that he was planning a mama-papa motel on top of one of the buildings. The merchandise in the stores was of unusually high quality. Apparently the tourists like it because the shops draw huge crowds daily. It is Monterey's chief tourist attraction; perhaps as famous as Pebble Beach Oceanfront Golf Course, a few miles away.

Should you ever visit California's West Coast, don't miss the innovatingly recycled canneries and the unusual merchandise that's sold there.

TROLLEY SQUARE IN SALT LAKE CITY

Trolley Square is almost as famous as Ghirardelli Square. It's Salt Lake City's main restoration and merchandising attraction. It has attracted national interest and it deserves it.

This is a situation where a maximum degree of guts and imagination were needed. Guts without imagination or imagination without guts would not have been enough. It took the magic wands of both to transform 270,000 square feet of old, dust-laden car barns into a wonderland of theaters, shops, and offices, transporting yesterday into today.

The developers bought the old car barns for $1 million, or a little less than $4 a square foot. What followed was an adventure in preservation and restoration. First, they sandblasted the old barn brick to its original vintage red. They had been covered with a thick layer of yellow paint for years. New floors were poured to cover old tracks. Overhead power lines were replaced with underground installations. Shrubs, grass, and flowers, landscaped to perfection, adorned courtyards. So much for the beautification.

Now comes the economic underpinning that pays for it all. Four movie theaters are now playing to enthusiastic audiences where the old, 20,000-square-foot machine shop used to be. The owners leased 8,000 square feet to what they claim is the largest old-fashioned ice cream parlor in the world. But that's just the beginning. They gave Trolley Square a most interesting mix of tenants: a self-service gas station, a savings and loan office, a farmers' market, an open-air fair, a bakery, a fish market, fresh fruit and vegetable stands, several distinctive gift shops, various health food stores, a leather outlet, wood carving and candle shops, several restaurants, book and greeting cards shops, a jewelry store, a pet shop, a beauty parlor, an optician's office, a florist, and a branch of the First Security Bank. The rentals from all these establishments are paying off the rehabilitation costs and fixed expenses, leaving a hefty, deserved cash flow.

Here is private urban renewal at its finest. Nothing is razed. Everything is shored up and preserved. Besides the immense contribution of revitalizing an old area, the entrepreneurs now have a real estate project that's going to provide them with substantial incomes for many years. Everyone gains when creative people with feasible ideas brainstorm buildings and make economic miracles happen.

HOW A HIGH SCHOOL BUILDING IN DECATUR, ALABAMA, WAS RECYCLED INTO APARTMENTS FOR THE ELDERLY

In order to cover as much of the recycling spectrum as possible, it's important to call attention to the mini-projects as well as the large, famous ones. One of these that can be duplicated in hundreds of small towns in America was done with a small schoolhouse in Decatur, Alabama.

What can you do with a high school that's no longer needed by the school system? Switch the accent from youth and convert it into apartments for the elderly. This is what an enterprising local businessman did after he bought the 54-year-old vacant building for $60,000. What was unusual about this project was that the owner did all the work himself.

He gutted the 29,000-square-foot interior, rearranged the walls into a mix of 28 efficiency and one-bedroom apartments, dropped the ceilings, installed new plumbing and electrical wiring, and built new bathrooms and kitchens. There was enough land for a parking lot and two patios. He preserved the original character of the building by doing nothing to it. The complete rehabilitation work was done in eight months. Elderly people are now enjoying apartments where classrooms, chemistry labs, and a cafeteria used to serve the young.

We can assume that the recycler's eight months' labor provided him with a cash flow of about $25,000 a year. Not bad for eight months' work.

QUAKER SQUARE, AKRON, OHIO—A MODERN SHOPPING CENTER IN AN OLD BUILDING

Quaker Square is a handsome complex of brick buildings housing modern offices, several of the city's newest restaurants, and a cluster of up-to-date specialty stores stocked with the latest in everything from fine jewelry to baking pans.

In fact, nearly everything about Quaker Square is new—with the major exception of the buildings. The complex is housed in 77-year-old structures that once constituted a Quaker Oats Company mill.

Raising capital for reuse wasn't easy, as five businessmen in Akron found out when they bought the old Quaker Oats mill for $325,000. The following year, the group tried to float a $3 million offering of limited partnership interests to finance the mill's conversion, but the investors were skeptical and the offering collapsed.

Late in 1974, an Akron accountant joined the Quaker Square group and advised them to rehabilitate one step at a time. First, they sold about $200,000 of the mill's equipment and used the proceeds to build a tavern and a few shops. The rent from these businesses gave the group confidence to apply for a loan once again. After trying several, only one savings and loan association with some experience in restoration loans was willing to back the new venture. It gave them an initial mortgage of $1.1 million and later increased it to $2 million. With this money, the group was able to complete the recycling.

It has become a huge success. Several million visitors are spending about $9 million a year in modernized old buildings. It turned out to be a safe mortgage for the savings and loan, and an excellent investment for the equity holders.

"I can understand why so many lending institutions turned us down," one of the group said. "Nothing like this had ever been tried before in Akron."

It has been the same elsewhere. Lenders had been reluctant to commit themselves because information about the feasibility of recycling projects hadn't been readily available to the general business community.

But, during the past five years, a lot has been learned about the recycling revolution. Lenders are looking at it longer now because there have been so many successful recycled projects throughout the country. In ten years, the revolution will become institutionalized and absorbed into the Establishment.

In most cases, recycling old buildings to new uses is less costly than new construction for reasons that have been cited. However, when a developer wants to give his project an extra flair that makes it more interesting than the austere, modern shopping centers, then the cost can go beyond new construction. For example, the Rouse Company, the real estate developer that converted Faneuil Hall, Boston's former public market, into a shopping-restaurant-office complex, estimates that the cost per square foot was higher than building a new shopping center of comparable size.

But the returns are worth the risks of the added expenditures in certain cases where extra cost is justified. The Rouse Company estimates that Faneuil Hall's retail sales will eventually be more than double the average from new shopping centers.

Each project is a new adventure in restoration, financing, and income projection. Many variables play on the rehabilitation theme. In the final analysis, only you are in charge of composing and directing the recycling symphony.

OTHER RECYCLING PROJECTS WORTH NOTING AND COMPARING BEFORE YOU PLUNGE INTO YOUR OWN

1. Old City Hall—Boston, Massachusetts: from a vacated city hall to modern office building.
2. Dancer-Fitzgerald-Sample—San Francisco: from a warehouse to modern advertising agency offices.
3. Office of Ferendiono-Grafton-Pancoast—Coral Gables, Florida; from historic buildings to modern offices.

4. Smith, Hinchman and Grylls—Detroit, Michigan: from loft buildings to architectural offices.
5. Saturday Review Industries—San Francisco: a 60-year-old brick building remodeled into publishing offices.
6. The Feather Factory—San Francisco: from an old feather-cleaning building to offices for graphic designers.
7. Office of Coca Cola—San Francisco: from unused space in a company-owned warehouse to modern offices.
8. Custom House Block and Chart House Restaurant—Boston, Massachusetts: two old buildings on Boston's Long Wharf converted into 27 luxury apartments and a restaurant.
9. Larimer Square—Denver, Colorado: a block of 19th Century buildings converted into a commercial mall, adjacent to downtown.
10. Old Town—Los Gatos, California: an old building transformed into a fine arts center.
11. The Garage—Cambridge, Massachusetts: an old garage building turned into a profitable retail center.
12. The Ice House—San Francisco: an actual ice house converted into showrooms for contract furnishings.

The list is endless. For a more detailed and illustrated collection of recyclings, I suggest you read *Recycling Buildings*, edited by Elisabeth Kendall Thompson, FAIA, published by McGraw-Hill, Inc. It doesn't tell you how to recycle for profit but it's a valuable architectural record book of some of America's most interesting projects.

8

HOW NONPROFIT ORGANIZATIONS AND GOVERNMENT AGENCIES CAN SAVE MONEY IN RECYCLING OBSOLETE BUILDINGS TO FUNCTIONAL USES

HOW A MONTESSORI SCHOOL SAVED $600,000

One cannot live by bread alone, nor can capitalism live by profit alone. Unless the haves help the have-nots, enlightened capitalism loses its light.

American capitalism is shining brightly because we have a lot of people who care and share. It's estimated that close to eight million men and women do some form of voluntary work worth several billion dollars yearly. The Salvation Army, Red Cross, United Way, and thousands of other nonprofit agencies care for those who don't have the means or health to care for themselves. Since that is still not enough, the government steps in to provide the rest.

This book's main thrust is recycling for profit. It's what makes capitalism work. However, if we can pass some of our expertise on to government and non-profit organizations, we can save them money and indirectly save the taxpayers' money—yours and mine.

Here's such an example: the saving of $600,000 for a nonprofit agency. It involved a Montessori School for special children that started with a few children in a church basement.

A young couple with several degrees in sociology and psychology between them started this school for retarded and Mongoloid children from the ages of one to five, to help mothers who were incapable of caring for them at home. Some husbandless mothers were as young as thirteen, while others either worked or had no concept of how to care for these problem children.

A friend of mine who is a professor of sociology, became the couple's advisor and helped them organize a board of directors to guide the school's activities. The professor put me on the board because he wanted my help in finding a way to build a school for 50 children and 25 teachers for about $350,000, a sum he thought several socialites on the board might be able to raise. The bids for a new school were about a million dollars—a price that was completely out of reach.

I looked at a dozen old buildings and ruled them out because of location or price, or else the structure didn't lend itself to use as a school. It was a good cause so I didn't give up. Eventually, I was led to an old bowling alley that a savings and loan association had taken in foreclosure. The original mortgage was $400,000. For years, the two-story, 20,000-square-foot structure had been gathering dust and taxes for the mortgagee. The savings and loan had tried to get most of the brokers in town to help sell it for half what had been invested in it, but to no avail. I of course knew that, and when I examined the sturdy concrete building and was satisfied that both the structure and location were right, I got the board's enthusiastic approval to offer $105,000, with $15,000 down and the balance of $90,000 on a land contract, due and payable in two years.

To my pleasant surprise, after I explained to the president of the savings and loan association that as long as he had to lose money, it might as well be for a good cause, he accepted our offer.

While the socialites on the board were soliciting foundations, corporations, and wealthy citizens for capital funds for the school, I was planning with the architects how to reuse the former bowling alley for classrooms and administrative offices, and negotiating with contractors on how to cut costs so the school could get the most for the least.

A year later, with dozens of people donating hundreds of hours to raise $350,000, and with my planning with the architects and negotiating with the contractors, all the pieces finally fell into place. The Montessori School was built. The volunteers raised the $350,000, but the total cost, including the $105,000 purchase price, was close to $400,000. The treasurer of the board, a banker, arranged a loan for the difference. The school qualified for both county and United Way funding, and is now an established community facility, caring for special children from 9:00 a.m. to 4:00 p.m., after which time they are transported back to their families.

At one of the board meetings, the executive director told a touching story about a four-year-old who stared at his teachers and the other children for six months, without making a single move to reach for anything or react to anyone. The teachers patiently tried to stir him into animation without success. One day he reached for a toy; there was a celebration. A few weeks later, his face creased into a smile. The teachers claimed another victory. Gradually, the child began climbing out of his mental well into the open. Without the school, that little boy would have remained mentally frozen. Loving care thawed him toward normalcy. Without it, he probably would have remained a human robot.

Other dramatic changes were related to the board from time to time. I felt an inner glow when a few of the youngsters would come up to me and put their little hands in mine on my way to a board meeting.

Recycling for profit is exciting; it makes money and renews neighborhoods. Helping the needy is a different kind of excitement. It's a spiritual glow that lights up our mundane activity and gives balance to our lives.

HOW AN ARMY BASE BECAME A COMMUNITY CULTURAL CENTER

Recycling for nonprofit can be as innovative as recycling for profit. A rare demonstration of this fact is shown in the transformation of a 130-year-old army base in San Francisco into the city's vibrant new cultural center.

Once the main point of embarkation for American forces in the Pacific, the base, known as Fort Mason, has become a national model for the imaginative and successful recycling of surplus military facilities.

Bordering the bay, the fort's former barracks and warehouses have been converted into various multi-use spaces for classrooms, workshops, galleries, offices, studios, a theater, a bookstore, a coffee house, a conference hall, a restaurant, and a bakery.

The conversion of the center's total space of 300,000 square feet in five buildings has cost $1.7 million to date, almost all of which has come from foundations and corporate and private donations.

The center is a nonprofit citizens' organization formed in 1976 to renovate, operate, and promote it as a cultural, educational, and recreational facility under an agreement with the National Park Service from which it leased the buildings (at no cost).

Fort Mason is self-supporting. More than 40 nonprofit organizations operate within the center on one- to three-year leases, while hundreds of other groups rent space on a one-time basis for specific events. Part of the attraction is that rents average about $3 per square foot per year, far less than comparable space would cost in a private commercial building. To qualify for space at this low rate, a group must be nonprofit and offer some free benefits to the public, or at minimal cost.

This imaginative renovation and use certainly filled a need because the activities at the center attract over a million persons a year who are involved in classes ranging from acting, dancing, singing, drawing, ceramics, writing, sensory awareness, childbirth preparation, stress management, energetics, and martial arts. There is also a constant schedule of lectures and various kinds of performances.

Let's render to profit what is due to profit, and render to people our obligations to people. If an obsolete building can be put to use to help society, we should develop it with the same gusto as when we're working for profit. Enlightened capitalism is getting and giving. When there's all getting and no giving, it disintegrates into inferior living.

HOW AN OLD VAUDEVILLE HOUSE BECAME AN ELEGANT CENTER FOR PERFORMING ARTS

Preservation contributes to the welfare of all the city's citizens.

When Loew's Penn Theater in Pittsburgh closed its doors in 1964, after providing film and vaudeville entertainment for 37 years, demolition seemed inevitable. The Golden Triangle was being built and old structures nearby were being pulled down and replaced by glistening metal-skinned towers. But an "angel" by the name of Henry J. Heinz II saved the buildings and millions of dollars for the community by recycling the abandoned movie house into Heinz Hall for the Performing Arts. The Pittsburgh community helped to create Mr. Heinz' wealth, and in his case, he pumped a lot of it back—$10 million worth. But without recycling, the Performing Arts Center would have cost twice as much, and the community would have had to make up the difference. And it wouldn't have had the charm that the $10 million of Heinz's money produced.

The hall, seating 2,730, now serves not only the renowed Pittsburgh Symphony Orchestra, but also the Pittsburgh Opera, the Civic Light Opera, the Pittsburgh Ballet, and the Youth Symphony Orchestra.

The neo-baroque opulence of the old movie palace remains, since the technical requirements necessary for revamping the building to its new use have been achieved economically and unobtrusively. In addition to restoring the Grand Foyer, the Grand Lobby, and the hall itself to a tasteful reflection of the late Twenties, the architects and their consultants revised circulation patterns and intermission lounges, provided three floors of offices for the various performing groups, added a wing containing enlarged backstage space, and finally, under the direction of Dr. Heinrich Keilholz of Salzburg, Austria, added a large acoustical reflector above the stage with other refinements for optimal sound delivery in a multipurpose hall.

The Heinz Hall for the Performing Arts is a perfect example of putting people ahead of hoarding profit—and enriching an entire community.

HOW A CARRIAGE HOUSE WAS CONVERTED INTO THE NEWARK COMMUNITY CENTER OF THE ARTS

There's not much profit in cultural activities, nor is there much culture in sterile profitability: they need and compliment each other. And so it's not surprising that an old carriage house that needed capital to turn it into the Newark Community Center of the Arts should get it from profit-making people who were culture-oriented. Grants from two foundations did wonders for the dilapidated carriage house and for the budding ballet dancers and musicians who were given a chance to develop their talents.

A large home is part of the facility located only a short distance from the carriage house. The space between the two will be developed into an outdoor theater when more money becomes available.

I haven't actually seen this nonprofit recycling project, but rather only pictures of it, showing little girls practicing at the ballet barre and a chamber music quartet performing under kleig lights showing what appears to be a new ceiling under a new roof.

Without volunteer work, philanthropy, and recycling economics, many a youngster's potential in Newark would have been stunted.

Money-making is fun. It's even more fun when we give some of it away and create fun for others.

HOW GOVERNMENT CAN SAVE MONEY BY RECYCLING OBSOLETE BUILDINGS

Local, and state governments are not in the forefront of the recycling revolution nor is the Federal government. Government should, at least, be not far behind, since it comprises one of the largest segments of the office market in most central cities. Moreover, many of the most interesting obsolete buildings are publicly-owned.

To maximize the potential for recycling of all structures, the government should, on all levels, consider building into its capital improvements a legislative mechanism for using available existing structures prior to deciding on new construction as an alternative.

As a first step, government bureaucrats must become aware of the potential benefits to be derived from recycling, the two most important being economy and preserving the architecture of old buildings, because a city loses its unique character by demolition. In the past, the almost exclusive concern with new construction inhibited the development of much interest in recycling. Moreover, many corporate and government egos have traditionally demanded new buildings for their headquarters and offices.

But we're entering an era of austerity, and government should begin recognizing the many benefits and hidden assets of old buildings that they had heretofore overlooked. Entrepreneurs have awakened to recycling's potential, but government, in most cases, is either still asleep or just waking up. To back up this contention, let me cite an example in my own city of Milwaukee.

HOW GOVERNMENT WASTED $29 MILLION OF OUR TAX DOLLARS

City and Federal officials decided that Milwaukee needed a Federal building of 300,000 square feet for office space to house U.S. agencies. The combined city and Federal egos were still immersed in the new-building syndrome of the past, and like corporations that spend billions to bolster their egos, our public bureaucrats decided to do likewise. They assembled land at high prices, razed old buildings, and sold the site to a private developer who was guaranteed that the General Services Administration (GSA) would lease 300,000 square feet from him for a specific period of time, at a high enough rental per square foot that enabled the entrepreneur to obtain conventional financing. While I'm not privy to what the U.S. Government is paying per square foot for rent, I know that, based on the cost of the land and the high cost of new construction, it would have to be in the range of between $15 and $20 per square foot. That's about three times as much as the Federal government would have had to pay if it had shrunk its ego and moved its offices a few blocks away to two old but sturdy buildings that could have been recycled, not into plush, but into adequately modern office space.

About seven blocks away, east and south of the Milwaukee River, two concrete buildings were for sale at $3 a square foot, including land, which could have been recycled at $20 a square foot into good functional office space. This would have enabled a recycler to lease office space to the Federal government at between $6 and $7 a square foot per year, and be left with an adequate cash flow for the work. And the Federal government would have saved hundreds of millions of dollars during the next 30 or 40 years of its lease.

This tells me that the Federal government has yet not caught the mood of the recycling revolution. Only here and there is it beginning to see the tremendous possibilities of saving money, energy, and neighborhoods, but not fast enough or on a large enough scale. It's a trickle instead of a torrent. To stimulate government to join the recycling revolution, I'd like to cite a few examples where its eyes have been opened to the waiting possibilities.

Ventura, California converted a Roman Doric courthouse that was no longer needed into a branch library.

Baltimore, Ohio renovated a warehouse to serve as a neighborhood community center.

Greenwich Village, New York adapted a Victorian Gothic courthouse for use as a library.

Boston, Massachusetts has converted a 19th-Century coal storage facility on the waterfront to a station for fire and police patrol boats.

Minneapolis, Minnesota acquired the old Federal courthouse there as surplus Federal property and is converting it to a complex of county offices and cultural facilities.

In Seattle, Washington city agencies, a post offices, the transit authority, and state government agencies all rent office space in the rejuvenated Pioneer Square.

In East Dallas, Texas the government leased half a vacant building and saved the unique structure from demolition.

In Milwaukee, the reverse will be true; the new Federal building will draw tenants away from recycled buildings and push them into neglect.

No doubt, there are many more instances of Government involvement in furthering the recycling movement, but it's miniscule compared to what it should be. Could it be that bureaucrats are not as imaginative as profit-motivated entrepreneurs? If true, that's part of the problem.

Then the solution should be to form a partnership between public and private efforts so that self-interest and public welfare mix creatively to reinforce each other.

Here are a few suggestions how the government can help the recycler-developer.

Where there are obstacles which hinder private acquisition, the government should serve as a middleman in buying, building, and selling it as a recycling package (just as Urban Renewal agencies sell land).

Have government provide public improvements as it did in Seattle's Pioneer Square with its period street lights, drinking fountains, walkways, street furniture, parks, and a pedestrian mall. An economic evaulation report on the city's original $1 million investment, which was later upped to $2 million, showed a $10 million increase in assessed valuation, plus increases in tourist dollars and employment (a sort of multiplier effect).

In its Waterfront Renewal Project, Boston provided street improvements, brick and granite sidewalk installations, period lights and landscaping to enhance warehouses being recycled into housing.

As with any desirable public objective, the recycling of obsolete buildings can be greatly simulated by various public financial incentives. Given the risks involved in some recycling circumstances, a public effort to reduce or share in the risk may be essential. Such incentive may be especially necessary where the probable alternative is the loss of a building. Here are several forms of help, used sparingly so far, which should be accelerated in many other parts of the country.

Assembling properties and their resale to developers for reuse at a lower price may often be the only route for a feasible recycling project.

Long-term leases of properties owned by the city or Urban Renewal agency to private developers can be a financial help. The development of the Old City Hall in Boston into a high-quality office and restaurant complex was made possible through such an arrangement.

The use of city or city-controlled Federal funds (e.g., General Revenue Sharing and Community Development Block Grants) can help to reduce rehabilitation costs for recycling.

Also the use of mortgage insurance programs, 221-D4, are still available, but at lower than 90 percent of appraisal, as are revolving loan funds at lower than current interest rates.

Tax increment financing can be used, whereby the incremental tax increases resulting from a project pay off public improvement bonds.

New York City's J-51 Program provides incentives for the conversion of non-residential structures (e.g., industrial loft buildings) to residential use by permitting a 12-year tax exemption on the increased assessment due to alteration.

These differing forms of government aid stimulate the maximum amount of private recycling investment with the minimum of public investment. However, where government can save money by recycling for its own use, it should do so with as much enthusiasm as the private developers who recycle for profit.

Recycling is a comparatively new phenomenon. Naturally, the older cities tend to show the greatest amount of interest, but the younger and smaller towns need not sit back and wait. Small town entrepreneurs should meet it head on, alone if necessary, and with government aid if possible.

WHO WILL LEAD THE RECYCLING REVOLUTION?

Private entrepreneurs will be at the forefront of the recycling revolution because they have the guts, imagination, and persuasive ability needed to package a recycling project. When any of the three essential components is missing, the chances for success fall sharply. Scholarship is no substitute for any of these. It will get you a good job in either the private or public sectors, but alone, without these three basic prerequisites, scholarship will not get a recycling project off the ground, although it is a definite plus.

In my city, included among the leaders of real estate recycling and development is a colorful character with a third-grade education who today has real estate assets worth $10 million; a high-school graduate who owns two of our main hotels; a former automotive repairman whose real estate recycling now nets him $100,000 a year; a former electrician who enjoys a $150,000 a year annuity from his recycling efforts; a two-year college dropout whose recycling has catapulted him into a $2 million fortune; an immigrant from Ireland with little scholarship but a lot of street savvy who now controls $30 million of recycled real estate; and a dozen lesser operators who, without formal education but possessing the three basics for recycling, are now earning three times as much as the average college professor or the typical salaried executive in the public or private sector.

Of course, I'm not anti-education. I'm not sorry for having received a B.A. in Economics from the University of Wisconsin. Many of my interesting and stimulating friends have more advanced academic degrees than I. But most of them don't have the boldness, imagination, and persuasion to risk the uncertainties of recycling, and I don't blame them. What's more, we need them badly to keep the infrastructure of private enterprise and public service running smoothly. The recyclers I know, with all their money-making abilities, couldn't do what scholars are doing. They're too volatile. They lack the scholarship and discipline necessary for the orderly functioning of organized society.

We need them both. We need the blue-blooded scholars and the red-blooded risk takers. Together, they reinforce each other: the scholars provide the stability while the risk-takers supply the action. That's what makes America great.

9

TECHNIQUES FOR MATCHING REHABILITATION TO THE CHARACTERISTICS OF YOUR CITY

KNOWING THE TYPE OF TENANT IN YOUR TOWN IS A VITAL PREREQUISITE FOR RECYCLING

It's obvious that it would be folly to recycle an old 500,000-square-foot factory building into a Ghirardelli Square in a sleepy town of 5,000 people. However, an overly ambitious architect in our city spent four years in the late 1960s, trying to finance a 250-foot observation-tower restaurant. He tried to emulate Seattle's Tower without realizing that Milwaukee is not Seattle; that it's a staid, conservative city with few tourists, not nearly enough to make it a feasible project. Milwaukee is not a regional center like Chicago or Denver. In spite of all the obvious reasons against its success, the architect bought the land and excavated a hole for the tower's foundation. That's as far as he got. He went into the hole financially (pardon the pun) for tens of thousands of dollars. He failed because the project was woefully mismatched for Milwaukee. He misjudged his city and the characteristics of its inhabitants.

Don't make a similar mistake. After you've found the right building in the right location, give a lot of thought to the characteristics of your city and its inhabitants, particularly the type of people surrounding your project.

If your apartment project, for instance, is located in the downtown area, slant the size and amenities toward couples or singles. Structure the rent schedule proportionately to the potential tenants' earnings. And, to cut rehabilitation costs, do what I did in Chapter 4: eliminate interior partitions except in the bathrooms and kitchens.

However, if you're recycling an architectural gem of a building, in an unusually good area close to downtown, and are planning to draw elderly wealthy suburbanites to live there (as recyclers are doing in Chicago) then plan more lavishly. Have larger apartments featuring more than one bathroom, unusual electric and plumbing fixtures, and an elaborate lobby, and provide expensive special service amenities such as valet parking, a doorman and meticulous daily cleaning of public areas. Of course, the rent schedule should reflect the higher cost of recycling and management.

The character and size of your city should determine whether you decide to rehabilitate at a lower cost for downtown workers or spend more to attract semiretired, elderly suburbanites or higher paid junior executives. Chicago could support all three types. In Milwaukee, a recycled building could only draw the white-collar office worker. You'd have to decide whether your city is ready for any or all of the three tenant types. You may have to take risks to find out. That's why, even if you know your city and even if you have unusual insights, there's still a bit of uncertainty. Of course, for me, that's what makes it exciting. Uncertainty should be a challenge to be met, not an obstacle to be avoided.

If you're refitting a building into stores, these are the things to consider. If it's in the downtown district catering to downtown working people, the remodeling should be austere in order to keep the rents low. More specifically, and this is important, be careful about leasing to tenants who have never worked in shops for others or who have never operated a store of their own. (More about that later). This may sound discriminatory or unfair, but you'd be doing yourself and them a favor by reducing their and your chances for failure.

Some cities have an overabundance of good merchants, others don't have enough. The West Coast, for instance, is a fertile field for new shop ideas and new merchandising techniques. But the same ideas and techniques may fall flat in staid towns where the merchants are not imaginative and the people aren't interested in moving out of their traditional shopping grooves. People who have deep roots in their town change more slowly than people in growing cities where newcomers comprise a large portion of the population, such as the Sun Belt. Cities in the Northeast or Middle West are less ripe for new ideas than those in the fast-growing warm climates. People on the move change more readily than those who stay put. Keep the differences in mind when recycling for stores. However, should you decide to try a new idea in a tradition-loving town, be sure to devise an educational program (see Chapter 4) and provide financial staying-power while waiting for your new idea to catch on.

If you recycle for office space in a town that isn't growing, it's more imperative that you gauge your prospects' demand based on local habits rather than on ideas that you've seen work elsewhere. Let me cite a personal example—a sad tale of misjudgment.

About 20 years ago, I was building the first hotel in West Allis, Wisconsin, a Milwaukee suburb of 50,000, and decided to try something new, much to my regret. No sizeable commercial building had been built there for several decades. There was no hotel or elevatored office space, only walk-up offices above stores, even for the doctors and attorneys. I decided to build modern office space on the first four floors of the 40,000-square-foot building, and about 60 hotel rooms on the three upper floors. For a year I tried to lease the office space at $3.50 a square foot, at a time when Milwaukee's rate for new space was $5 a square foot. Not a single prospect showed any interest.

"Why should I pay $3.50 a square foot," was the typical reply of businessmen and professionals, "when my customers don't mind walking up to my offices where I'm paying only $1.50 a square foot?"

"Don't you owe it to yourself to work in elevatored space where you can enjoy your work day in a pleasant, air-conditioned environment?" I asked persuasively. "And don't you owe a pleasant environment to your clients and patients?" I gave them my best selling efforts while the building was under construction. The result: zero!

Inadvertently, I mentioned my problem about not being able to sell office space to my plumbing contractor. He made a suggestion that saved me a lot of money. "For about $10,000," he said, "you could stub in plumbing in the office floors so that if you can't get office tenants, you can convert the space into hotel rooms. It'd be good insurance."

How right he was. Since I was unable to procure office tenants, I proceeded to partition the lower floors into hotel rooms, based on the location of the stubbed plumbing outlets. Because of the plumber's foresight, I was able to "recycle" the almost completed office area into hotel rooms. I subsequently sold the 125-room hotel, which has been a success for the last two decades.

The point of the story is not to take for granted that, because tenants will upgrade in one town, they will in another. A little preliminary exploration of tenants' attitudes pays big dividends. Yet, on the other hand, you have to be careful not to be easily disuaded.

I learned another lesson at the tail end of the recession in 1975, about recycling an old building into office space. I thought there would be a demand for low-priced offices in Milwaukee because of the recessionary atmosphere at the time. The building was four blocks south of the downtown's main street, but it had a passenger elevator, high loft ceilings, and lots of window space. True, the lobby had a forlorn look and the interior showed its 60 years, but I gave it some cosmetic attention (it would have been foolhardy to go into extensive remodeling) and proceeded to rent the space at only $2 a square foot. You'd think that, in a metropolitan area of over a million people, there'd be enough small businessmen who'd grab at this low rate. It didn't happen. After a year of sustained advertising, I was able to lease only 80 percent of the building, and only at an average rate of $1.50 a square foot.

I had misjudged the market, but I was saved by playing it safe and spending only a nominal amount for rehabilitation.

In another city, office space at this low price, even in a third-rate location, might have been quickly snapped up by marginal small businessmen.Or, in yet another city, it might not sell at all. That's why knowing the habits of the tenants in your particular town is so important. One of the tell-tale signs to pay attention to is the amount of similar offbeat space that's available. If there are many vacancies, don't buck the trend. If the vacancy factor is low, cosmetic recycling could be a bonanza. This type of recycling has spawned many new millionaires in many cities across our land.

WHY REHABILITATION IS ADVANTAGEOUSLY DIFFERENT IN A TOURIST TOWN

Anything goes in a tourist town. There's more flamboyance in the merchants, in the merchandise, and in the way people spend their money. Tourists, away from home, are psychologically programmed to spend more, to seek out the unusual. The shopkeepers of tourist towns know this and fill their shops with dazzling decoration and unique items. This gives their merchandising an extra dimension, and gives them the rationale for marking up their unusual inventory for maximum profit.

Recycling an old building in Carmel, Monterey, La Jolla, Santa Barbara, or Palm Springs, requires far greater imagination than doing so in towns that cater only to its rooted inhabitants.

On Victoria Island, across the bay from Vancouver, British Columbia, a gravel pit was recycled into a botanical garden where hundreds of thousands of tourists visit yearly. The project paid profitably in Victoria, but would it have played in Peoria? No! A big gun deal in one town could be a pop gun deal in another. A tourist town is special and the recycling methods and expenditures have to match its characteristics.

You'd be making a mistake, for instance, converting an old building in a booming tourist town into apartments or offices. If the location is right, you'd get far more rent per square foot converting it into shops. And your recycling costs would be less for a good reason. Merchants are extremely imaginative in tourist towns and prefer to plan their own remodeling and decor, rather than relying on the owner's plans. All you need do, then, is provide the basic space—they'll do the rest.

On St. Thomas in the U.S. Virgin Islands, a duty-free port in the Caribbean, a recycler geared a tourist attraction to maximum profit. He bought several hundred thousand square feet of old warehouses where, several centuries ago, the infamous pirate, Bluebeard, stored his booty. The developer recycled it into a bazaar of hundreds of little shops. He went to great lengths to preserve old characteristics of the warehouses, and thus saved hundreds of thousands of dollars. The flamboyant merchants did the rest.

My wife and I had to meander through crowds in each store—shiploads of people browsing, bargaining, and buying watches, jewelry, pottery, native wood art, cameras, spirits, and hundreds of other items that they probably wouldn't have bought at home. The point of the St. Thomas example is that the owner used recycling ingenuity by first seeing the profit possibility in converting centuries-old buildings into an international mart, and second, doing it economically by letting the merchants have the fun of designing and paying for their own remodeling. From what

I've observed, both the lessor and the dozens of lessees were highly successful, because tourists are mesmerized by the unusual and buy more than they need when vacationing. The St. Thomas recycler knew what he was doing and cashed in on his idea.

In Carmel, California, my wife and I found the most interesting boutiques in old houses off alleys, where merchants in typical American towns would never have dreamed of leasing space. But in tiny Carmel, where the tourists outnumber the native population on almost any given day, any old building located anywhere near the mile-long street of stores fetches much more rent than residential or office space. In tourist towns, therefore, store space is king. In sleepy towns, it's the most marginal and unwanted.

In Venice, the remarkable St. Marks Square is where tourists and pigeons mingle in noisy confusion. It's the centerpiece of a city laced with labyrinthine canals and waterways, surrounded by century-old multistoried buildings recycled into stores. My wife and I visited some of the upper-floor shops. They were magnificent. Because the merchants dealt in some of the finest glassware, art, and clothes in the world, the environment was elegant compared to the bazaar atmosphere of the warehouses of St. Thomas Island. The buyers were wealthier, the salespeople more cosmopolitan, and the decor more elegant. And the rent in these recycled buildings must have been sky high because of the tourists. Tourists create real estate value, and the wealthier the tourists, the more value they create.

A garage in Palm Springs, California, several miles from its downtown, was recycled into a small Chinese restaurant by a couple who escaped communist China. There was room for only 25 diners. What the tiny restaurant lacked in chic, the Chinese couple, who were friends of Madame Chiang Kai-Shek, made up in fine cuisine and interesting conversation. They did well in spite of their meager quarters because it was located in Palm Springs—a tourist mecca. They could never have made it in a recycled garage in say, Cincinnati.

In Lausanne, Switzerland, one of the world's tourist havens, there isn't a scrap of old property that isn't used for either a shop or restaurant. Properties that are wasting away in Milwaukee, Kalamazoo, Cleveland, or Peoria would be considered relatively new by Swiss standards. In Lausanne, they would be renewed and trimmed with geraniums to entice hundreds of thousands of travelers to spend their money there. Obviously, what can be done with old buildings in Lucerne cannot be done in a town without tourism in America. The tourists make the difference.

For example, in the tourist quarter of Quebec, my wife and I didn't find a storefront that didn't feature either unusual merchandise or an unusual restaurant. Perhaps by design, in order to accentuate the city's old character, the storefronts were left with as much of the derelict look as some of the old-fashioned storefronts in the small towns of America. However, what was derelict at home to American travelers was displayed as Old World charm in Quebec. That's why these antique buildings, which looked like sorry replicas of some of the neglected buildings in America, were excellent real estate investments in Canada: because of tourists.

In contrast to Quebec's old, left-as-is store fronts, Rodeo Drive in Los Angeles has some of the most outstanding shop facades in the world, and their unbelievably expensive interiors match the grandiloquent exteriors. The rent per square foot is also among the highest on earth. Why the difference between Rodeo's opulence and Quebec's quaintness? Because the merchants know how to size up tourists and get the most out of them. They play different tunes to different tourists. Only the skeleton of Rodeo's old buildings are used—the rest are fleshed out with the utmost snob appeal because the wealthiest of the wealthy shop there. The ultimate in snobbery is when some of the shopkeepers open by appointment only.

When my wife was looking at clothes in a Rodeo Drive shop (which I hoped she wouldn't buy), to pass the time away, I walked into a men's shop next door. Jackets were priced from $400 and up; suits were $600. On a table near a pile of shirts was a "Sale" sign. Forgetting where I was for a moment, I picked one up and said, "I'll take it."

As the salesman was wrapping it, I asked, "By the way, how much is it?" In Milwaukee, the price would have been about $15. He casually replied, "$75." I was stunned but too embarrassed to back out. Fortunately, my wife was smarter—she looked but didn't buy.

I enjoyed quaint Quebec more than nightmarish Rodeo. Its shops reminded me of Picasso's surrealistic art. American moguls and Arabian sheiks apparently like to be suckered in by the weird, lavish come-ons of the suave merchandisers. Real estate values on the street have skyrocketed, and so has the chic "art" of ostentation—all because of tourism.

Twenty-five years ago, my wife and I were vacationing in Montego Bay, Jamaica. The British owner of our hotel said to me, after we became friendly:

"George, if you're looking for a safe speculation, I'd advise you to buy that old building I showed you at the edge of Montego village. Stores are moving out that way, and in a few years, you'll quadruple your money." I listened and smiled.

"First of all," I said, "a safe speculation, as you describe it, is a contradiction. But I know what you mean. Second, since I have a theory about real estate that's peculiarly personal, I don't invest anywhere except in my own city. The theory has worked exceedingly well for me. My city has been good to me, and if I'm going to invest money in real estate, I want to pump it back into the businesses and economy that participated in my success. It's a long, philosophical answer, but also a practical one. I guess you know what I mean."

"I do," he said, "and I applaud what you're saying. I never thought of it that way."

The value of the building my friend alluded to probably did quadruple in price over the next several years because Montego Bay became a world-famous resort. But then something happened—hostility grew on the part of the natives toward tourists. And when Jamaica got its independence and a leftist government was elected, the torrent of tourists dwindled to a trickle.

The value of recycled Montego Bay real estate plummeted. My British friend sold his hotel, and several of my Milwaukee friends who owned expensive homes on the outskirts of Montego Bay sold them at a loss. As many people cashed in on the tourist trade as those who now took losses because Montego Bay was reverting to the quiet village it once was.

The leftist government was defeated recently by a conservative one, and one of its aims is to encourage tourism once again. If it succeeds, Montego Bay's real estate values will rise once more. Tourism will make the difference.

Let me conclude this discussion on the difference between tourist and nontourist towns by showing the mental gymnastics I had to go through before deciding not to recycle a beautiful old building across the alley from the "Chalet At The River," which I described at great length in Chapter 4. There were many compelling reasons for buying and recycling it, but I turned it down only because Milwaukee is not a tourist town.

In LaJolla, Santa Barbara, Carmel, or Monterey—all tourists towns—this building would have been snapped up for recycling in a hurry, but not in my town.

While the exterior was an architectural pearl of yesterday's ornateness, the interior was an empty shell bereft of functional elevators, plumbing, heating, and sufficient electrical power. The most serious negative of all was that it was a mill-constructed building.

This was my problem. While it was tempting to buy the four-story, 60,000-square-foot building because it could have been an extension of my "Chalet At The River," with all the management advantages of its proximity, I nevertheless had to look carefully at the economics of recycling it. In addition to the shortcomings of its utilities, the exterior walls showed buckling and the interior floors sloped in many directions. I still might have given it serious consideration if the price had been right, say $5 a square foot. Instead, it was owned by a millionaire who had the affrontery to ask $700,000. The price dissolved my interest.

It's not wise to recycle for the love of it. It's an important part, but you've got to see a profit at the end or the dream collapses. My quick reckoning showed an expenditure of a million dollars to put it in rentable shape. In a tourist town, this ornate structure could have been turned into a four-floor galleria of shops with a skylight to diffuse daylight on each floor. And imaginative merchants would have found unusual merchandise to sell to tourists at high prices so they could afford to pay the high rent, which in turn would amortize the high cost of rehabilitation. But in Milwaukee, with little tourist money available, there's only a limited sales volume, making it difficult for the lessee to pay the high rent necessary to amortize the expensive recycling.

Had there been a way to wring out half of the $1.7 million total cost of the project, the consequential lower rent structure might have made the galleria idea feasible even in Milwaukee. But there was no way, and the code problems in a mill-constructed building foreclosed the economic feasibility of turning it into apartments. As of this writing, I see no way of saving the old, well-located structure. My guess is that it will be razed and the site turned into a parking lot.

In a tourist town, the high shop rentals would have saved it; in Milwaukee, no. These examples should underscore the economic differences between tourist and nontourist towns. You'll be making a mistake to ignore them.

THE FUTURE OF SMALL-TOWN REHABILITATION

Howard Ruff, in his *The Ruff Times Newsletter* that deals with money matters and economic predictions, has been telling his readers over and over again that our future growth will be in the small towns and villages of America. The trend is already visible, he says, and it will be accelerated in the near future.

I agree. Although there are efforts in many parts of the country to bring people back to the city, nearly all large cities are losing them to the suburbs and small towns. There are many reasons to get out of the big cities: crime, noise, hassle, hurry, crowds, pollution, and the general deterioration of life. In the battle for people, the big cities will win some, but the small towns will win more. If you agree with the trend, you'd be wise to move with the times.

You must differentiate between stagnant and growing small towns. Several variables determine whether a town is going to grow, remain as it is, or shrink. The most important factor is the stock of people in the town—do they want the town to grow, and do they have leaders who can affect growth? Often a handful of go-getters can make the difference: a local newspaper editor, a banker, a town planner, a real estate agent, or a combination of them.

Another growth-promoting factor is the availability of a labor force to serve a new industry, a large medical clinic, or any other commercial enterprise. In LaJolla, California, the Scripps Medical Clinic and the Salk Institute have contributed immensely to the town's burgeoning growth.

Prospering nearby recreational centers promote small town growth. Door County in Northern Wisconsin is a narrow finger of land projecting between Lake Michigan and Green Bay. Fishing, golfing, and the pleasant breezes that constantly blow across its four-mile wide isthmus during the summer bring many tourists from Chicago and Milwaukee. Small villages like Bailey's Harbor, Fish Creek, Allison Bay, and Sister Bay thrive on this tourism. Local leaders have banded together and promoted the entire area as an art and antique center. As a result, many little shops have sprouted in many old buildings: art galleries have appeared in barns, antique shops have opened up in old, spruced-up houses, mini-malls featuring mini-shops have sprung up in large stores that had previously been vacant. This recycling also stimulated construction of vacation homes, condominium projects, motels, and restaurants, which, in turn, increased the population of the small towns. The area leaders are now beginning to promote winter sports to buttress the summer recreational season.

As a result, real estate values in the small towns of Door County have gone up, and they will continue to do so. The Maxwelton Braes Resort, in the heart of the county where my wife and I have vacationed for the past ten years, is a 120-acre facility that has a champion 18-hold golf course, a 25-room lodge and restaurant, and about 50 rooms in a dozen cottages in the midst of a lush wooded area. It will not remain a resort much longer. The elderly owners have it up for sale, and I can visualize a developer buying it and increasing the population of Bailey's Harbor, which adjoins it, by several hundred people. Obviously, Door County is in the path of growth. Recycling in any of those villages will not make a fortune, but will ensure enough for a pleasant life.

Here are some factors to consider before investing in small-town recycling. Does the town have dependable, good government? Does it have a stable stock of people who are pluralistic and community-minded citizens that value freedom for themselves and for others? Is the town clean, aesthetic, and a pleasant place to live? These and other favorable factors will attract not only industrial and white-collar workers, but also well-to-do, semi-retired and fully retired individuals to spend their money and the rest of their lives in such attractive towns.

It's profitable to recycle in these towns. A nursing home would be a logical development, and if a main highway passes through the town, a mama-papa motel would be an excellent project if an old mansion or some obsolete building can be bought cheaply and recycled imaginatively.

The newest and most profitable idea to try in a growing small town is a factory outlet. If the leaders of a small town want growth, they should look for enterprising recyclers. The chances are, if the town is right, the developers will find it.

Here is just such a story of growth leaders and developers finding each other. What makes this story helpful for beginners is that the developers were short on experience but long on guts, imagination, and persuasiveness. They were two young men, barely out of their twenties, who joined hands with the town officials and created a factory outlet that's become a model for the Midwest.

The key for having a successful outlet in a small town is that the town be located 20 to 30 miles from a large population center, connected to this center by a major highway. This was exactly the situation of the small town of West Bend, Wisconsin, that had the combination of the right town, cooperative public officials, and two imaginative young men.

West Bend helped the two men fund a tax-free revenue bond of $1 million at 12½ percent, for a new, 50,000-square-foot building, which was to be divided among a dozen manufacturing firms that would sell their products at approximately half the price for which their retailers sold them in the big cities. The outlet was located half a block from West Bend's main street. As extra incentives to the two young entrepreneurs, the town leased the land to them for a mere $10,000 a year for 50 years and, in addition, provided 300 free parking spaces.

In West Bend, there are about 100,000 square feet of doddering stores in doddering buildings near the new structure, and the developers' next move will be to recycle those stores into an expanded factory outlet to make it a giant regional discount mart that will attract customers all the way from Chicago.

The two bold young men formed an unusually effective team—one is an excellent builder, the other a superb salesman. The new building is now finished and 100 percent occupied and, from what I've been told by one of the young men, they expect to split a lifetime annuity of $150,000 with no investment of their own. And that's just the beginning. There are the old buildings of West Bend still beckoning for action, and I'm sure they'll get it.

This project would not have been successful without guts, imagination, and persuasiveness—the three basics. In this case, the zeal of youth gave it an extra dimension. West Bend and the youthful developers have caught the crest of a new idea and they're riding it into a bright future.

While the exodus to small towns is gaining momentum, it is not the case everywhere. There are spots of resistence because many small-towners don't want growth. They fight it.

A friend of mine and I built new apartments, mama-papa motels, and small office buildings in about 30 small towns of Wisconsin. We were applying for a permit to build a new, 16-family building in Ripon, and a group of irate citizens came to a hearing to oppose it for no other reason than that they didn't want to change the traditional character of their town. The reader might be interested in knowing that Ripon was the birthplace of the present Republican Party.

I received a letter from one of Ripon's citizens, which read as follows:

"Please don't build in our town. We're happy with the way things are. We don't want to be citified with new apartments. Build somewhere else, where they want you."

Of course, there were as many Ripon people at the hearing who wanted the new apartments, there was a need for them, and we got our permit. The Ripon officials were pleased with the new building, and they induced us to build a 40-room mama-papa motel.

We should try to understand those who are content with their small towns, who don't want change. They're frightened by the erosion of character in large cities. But they can not stop the stampede. The exodus to small towns has begun, and it will run its course.

The answer to character building, in my opinion, does not lie in a back-to-the city movement, or flight from it. Human nature can't be changed by bigger cities or bigger towns. It can only be changed by a moral revolution in the hearts of the people. What counts more than the size of cities or changing institutions is finding something big to live for. We've tried to find it in success, sex, and science—they're important, but not important enough. That's because deep in our heart's there is a yearning to live for something big. So far, we haven't come up with anything greater than making God the centerpiece of our lives. That's why we need to add spirituality to our human goals to give direction and balance to our lives.

When that's added, more people will care enough, share enough, and have enough.

Please pardon the short sermon. It is a good transition point to switch from recycling buildings to recycling our human nature—the most difficult challenge of all.

HOW TO SIZE UP TENANTS FOR RECYCLED BUILDINGS

Rehabilitated buildings attract a different grade of tenants than new ones. There are several reasons for this. The rents in resuscitated buildings are lower and, as a result, they lure both the wealthy bargain hunters and the marginal inexperienced dreamers.

They're a motley lot, these tenants who are enamored by recycled space. Let me deal first with the successful ones who like to exercise their astuteness by taking advantage of bargain rates. I crossed swords with one of them when I recycled an automobile dealership into a mini-mall of small shops.

He owned 70 theaters throughout Wisconsin and wanted to lease 3,500 square feet for a twin movie theater. He saw the potential of the neighborhood more clearly than I because, a year after he opened, he told me that, seat-for-seat, the theaters in my mall were the best revenue producers of any in Wisconsin. But what I had to go through to get him! As it turned out, I didn't get him—he got me. I spent about $20 a square foot to remodel space for other tenants in the mall, but he made me spend $40 even though his rent was no higher than theirs.

"I'm a draw," he said. "My theater patrons become your mall customers, especially your two restaurants. That's why you can afford to spend more on me than on them."

He was right. He used the most potent argument to his advantage. I did well, but he did better. I had several other battles with the financially aware, and in most cases, they came out better than I. This is not meant to condemn them, but rather to underscore their characteristics and to point out that once they're in, they become trouble-free, desirable tenants. It's getting them in that's difficult.

The marginal ones are different: they're easier to deal with at the beginning, but they become more troublesome at the end. They're not sagacious, they don't negotiate as cagily as the successful ones and, in their anxiety, risk too much on too little experience.

A young married couple opened a Hallmark Card Store in my recycled auto-agency mall with their last and only $30,000. They were pleasant to deal with and insisted on leasing more space than they needed. They also spent too much money embellishing their store. But whether there wasn't enough traffic, or they didn't carry the right merchandise to complement their card inventory, their business floundered. They lost money and had to close shop.

But some inexperienced young people make it. And it's not easy to determine who will and who will not. A young couple in the same building leased a 1,000-square-foot store to sell art and picture framing, and within a year did so well that they doubled their space when their next door neighbor folded. The art-selling couple is well on their way to entering the successful category. With their earnings, they bought a small downtown building and opened a second store.

Inexperienced tenants test our compassion. Because of the comparatively low rent in revived buildings, young prospects with low-capital flock to them. Their starry-eyed notions of business make them unacceptable risks, but what do you do when they say, "We've got to start somewhere. Please give us a chance"? It's not easy to turn them down, especially when they're young, eager, and pleasant.

I've made some bad commercial blunders when I led with my heart instead of my head. I leased space in the same mini-mall to a friendly, bearded young man and his teen-aged wife who claimed to be experts in making custom jewelry. I built a small manufacturing shop in the rear of their space and spent a bit more than usual to decorate the front selling area, all for $175 a month rent. For several months they did well—well enough to move out of their parents' quarters and rent a small apartment of their own. Whenever I walked through the mall, I stopped at their store and left a few words of encouragement. They responded gratefully. I felt I was doing a good deed because I was giving a young couple a chance to get into "the Establishment" for a "piece of the action," as they called it. But my inner glow didn't last too long. They slid into rent arrears and became less pleasant toward me and my manager. But I was lenient. I waited patiently for them to catch up, and wanted very much for them to succeed. But my concern didn't help. After four months of rent loss, my manager found an empty store one day. They either moved to some other location or left town. They terminated their lease and, of course, I didn't bother to sue. I took my loss and chalked it up to a goodwill gesture that didn't turn out the way I had hoped.

I've had a dozen such experiences, but I'm not sorry because in trying to be understanding and helpful, I've also had some marvelous successes. One of them involved a young man who operated a record store under the name of Dirty Jack's Record Shop. He was in a third rate, dirty neighborhood (pardon the pun) and wanted very much to get into my mall. I found him surprisingly intelligent. We had gotten into a profound philosophical discussion and he tested my knowledge to the utmost.

"Look," he said, "I don't have a lot of money, but I know my record business. I think I'll do well in your mall. I won't haggle. I'll pay what you ask. Is it a deal?" He was so unlike the astute theater tenant who went for my jugular.

"It's a deal on two conditions," I said. Change the name of your store from Dirty Jack's to Jack's Record Shop, and stop selling marijuana paraphernalia. You see, I know something about you."

He smiled. "The name and the marijuana stuff were just ploys to get me started. I won't need those anymore if I move into your mall. I'm ready to meet your conditions, so I'll clean up both."

He did as he promised and he's now a successful merchant. He was among the first to pay his rent on time, and has since doubled his space. Ten years from today, he'll jell into a solid section of society and "Dirty Jack" will become a faint memory.

I can point with glowing satisfaction to several other dramatic instances where starting-from-scratch tenants in my recycled projects became successful. My conviction is that successful businessmen have an obligation to take some acceptable risks to help unsuccessful people become successful. So what if we fail in a few instances; the successes make up for the losses. Of course, we need not be foolish about it. We can't take on too many or we, the helpful, and they, the helpless, will fail together. But if, by taking some risks, we give enterprising young people a chance to succeed, we help build new points of commercial power. The rippling effects of such help strenghtens capitalism and democracy.

There's another type of tenant you should know about and recognize. I call them "therapy" tenants—people who open up stores primarily to do something interesting, not to make money. Bored wives of wealthy husbands, or retired businessmen who don't have enough to do and become stagnant are typical examples. These are good tenants because, even if they don't make a profit, the rent is paid promptly. Naturally they try to stay in the black, but even if they break even, they're satisfied. And of course, if they make a profit, the therapy is that much more effective.

Some, like two doctors' wives I know, actually became successful. They started their gift business in a recycled store as a lark but soon discovered that they had good business sense and unexpected profits came their way. But the more meaningful profit was the self-worth the women began to feel as they became more interesting to themselves and to others as their business grew. Working with people removed their bouts with boredom; activity is a great healer.

Every project will have a few unreasonable tenants. Watch out for them. I didn't and lost. I leased 3,000 square feet to a restaurateur who specialized in preparing bratwurst delicacies. He bought the "brats" (a specially-seasoned German sausage) from a special place in Sheboygan, Wisconsin, and with a great deal of promotional zeal, began touting his Bratburger Restaurant.

Several months later, I leased another 2,000 square feet to a suave restaurateur from out of town who was starting a chain of fish restaurants in Wisconsin and chose my recycled automobile agency for the location of one of them. He inserted a clause in his lease to have the exclusive right to sell fish. I agreed, because I had no intention of having any more restaurants in the mall. But, as you'll see, I didn't think ahead.

Within six months, my out-of-town fish specialist was losing money in all five of his new fish restaurants, mine among them. As luck would have it, the brat restaurant was also losing money and, in desperation, began offering Friday Fish Fries (a popular Friday night fare in Milwaukee) to bolster his trade. But by this time, the out-of-town chain operator had already closed all of his restaurants, including mine. He was experiencing a nightmare of losses, and although he was foolish to start too many restaurants in too short a time, he was smart enough to cut his losses early. I found out, though, that he was as unreasonable as he was smart.

I had a 20-year lease with him backed by his personal signature with a lot of assets behind it. I felt safe, even though he was four months in arrears. He had spent $100,000 in remodeling and fixturing his restaurant, and I felt sorry for him, but he didn't feel sorry for me when he hired a lawyer and informed me that he was not only terminating his lease, but also suing me for $100,000 to recover his restaurant improvements. We had been friendly during all our dealings, and I was shocked at his turning on me.

I had reconciled myself to terminating his lease and holding him harmless because I dislike litigation, but he had a technicality in his favor—the Bratburger was selling fish, even though these minuscule sales had absolutely nothing to do with his fish restaurant's failure.

"Al," I said when I was informed of the lawsuit, "you know as well as I that the fish the brat restaurant sold made a tiny dent in your business, and besides, you would have closed the mall restaurant for the same reasons you closed the four others. You were new in our town and you misjudged the market. I'll be fair. Take out all the moveable equipment and I'll terminate your lease and forget about the four months' rent. You've made a mistake and I'm willing to share part of the loss."

"No, George, you've made the mistake of breaking the exclusive right in my contract to sell fish, and I want $100,000."

My friend became my adversary. It was an unpleasant experience, and the first time I had ever been sued. He had pounced on a technicality; I had no idea that my brat tenant was going to sell fish. That was my big mistake. The out-of-town plaintiff knew as well as I that the Bratburger's several hundred dollars of fish sales a week did not cause his failure, but when the judge indicated that there was a technical violation, my attorney advised a negotiated settlement. I'm ashamed to reveal the thousands of dollars I lost in this lawsuit. In my heart, I knew that my opponent was completely unreasonable. In 99 cases out of 100, my fair offer would have been acceptable. I was unfortunate, however, to catch the one who was not only unreasonable, but also wealthy and smart enough to blow my tiny blunder into an unreasonable demand for damages.

So as not to be unfair to the wealthy, I want to relate an incident showing that the poor can be just as unreasonable as the rich. Partly out of compassion, I leased a 100-square-foot boutique for $75 a month to a retired woman who wanted to run a tobacco shop. Her lack of experience was surpassed only by her lack of capital. She opened her tiny shop with a few hundred dollars of inventory. Instead of being satisfied with just making ends meet and joining the "therapy" category of tenants, she thought she should make a profit. I didn't blame her for wanting it, but I was greatly disappointed at her unreasonableness. After she had been floundering for a few months, she noticed that one of the restaurants in the same recycled mall had installed an automatic cigarette machine. She was irate. How could I let him cut into her business? She was quitting and wanted damages. I told her I'd try to have the restaurant owner remove the cigarette machine. No, she said, it was too late. She not only wanted to terminate her lease, but also demanded the several hundred dollars that she had spent to fix up her shop.

With the fish restaurant experience behind me, I terminated her lease and paid the several hundred dollars. I didn't blame her as much as I did the suave fish merchant. Her unreasonableness stemmed from a lack of fairness due to a lack of business knowledge; his source of uneasonableness came from a maneuvering mind with too much knowledge and not enough fairness. I realize, of course, that I'm only expressing my side of the story.

There are only a few unreasonable tenants. Most are fine, honorable people. Their various points of view and many-faceted personalities have given me many opportunities for educational and inspirational growth. I've met many splendid people in my commercial dealings, many of whom were more interesting than the characters I've met reading some of the best novels.

THE DIFFERENCE BETWEEN HUNCH AND OBJECTIVE ANALYSIS—HOW TO USE EACH IN A RECYCLING PROJECT

Supposing you have the three prerequisites of boldness, imagination, and persuasiveness before going into a recycling project—what about getting the underlying facts before you plunge into it? Should you lean more heavily on hunch, or on an objective study analysis? You need an extra dimension of good judgment before deciding whether to use one or the other. But your answer might be, why not use both? My answer is that, even after you've arrayed all the pluses and minuses the way Benjamin Franklin used to, it still takes a flash of intuition, or hunch, or whatever you might call it, to make the final decision.

That's the way I do it—I need the prod of intuition. But it's not the way many others decide. A very smart man I knew was persuaded by an in-depth objective study to remodel a building into a department store because it was several blocks away from a huge shopping center. The facts for the project were overwhelmingly in its favor, but it flopped. Both the recycler and the merchant lost. The undetected underlying cause was the weakness of the shopping center that was to have been the magnet. The study was built on an assumption—the strength of the center. When that didn't materialize, all the pluses of the study turned into minuses. A developer using intuition might have given more thought to the shopping center's potential. This would have involved a three-dimensional view, rather than a linear one.

On the other hand, here's a success story that didn't involve a recycling project, but proves the point that hunch is often superior to studied objectivity. A friend of mine, Yoesel, about whom I've written in my previous book *How Real Estate Fortunes Are Made*, decided 20 years ago to build a $3 million shopping center next door to a large, successful one that already had the who's who of Milwaukee merchants for tenants. Here's how he made his decision.

"I was driving by Southgate," (the large, successful center) he told me, "and I said to myself, I'm going to buy that piece of land next to it because this is too good a neighborhood for Southgate alone."

This was a man with a third-grade education talking. He was practically illiterate because he dropped out of school at the age of nine and started selling newspapers to help support his parents. Not only did he not make a survey to see if another shopping center next door to Southgate was feasible, but he probably wouldn't have been able to comprehend a complicated report if he had ordered one.

Playing his hunch, he built Point Loomis, which became a tremendous success. He recently sold it for a $3 million profit. I want to quickly add that, besides intuition, which is a quick sum-up of good judgment, he had guts, imagination, and persuasiveness in overflowing abundance. And to prove that his hunches were as dependable as elaborate feasibility reports, he built Brownport, a $7 million shopping center that others thought a wild gamble. Point Loomis, they said, was a lucky fluke. Now he's going to get burned. But Brownport became even more successful than Point Loomis. All this (and I might add, several smaller recycling projects) was done without a dime spent on feasibility reports.

But you might counter that he was an exceptional case. True. Not too many of us have his uncanny, x-ray business vision. And because of it, I suggest you use a combination of feasibility and hunch. By that I mean the following: in assessing a recycling project, collect all the pro and con data you can, but do it yourself rather than rely on some professional agency that might entrust the gathering of information to some inexperienced person who might provide linear statistics rather than three-dimensional insights. By that I mean that I would rather ask a dozen knowledgeable people about the potential of my project rather than rely on dry information.

In a recycling project there are few precedents, and even the few precedents have too many variables upon which to predict the outcome. In my "Chalet At The River" rehabilitation, I would have been foolish to spend three to five thousand dollars for a feasibility study when there were about a dozen unknowns that had to be decided more by common sense than statistical data. I did what I suggested a few sentences earlier. I asked several dozen people from artists to businessmen what they thought about recycling a 70-year-old downtown furniture warehouse into apartments featuring shops in living quarters. Some thought it was a marvelous idea, others thought it was crazy. In each case, I had them give me reasons for their opinions. That's where I learned a lot. Each hit a different facet of probability, and their collective perceptions became a treasury of information. It was a mixture of psychological, economic, and sociological reasoning that I couldn't have arrived at by myself. It was a conglomeration of hunches out of which I finally fished out my own. There were plenty negatives and plenty positives, and finally, because I had the three necessary prerequisites, I plunged into the unknown with more zeal than if I had been certain of the outcome. There's a certain intrigue in uncertainty. If it's prudently assessed so that you don't leap foolishly into certain failure, then a project takes on the romance of writing a novel and not knowing whether it will be published, or working on a painting and not being sure that it will be acclaimed.

I want to make it clear, however, that you are not to disregard the obvious: the gathering of knowledge and insights that form a springboard for intuition. Before a hunch is formulated, it's certainly helpful, for instance, to become aware of the differences between the opportunities in tourist areas, large cities, and staid towns; the kind of people in each and their income range; the building's location, structural assets, and liabilities; and the project's feasibility. This is what this book is about—giving you a base of knowledge and insight from which you can get closer to that "feeling in your bones," that you're on the right track. That's what hunch is all about—a subjective feeling that you're going in the right direction.

I've been involved in several dozen fairly large, successful projects, and I've yet to pay my first dollar for a feasibility report. This is not to say that others using feasibility studies have not done well. It's a matter of attitude, style, and conviction. If I've given you something to think about, then my long dissertation on hunch versus objective study will have been worthwhile.

In the final analysis, the buck stops with you, whether to lean more on hunch or statistical data. You're the final judge.

10

MY EARLY RECYCLING PROJECTS REVISITED—TECHNIQUES OF YESTERDAY ARE STILL SUCCESSFUL TODAY

Come along with me and revisit some of my early remodelings—the successes and the failures. Let's see what we can learn from the perspective of hindsight to help us get a better grasp of foresight.

I don't believe in the cliché that history repeats itself. Nothing is ever the same, not even two snowflakes. The past should only be used as a guide, not to be repeated, because repetition stifles innovation. It takes the fun out of work.

I therefore advise you to use what I've done only as a springboard to express your own recycling individuality. Improvise and move beyond me, as I've improvised and moved beyond others. As a Japanese artist once told his students, "To improve upon what a teacher has taught is the teacher's greatest compliment."

I REMODELED EMPTY SPACE ABOVE A GARAGE INTO A TWO-ROOM FLAT—38 YEARS AGO

I started small. After being out of college and out of work for several years, I got into the real estate business out of desperation. I wanted to be a journalist but I couldn't get a job. I tried to be a novelist, also without success. So ended my writing career—before it began.

And that's when my recycling career started. An elderly gentleman who was disposing of his real estate took a liking to me and offered to sell his duplex and coach house at the rear of the lot for $2,000, with only $100 down. I bought it because, when I ran up the stairs to see the upper story of the coach house, I quickly saw another source of income. I spent $200 repairing the old plumbing and heating, and rented the two rooms for $20 a month. With the increased income, I resold the property a year later for $4,300.

I learned something early in my new career that helped me develop an interest in recycling. I took several evening courses in real estate, and among them was a course in appraising. I quickly learned that what made the most sense, out of the three main methods used to determine property value, was the *income approach*. Numbers two and three were: *cost of reproduction less depreciation*, and *comparative market value*. Number two was too general and often misleading, and number three was not a dependable guide because two properties are never alike. But when we can project the income stream of a property for ten or fifteen years, that's what gets the closest to the heart of value.

With that conviction as my guide, I began to see very early how creating new income in old property skyrockets its value. I've never wavered from that basic theory. It has helped me make a lot of money, and it revitalized many neighborhoods. As a pioneer in rehabilitation, I know that the added-value theory through increase in income is the driving incentive behind today's recycling revolution.

It was a logical theory when I started, and its logic is even more relevant today because of the high cost of new construction.

I CHANGED A ROOMING HOUSE INTO 11 APARTMENTS—37 YEARS AGO

While I was forming an organization to sell residential real estate, I concomitantly looked for old, under-used properties that lent themselves to increased income.

With my limited capital, I tackled my next project: a huge rooming house that was half empty, in a shabby neighborhood on the south side of our city. I bought it for $5,000 with $500 down and hired an unemployed carpenter to convert it into 11 small apartments. In appreciation for giving him work, his productivity soared. Singlehandedly, he remodeled the maze of grimy rooms into 11 clean, three-room apartments—in only three months—and they rented as soon as they were finished. I spent $3,000 on this rehabilitation, and sold the property for $13,000 to an investor based on its income. In my spare time, I earned $5,000 in less than six months while I was building my sales organization. I'd like to add the interesting financial fact that my net profit from my real estate brokering that year was not much more than the earnings from that one project.

I haven't visited the remodeled coach house nor the 11 apartments for a long time, but I'm quite sure that, with the housing shortage today, tenants are still occuping them.

These are not very exciting projects, but bear with me as I chronologically unfold my personal recycling evolution. I promise it will get more interesting as you read on, and if you do, I'm sure you'll better understand today's recycling revolution.

I had no access to recycling literature—there was none. I had to grope slowly, with my own instincts. You're more fortunate. You can share my experience, build on it, and move beyond.

I LEARNED SOMETHING OF GREAT VALUE WHEN I RECYCLED 8 APARTMENTS INTO 16 UNITS—35 YEARS AGO

When you can get as much rent for a sparkling clean, four-room apartment as you can for an eight-room neglected one, you've got a potential bonanza in the making. Hundreds of millions of dollars have been made by remodelers all over the country who recognized this important economic fact and did something about it.

My eyes lit up with expectation when a bedraggled eight-family was offered to me for $25,000 in an excellent location. As I was walking through it, my mind was already arranging each huge flat into two small apartments. I bought it at once, and put my carpenter to work as soon as I cleared the building of its tenants. With very few changes except eight extra bathrooms, I got as much rent for the eight smaller, front apartments at $90 a month as the previous owner was getting from his eight larger units. Half of the former tenants rented the newly remodeled, smaller apartments. The eight four-room rear units, at $80 a month, added about $7,500 additional income a year. Capitalized at 10 percent, I added approximately $75,000 value to the building, based on the income approach. I spent only $10,000 for remodeling, so that at a total cost of $35,000, I was getting about $16,000 a year in rent and netting $11,000 after fixed expenses and before debt service. That was about a 30 percent return on my $35,000 investment. Not bad when the interest rate at the time was only 5 percent.

This was not a particularly innovative idea, but it stretched my imagination. Although it was a small project, it was a giant step toward a fuller realization that recycling old buildings could become a vehicle for building a high return investment portfolio with very little seed money.

REVIVING A DYING DOWNTOWN OFFICE BUILDING—34 YEARS AGO

There's a big jump from residential to commercial recycling. First of all, you're dealing with more sophisticated sellers and tenants. Also, the remodeling is more complicated and the financing more difficult. But the rewards are greater, and there's less competition because there are fewer entrepreneurs who are bold enough to tackle the greater hazards of commercial recycling.

Across the street from Milwaukee's City Hall was a 40,000-square-foot, five-story, barely breathing office building in dire need of resuscitation. It was half empty, with the other half occupied by tenants who were paying a dollar per square foot a year—if and when they paid it. The location was as prime as the building was poor. It was an intriguing challenge for a young man who had tasted residential recycling success and was now eager to confront a more difficult problem.

The owner of the Pereless Building, as it was called, was obviously losing money and both he and I were at a loss to arrive at a fair price. Not one of the three appraisal standards—cost of reproduction, market value, or income approach—applied. What would have been a simple solution for me now seemed insurmountable then. Putting all my limited ingenuity to work, I came up with a solution that satisfied the seller and, more important, myself.

I had an organization of ten residential salesmen at the time, and had produced several million dollars worth of home loans for the president of a savings and loan association. He had never made a commercial loan before, so he was skeptical when I said:

"Bob, I can buy the Pereless Building for $70,000 cash, and I'd like a loan of $60,000.

"It's a dog. Why would you want to buy it?" he asked.

"Because I think I can lease it up to produce $60,000 a year rent," I replied.

"But you're asking for an 85 percent loan. Even on residential, I don't go higher than 70 percent. Commercial is riskier. I might consider 60 percent, and that's only because I know you've been a successful remodeler," he answered.

"But, Bob, I need the $60,000 loan because I intend to spend $30,000 rehabilitating it. That would make it a 60 percent loan," I countered.

And to clinch the argument, I added, "I'm willing to put it in writing and certify the $30,000 expenditures."

After another half hour of persuasiveness as to the feasibility of the deal, Bob said, "I'll O.K. the $60,000 loan, but you'd better produce, because while I'm allowed to put 5 percent of our assets into commercial loans, I'll be severely criticized if I start off with a bad one."

"Let me do the worrying, Bob. You don't have to," I said.

Within a year, I spent $35,000 in selective cosmetic remodeling. (I say remodeling, because the word recycling had not, as yet, entered the real estate vocabulary). I upped the rent from $20,000 to $70,000 a year, and I was netting $40,000 after fixed expenses. That's about 40 percent return on cost, so it turned out to be a highly successful project.

But the Pereless Building was not destined to live long. Ten years later, the second largest bank in Wisconsin was assembling land for a $35 million home office building, and the Pereless was right smack in the middle. I was in the driver's seat, enjoying the sweet fruits of my risk-taking when the bank's real estate broker approached me on the sale of my property. I knew of the bank's plans and the broker knew I knew. I was in an enviable position.

"Place a fair value on it," he said, "and we'll buy it for cash. But I hope you're not going to be one of those hold-up guys who are difficult to deal with. Make it fair."

"Give me a day to think about it," I said.

The next day he called. "Two hundred twenty-five thousand," I said.

"We accept."

And that was the end of the Pereless Building. On its site, together with several other parcels of land, now stands the Marshall and Ilsley Bank Building.

I had a funny feeling when I saw the Pereless being demolished, even though I earned close to $300,000 from the cash flow during the time I owned it, together with the profit from the sale.

WHEN I WAS BAFFLED ON HOW TO BUY A 100,000-SQUARE-FOOT STORAGE BUILDING, I HIT ON SOMETHING NEW—33 YEARS AGO

No two deals are ever alike. That's why real estate is so fascinating. This is especially true in trying to determine the profit potential of recycling a building from a lesser to a higher use. Sometimes the problem defies solution. That's when imagination can stretch the mind from the known to the unknown.

About 33 years ago, a successful candy salesman decided to get into the real estate business. He bought a vacant, 100,000-square-foot, six-story grocery warehouse and began looking for tenants. He couldn't find any. A year passed and his building remained vacant.

One evening, the lecturer in my appraisal course was discussing the advantages of a 99 years lease. As he was talking, an idea clicked in my mind. The next day I arranged a meeting with the candy salesman.

"I learned something about a 99-year lease last night that could make sense for both of us. I know you're one of the greatest candy salesmen in America, but selling space is something else. Why don't you stick to selling candy and leave the leasing to me? What I'm trying to say is that you can lease your building to me for 99 years and get a steady income, instead of losing money in a vacant building."

Several days later, we met again and agreed on the following terms: I was to form a shell corporation, which was to sign a 99-year lease on the basis of $28,000 a year for the first 15 years, $20,000 a year for the next ten years, and $15,000 a year for the remaining 74 years of the lease. I agreed to pay two years rent in advance.

Paying that $56,000 rent in advance triggered his acceptance. Why not! He only paid $100,000 for the building. I borrowed the $56,000 from my bank, and gave my equity in the building and my personal signature as collateral.

As I look back now, the candy salesman and I structured the 99-year lease amateurishly. The rental should have started at a lower level and increased gradually, instead of the other way around. But who heard of inflation then! Looking at it another way, the advantages were equalized. He gained in the short run by getting all his money out of the deal in a few years; I gained doubly in the long run by having the rent come down as inflation went up.

But so far, we've only dealt with finance. Now comes the nuts and bolts of the conversion—how to create a profit.

I learned that the Army Reserve Training Center was looking for space near the downtown area. My building was at its edge. I contacted the top brass of the procurement division and pointed out the building's salient selling points. The captain was impressed, but I didn't get the final O.K. until a brigadier general flew in from Washington and approved the space. We signed a lease for 60,000 square feet at $35,000 a year for five years.

My banker and I now breathed more easily as my collateral grew stronger. Within 60 days, I leased the remaining 40,000 square feet to a plastic manufacturing firm for $35,000 a year. I was left with about a $25,000 a year cash flow, after all fixed expenses and lease rental. I used the prepaid rental of $28,000 to pay off the bank and the additional $25,000 overage to pay off the $125,000 loan I had used for installing new plumbing, heating, electric fixturing, and partitioning.

After five years, the army moved to a training center of its own and, by coincidence, the plastic firm went bankrupt at the same time. I had a vacant building again, no money in the corporation, but also no debts—I had paid off the bank and had amortized the $125,000 remodeling loan from the profits of the last five years.

I was now faced with a potential loss of about $45,000 a year: $28,000 leasehold rent and $17,000 fixed expenses, but I also had a building with $125,000 worth of improvements it didn't have when I originally leased it. Here again, the talent to lease space loomed as the main factor between success and failure. I keep stressing this because it's at the heart of risk-taking. The less ability you have at leasing, the greater your risk.

Besides knowing how to negotiate a prudent lease, you have to know where and how to find prospects. In addition to the various promotional plans described in Chapter 4, you should be active in your community and keep your eyes and ears open for tidbits of information that might flush out potential tenants. I don't drink alcoholic beverages, so I miss out on gossip leads that one can pick up at bars. However, I make up for it by attending many civic affairs. At one of those meetings, I received a tip that the General Merchandise Company was bursting to expand. I called the president and told him that he was in a position to get a tremendous space bargain. The owner of the firm was the kind of man who "smelled" a bargain even before he saw it.

"It sounds good," he said, after I explained what I had. "I'll take a look."

He liked it, and being a successful man, he rammed through an extremely favorable lease for General Merchandise.

"You tell me you were netting $25,000 a year before you lost your tenants. But now you have a vacant building and based on the $28,000 you pay to your lessor plus other expenses, you're losing between $40,000 to $50,000 a year. Right? Well, I'll absorb the $28,000 and all the the other expenses and let you net $10,000 a year."

I squirmed for more but there was no way. We signed a ten-year lease on his terms. It wasn't too bad a deal for me because, without a dime of my own money, I was still netting $10,000 a year. In addition, the company spent about $100,000 improving my building. It modernized the two elevators, built new partitions, added light fixtures, etc.

Seven years later, General Merchandise decided to give up its space because of a merger with another company. I was left with a vacant building again, but this time I had a millionaire dangling for three remaining years on the lease. I could have sat back and collected $10,000 for another three years, but that's no fun. There's no action in it. Since it was costing General Merchandise $55,000 a year to remain on the lease, I offered to cancel it for $80,000. They accepted at once, and it was good for both of us.

With the $80,000 cash profit in my pocket, but faced with a potential loss of about $50,000 a year, I began a new round of thinking to see how I could put the building to a higher and better use.

Two unrelated things then happened, which enabled me to lease the building for the third time. One started with a spur-of-the-moment idea. I had occasion to pick up a sundry item at a wholesale medical supply company, and noticed that the firm was operating on six floors of a 20-foot-wide building that had no parking and poor loading facilities. I asked to see the president of the firm.

"You're in awfully narrow and vertical quarters," I said. "Shouldn't you be on one floor?"

"I sure should," he said. "But I own the building and I'm stuck with it. No one will buy it."

"You've just sold it," I said seriously.

"To whom?" he asked.

"To me. There's only one catch," I said, "I'll buy it providing you become a tenant of mine in a building I control several blocks away."

"I hope you're not kidding," he said, "because I'm interested."

Within months, we signed a lease for 35,000 square feet at $18,000 a year for ten years. I paid $40,000 for his 10,000-square-foot building. I resold it for $20,000, but it was profitable to take a loss in order to gain a tenant good for $180,000 over ten years. At times, it's prudent to take one step back in order to take two steps forward.

While attending a board meeting of a nonprofit agency that deals with rehabilitating retarded people through work therapy, I heard complaints from the director that their space was too cramped, cut up into too many sections of the building, and generally inadequate. After the meeting, I suggested to the director that he look at my building.

"But our budget is low and our demands are high," he replied. "We can only pay 50 cents a square foot, heated. And we need many functional amenities catering to the infirm, and no money to pay for them."

"There's no harm in looking," I said.

"Certainly not," he replied.

The director looked, and liked the building. But while the medical supply tenant took two floors as is, the director of the agency agreed to lease four floors for $32,000, providing I remodeled them to fit his needs. I agreed, and before I was through, he used up all of my $80,000 profit from the General Merchandise lease. It was not a particularly good deal for me, but it was for a wonderful cause. Several months later, I leased the basement for $6,600 a year to bring the total rent to $56,600 a year. But by this time, my leasehold rent dropped from $28,000 a year to $20,000, and my net return came to approximately $17,000 a year.

Now both the building and I were getting tired. I sold my leasehold interest several years later, for $100,000 with nothing down, to a very good friend of mine, with the provision that if for any reason he decided to drop the deal, he could do so without any collateral consequences. He was to pay me $10,000 a year, including interest and principal, until the entire $100,000 was amortized.

For six years my friend was making the payments regularly, until the medical supply company became financially sick and folded, and the rehabilitation agency decided to move to larger quarters.

"George," I heard my friend say on the phone one morning, "I'm turning the building back to you."

For the fourth time I had a vacant building! I tried to sell it to my 99-year lessor for $100,000. He wasn't interested. I could tell by his conversation that he was more interested in getting it for nothing if I let go of my shell corporation.

It was 1973 now, and America was in a recession. I decided to give the building another recycling shot by turning it into low-priced office space. By now, the premises were greatly improved, with excellent elevators, good lighting, new plumbing, and adequate heating. I found that not enough businessmen, even down the financial ladder, wanted to locate off the beaten path as this building was. However, after a blitz advertising campaign, I got 80 percent of it leased for $130,000 a year. And, as Milwaukee's downtown began to move southward, the building's potential began to move up.

I sold it two years ago to an up and coming young real estate operator for $100,000 in cash and the balance on a complicated rent performance formula, which, when the water is squished out of it, will bring another $200,000.

As of this writing, the building is on hold. That is, the yearly rental is still $130,000, but any month or year, with a lucky break, it could be converted into modernized office space to yield $500,000 a year. The reason for this optimism is the new 1981 tax law (explained in Chapter 4) which can reduce interest rates from 16 to 6 percent due to investment tax credits and accelerated, 15-year depreciation allowances. When the recycling revolution sweeps into Milwaukee with full force, the present owner could make more in one year remodeling the building than I've earned during the some 30 years I owned it.

HOW I LOST $2 MILLION THROUGH LACK OF BOLDNESS—32 YEARS AGO

What follows is a short narration (as I look back with my accumulated recycling wisdom) showing how foolish I was to turn down an opportunity that comes once or twice in a lifetime.

A smart real estate man, who was more interested in sailing than work, bought the 100,000-square-foot Mitchell-Mackie office building in Milwaukee for $100,000. To the connoisseur, its architecture conveyed the elegance of the Old World, but to the layman at that time, it appeared to be nothing more than an old gray brick building with lots of gingerbread. It was the same story as with many other old buildings—half empty and the interior in shambles. Under its shabby gray brick was an architectural pearl, but attitudes were different then. Anything old was bad, anything new was good; and although I didn't subscribe to that false syndrome, I was unfortunately influenced by it.

The Mitchell-Mackie needed a lot of renovation and a lot of money to turn its operating statement from red to black. Yet its owner asked $200,000 for it, and at that time it was out of my reach. This happened soon after I had signed the 99-year lease for the grocery storage building with the candy salesman. I tried using the same idea on the owner of the blighted office building and almost succeeded.

The sailing enthusiast was finally reconciled to the fact that he couldn't get $200,000 in cash and was willing to settle for a 99-year lease at $25,000 a year, provided I sign it personally and, as additional security, convey my equity for ten years in a $100,000 apartment building I owned. I could keep the income but not mortgage the building. But no, he was not interested in having a shell corporation sign the lease the way I arranged it with the candy salesman. That stopped the deal. I was too concerned about putting my 16-family in hock for ten years and mortgaging my future with a yearly $25,000 debt in the event I failed.

A foresighted attorney bought the Mitchell-Mackie for $200,000, soon after my deal fell through, and gradually over a period of several years, renovated it so that he was able to keep the existing tenants and attract new ones. Ten years ago, he turned down an offer of $1 million, and today, it would easily bring $2 million. This was in addition to the several million dollars the building earned for the owner during the last three decades.

In retrospect, as foolish as my decision was to turn down the recycling challenge because of the personal liability factor, I want to caution the reader that it's still a danger to be considered carefully. While I missed out on millions because I refused to sign personally, it could have gone the other way and become a financial burden for the rest of my life.

A few years ago, a very good friend of mine was offered a choice between taking a limited partnership liability position with a limited return in a $75 million apartment project, or signing personally as a general partner to the extent of $1 million with a much larger return if the project succeeded. He chose the latter and lost $1 million, the extent of his wealth. Signing personally is a treacherous business. That's why corporations were born—to limit a businessman's liability.

The Mitchell-Mackie loss did bring some gain. It sharpened my prudence and increased my boldness. The right combination of prudence and boldness is what fuels action. The Mitchell-Mackie failure, as we shall see, triggered a dozen successes. But never again did I have the opportunity to make so much with so little risk.

HOW I RECYCLED A WAREHOUSE TO MANUFACTURING SPACE WITH DEFT LEASING AND FINANCING —26 YEARS AGO

Fortified with increasing boldness, I stepped into deals where the fainthearted feared to tread. I was shown a huge, 200,000-square-foot warehouse in an industrial area, opposite mountains of coal alongside the mouth of the Milwaukee River. It looked desolate by day and eerie at night—a radical departure from the old, smaller buildings I had been used to viewing in residential or commercial neighborhoods.

The challenge was to recycle the warehouse into light manufacturing space, something with which I was not familiar. I was to provide heat from a boiler that was as big as a house, and whose machinery looked as strange to me as something that would baffle anyone who knew nothing about it.

But I was intrigued by the enormity of the building. The owner, who used only 30,000 square feet of it for manufacturing machine gun shells for the government, was anxious to sell it.

"I had it sold for $400,000 with $50,000 down," the owner told me, "and a closing date set six months later. But because the buyer couldn't find tenants for the remaining 170,000 square feet of warehouse space during the six months, he dropped the deal and lost his $50,000."

I appreciate your forthrighness," I said, "and I'm going to match yours with mine. It's a risky deal but I think I can handle it, providing you reduce my risk and I reduce yours."

"What do you mean?" he asked.

"This is what I mean. Sell me the building for $250,000, and I'll lease the 30,000 square feet you occupy for ten years at 75 cents a foot, or $22,500, with this interesting kicker. Since I know that the government can cancel your shell contract at any time by giving you 30 days notice, I'll include a clause to cancel your lease in 30 days, concomitant with the government's clause."

"I don't like the $250,000 price, but I like the cancellation offer. I'll sell providing there are no other strings attached," he replied.

"There won't be any," I said.

I took a three-month closing date, during which time I beat the bushes and flushed out the Gleason Corporation, a successful materials handling manufacturing firm, whose astute president beat me into leasing him space at the bargain price of slightly less than 40 cents a foot, heated, or $35,000 a year for 90,000 square feet. On the financial strength of the two leases, I was able to obtain a $225,000 mortgage. I only had $25,000 in the deal, and was breaking even after fixed expenses and debt service. My cash flow profit lay in leasing the final 80,000 square feet of vacant space.

My boldness paid off. Few would have taken the chance I did, but it was a prudent move because of the confidence I had in my leasing ability.

I now began to stretch my imagination to get away from my break-even position into one of profitability by leasing the remaining 80,000 square feet.

I didn't have to look far. Cutler-Hammer, Inc., a multimillion dollar corporation, practically surrounded my building with its various plants, yet its management had never shown an interest in the building. I had a hunch that sooner or later a situation would develop where Cutler-Hammer might need some extra space.

My intuition was right. Five months after I bought the building, Cutler-Hammer's management communicated, through its broker, an interest in the 80,000 square feet. I leased it to them for $30,000 a year. I was now enjoying over 100 percent return on my $25,000 investment.

There wasn't much creativity in merely pocketing $30,000 a year profit. I needed cash with which to do more recycling. A unique idea had made it possible for me to buy the building, and now I was dredging my mind for a creative idea to sell it. When you knock, doors open. I knocked on the nearest door—Cutler-Hammer, Inc. I called its broker and told him that his client ought to buy the building for the following persuasive reasons:

1. I was willing to sell it for $365,000 with *nothing* down.
2. I pointed out that the $56,500 rent from the 120,000-square-foot tenants would pay the interest and principal on the $225,000 mortgage and all fixed expenses, and that his client would then have free rent for its 80,000 square feet.
3. It would save $30,000 a year.
4. Furthermore, I arranged for Cutler-Hammer to be able to expand its operation in the building by getting Gleason, who now occupied all of the 120,000 square feet, to agree to vacate its space any time during its lease if it got six months' free rent. This turned out to be a key selling point.
5. And then I came up with the most important argument of all. There was talk of an expressway cutting through a part of Cutler-Hammer's buildings, in which case they might need my entire building.

The broker must have done an excellent job of convincing, because his client promptly accepted my terms and, soon afterward, gave notice to Gleason to vacate and occupied the entire building.

I had a good reason to sell the building with no down payment. Cutler-Hammer's signature made bankable my equity between what I owed to the savings and loan association and what it owed me. Furthermore, I had a hunch they would not remain a borrower for long. I was right again. Within six months, they paid the entire $365,000 in cash; I paid the balance I owed to the savings and loan, and pocketed a profit of about $150,000, plus what I had earned during the time I owned it.

Within several months the profit began burning a hole in my checking account. My mind began racing and I was up and away looking for another recycling project.

I STARTED A RENAISSANCE OF NOSTALGIA WHEN I SAVED A 75-YEAR-OLD BUILDING FROM THE WRECKING BALL—27 YEARS AGO

At the turn of the century, farmers hitched their horses alongside the Steinmeyer Building. It was a farmer's mart then, a sort of Gay-Nineties supermarket. After the farmers sold their wares in the city, they would stop at the Steinmeyer to buy groceries before returning to their farms.

Twenty-seven years ago, the building was a shabby relic of its glorious past. Today it is a hundred-year-old centerpiece in two square blocks of buildings that have undergone a renaissance of bringing back the nostalgic past to the busy present.

I started this renaissance by buying the 50,000-square-foot, mill-constructed, six-story Steinmeyer for $130,000. The owners were glad to get it because the rent from the first two floors was $20,000 a year and the expenses about the same. The upper four floors were vacant, and when I walked through them, I could still smell the acrid aroma from the old coffee grinding machinery that had been gathering dust for decades.

Twenty-seven years ago, the Steinmeyer at first glance was a poor buy. It was in a rundown, congested area, surrounded by characterless, blighted buildings. That's the way the location was perceived at the time—simply a slummy section at the edge of downtown. But I had a different vision for the Steinmeyer and its adjacent neighbors—a vision that eventually revitalized a small enclave of buildings four blocks from our city's prime location, and a block away from the Milwaukee Journal's newspaper plant and offices—the key to my vision. I needed its promotional help.

I cleaned the grime off several bricks and found, to my surprise, a rich red that I pictured would make an interesting contrast to the gray terra cotta adorning the lower floor and its ornamental arched windows. Sandblasting the exterior was the answer. That was my first foray into it, and I've been sandblasting paint off old buildings ever since. When I restored the Steinmeyer's original naked red, it became a conversation piece among all the building owners in the area. That was the beginning, but it was apparent to me that I wouldn't be able to make an enchantress of this 75-year-old dowager by just removing the old makeup and powdering her face. She needed a new hairdo, a face-lift, and a few internal operations to make her attractive and healthy.

At that time, my mind was not yet honed to merchandising old architecture as a form of uniqueness. That's why I made the mistake of changing the lobby's old look and foolishly spent money on fluorescent lighting fixtures, fissured acoustical tiled ceilings, asphalt tile floors, and removing faded wood paneling. I mistakenly tried to create a modern contrast to the more beautiful old look of the building's exterior. However, I did one thing right—I converted the old freight elevator into an automatic, self-operating passenger type. That was a much needed and prudent functional change.

Now I was ready to begin renting space at one dollar a square foot per year. I knew I couldn't attract doctors or lawyers. Instead, I directed my sales campaign toward printers, charitable agencies, artists, manufacturers' reps and the like.

The low price and my concentration on selected low-paying tenants paid off. I leased 5,000 square feet to a group of commercial artists who were captivated by the north light and the Gothic windows. The Wisconsin Heart Association needed lots of space but had little money in its budget for rent. Its officers admitted they were getting a bargain when I accepted $600 a month for 7,000 square feet partitioned into private offices, with acoustical tiled ceilings, asphalt tiled floors, and flush fluorescent lighting, a plush item at that time. A fur auction association needed 7,000 square feet at periodic times of the year to show their mink pelts to customers, and could not afford to pay more than $500 a month for open space. I partitioned off almost an entire floor and they were delighted with it. I was even able to lease 2,000 square feet to a casualty insurance agency because it couldn't resist my low price.

Within a year, I filled the building to a gross rent of $60,000 a year. I spent $130,000 for remodeling, in retrospect, some of it for show rather than function. But I was learning. The 75-year-old "lady" was bursting with pride. My leasing success gave her a new lease on life; she was active again. Though she was not as beautiful as when the farmers wooed her three quarters of a century ago, she was attracting the attention of the owners of the neighboring buildings.

The invigorated Steinmeyer was netting $30,000 a year, and when, a few years later, I received an offer of $285,000, I accepted. I earned about $50,000 during the time I owned it and $25,000 on the sale price. Not a howling financial success story after all my remodeling and leasing work, but it triggered other benefits beyond recycling one building.

The owners of a dozen buildings on both sides of the two adjacent blocks liked what they saw in the Steinmeyer and began to restore their own 75-year-old "ladies." In addition to exterior changes, many of them needed plumbing and heating transplants to join the mainstream of activity. The Usinger Sausage Company sprouted into a bit of old Switzerland, and a three-generation restaurant embellished its exterior with Teutonic crests and shields to enhance its aura of German *gemuetlichkeit*. And the Milwaukee Journal, when it bought the Milwaukee morning newspaper, the Milwaukee Sentinel, spruced up an adjacent,half-vacant, 75-year-old building, and filled it with administrative and editorial offices. The Journal Square, in melding the old with the new, created one of the most aesthetic restoration projects in the country.

Today, there's a beautiful old vine-covered bank turned into an Historical Society on a triangular lot half block away that adds to the European scene. A two-acre park along the Milwaukee River just a block away has been created to blend with the nostalgic renaissance of restored old buildings in which the Steinmeyer played a stellar role.

I checked recently with the manager of the Steinmeyer about its present gross rent and the type of tenancy. It had been upgraded, but mostly with the tenants' own improvements. Publishers, advertising agencies, media communicators, and documentary studios are paying the owner $150,000 a year rent. It had been an excellent investment for the owner for almost three decades. When I asked the manager about the building's structural condition, he said:

"The Steinmeyer has another hundred years of life. Its foundation hasn't budged an inch."

Will the area remain revived for another 100 years? That depends more on the owners than the buildings. In Switzerland, they don't let buildings die. Their collective cultural attitude won't permit it.

We're finally turning in their direction. The Steinmeyer was a practical example of owners who caught the recycling spirit and, by reinforcing each other, changed blight into light, neglect into preservation.

WHY MY RECYCLING EFFORTS DIDN'T CATCH ON SIX BLOCKS FROM THE STEINMEYER—25 YEARS AGO

Why does one country advance materially and spiritually while another doesn't? The answer, of course, lies in the difference between the nation's stock of people. It's the same in cities, communities, and even in a small enclave of buildings. The kind of owner makes the difference.

On the northwest corner of Seventh and Wisconsin Avenues, Milwaukee's main downtown thoroughfare, two buildings were joined to comprise 80,000 square feet and became known as the Welch Building. One was a former auto dealership and the other a light manufacturer. Four of the seven retail shops on the first floor were rented, and half of the upper floors were vacant. Printers and light manufacturing firms were sprawled in disarray on various floors. I saw an opportunity to upgrade the neglected buildings for three excellent reasons: they were on the corner of Milwaukee's main downtown street, they were four blocks from its prime location, and they were two blocks from the city's largest hotel.

The buildings were ripe for recycling, and to my good fortune, the owner was ripe for letting them go. He was a wealthy, 75-year-old retired president of a large Wisconsin corporation, who was more interested in his Florida vacations than doing anything with his property. His apathetic management held the rental down to $40,000 a year—slightly more than his fixed expenses. Yet he had the *chutspah* to ask $500,000 for his properties.

"Why?" I asked after he admitted that his real estate was losing money.

"Because it's a great site for future development."

Sensing that I couldn't budge the sophisticated executive from his price, I took another tack.

"How do you intend to invest your money if you get your price?" I asked.

"In mortgages," he answered. "Perhaps you'll help me find a few good ones," he added with a twinkle in his eyes.

My train of thought was taking on momentum as I asked, "How would you like to sell your buildings, invest your money at the same time, and as a sweetener, not have to pay income taxes while doing it?"

"It sounds good. But what are you driving at?" he asked.

"Well," I said, "listen carefully. See if what I have to say doesn't make sense, both for you and for me, and won't satisfy Uncle Sam."

"All right, go ahead! But it'd better be good, because I'm pretty good at tearing schemes apart that don't make sense, and what I can't tear apart, I've got an attorney who can."

"Here it is," I said. "You lease the building to me for 50 years, on the basis of a $500,000 value, capitalized at 4 percent interest or $20,000 a year. This is $20,000 more than you're getting from your buildings at the present time, since your expenses are about equal to your income. And you pay income taxes on the rental income only as you receive it. You pay no taxes on a sale, yet, in effect, it is a sale. What I'm saying is this: you are, in effect, selling your building for $500,000 and simultaneously investing the money with me at 4 percent, using your own buildings in which you have a lot of confidence as your collateral. Price-wise, return-wise and tax-wise, it makes a lot of sense for you, doesn't it? But it would not be a good deal unless this plan also makes sense for me, and it does. Here's how.

"I believe that if I spend $75,000 in remodeling your buildings and renting the vacant space, I can bring the rental up to $80,000 a year. Thus, after $40,000 expenses and paying you the $20,000 a year rental, there will still be $20,000 left for me. That would be a good return on a $75,000 remodeling investment."

Would you guarantee to spend $75,000 within, let's say, two years as a condition to the deal?" the owner asked with a spark of interest.

"I'd say it's fair," I said. I knew I couldn't bring the rental up to $80,000 unless I spent at least $75,000.

We closed the transaction with no money exchanging hands, and I was in control of a $500,000 piece of good downtown property.

My imaginative financing had worked; my first recycling step was successful. My second step was equally successful. Using direct mail advertising, selective solicitations, newspaper stories and advertising, I obtained tenants on whose additional income I was able to borrow the money needed for remodeling. Actually, I spent $100,000 and got the rental up to $85,000, mostly from attorneys, labor unions, and advertising agencies.

The third step was unsuccessful. My rejuvenation of the building didn't cause a stir among the adjacent building owners. They were a different breed. Unlike the owners near the Steinmeyer, these had no spirit of cooperation or interest. While my building teemed with new life, the adjacent ones slid into greater neglect.

Several years later, I sold my 50-year leasehold interest for $50,000 profit. There was a change of ownerships several times after I sold it, and in preparation for the writing of this book, I visited my old recycling project.

I was disappointed. The attorneys, unions, advertising agencies, and other users of office space had long since moved out. One of the buildings had been razed, the other had reverted to light manufacturing, and the blighted surrounding buildings had deteriorated into further neglect. My restoration effort didn't spread. Instead, it was contained by indifference.

A new, 20-story office building has since risen across the street, after an entire block of still useable properties had been razed for it, but the surrounding old buildings were not helped by it, and hence sank deeper into blight.

I have stressed elsewhere that the new does not help the old unless the old is renewed into functional offices, apartments, or shops. Because the owners within several blocks of my remodeled Welch Building didn't band together to restore their buildings the way others had around the Steinmeyer, the area deteriorated, the owners continued to sustain losses, and that part of downtown slipped a notch deeper into decay.

HOW I LEARNED TO MERCHANDISE OLD CHARM —24 YEARS AGO

Revolutions burst forth suddenly, but behind them are slowly cumulative, evolutionary forces. Evolution always precedes revolution.

The present recycling revolution came out of evolutionary necessity: economic, social, and aesthetic reasons that could no longer be held back. In the process, I and thousands like me, began to learn the importance of merchandising the ornamental charm of old buildings rather than tearing out their old architectural features and replacing them with new ones.

I learned this lesson gradually, but it was quickened when I recycled the Bresler Building. It taught me a valuable lesson in preservation and restoration.

Bresler Galleries, for whom the building was named, was a mecca for art-lovers for half a century. Some of the leading artists of our country showed their paintings there, and its picture-frame department was nationally known. It's craftsmen framed many world-famous paintings. The three-floor, 25,000-square-foot building was located on Milwaukee Street, the artiest street in our city. In its heyday, Bresler Galleries occupied all three floors of the building, but as time went on, its business had dwindled to the point where it was occupying only half of the first floor and paying only $350 a month rent. The rest of the building was vacant.

The elderly owner wanted $120,000 for it, and of course, based on income, no one wanted it. My offer of $75,000 was quickly turned down. Unless I was ready to pay $120,000, the broker told me, the owner would definitely not sell.

I was listening to a real estate appraisal lecture one evening when the following statement changed my mind: "Each city has unique locations which cannot be duplicated in any other part of the city. These unusual locations are like diamonds: they are rare."

My mind quickly raced to the Bresler Building. Its location was unique. Many quality shops in the city were on that street. A high-fashion woman's apparel shop next door, I found out, did

$750,000 a year in sales—a huge gross volume in those days. The next day, I called the broker and offered $120,000. It was accepted. The lecturer, in effect, sold the building for the owner. The broker failed to call my attention to the word, "rarity." He missed the most dynamic selling point of his listing.

The owner of Bresler Galleries, upon learning that the building was sold, became frantic. He knew that his $350 monthly rental was very low, and that it would be raised considerably. When I told him that I had to pay a stiff price for the building and that his rent for his first floor store and the entire basement area where his frame department was located would have to be $750 a month, he told me he would have to go out of business.

I felt badly, but not for long. Friends of art came to his rescue. A group of wealthy art-loving women formed a corporation and backed the Bresler Galleries with new capital. We signed a seven-year lease at $750 a month.

I was delighted when my artsy tenant told me that he didn't want any changes made in his store. I thought it had a shopworn look and I was ready to spruce it up, but he said no. What apparently looked dilapidated to me, looked artistic to him. I learned my first lesson in art—old can be beautiful.

The second floor had about 5,000 square feet of net rentable area. Half of it had a Florentine motif, with a red clay tile floor from which oozed white specks that an artist friend of mine called "an interesting patina." A window opened from that space into a small patio enclosed with black corrugated iron. This area, which had been vacant, no longer looked decrepit to me. Even the dusty fresco-plastered ceiling had appealing interest. There was only one logical thing to do: look for artists who would appreciate its neglected uniqueness. That triggered a prudent search, and when you search prudently, you find, as I did. A group of artists became enthusiastic when they viewed the space.

"Why didn't we know that such unusual beauty existed in Milwaukee?" they asked.

"Because it's been hidden for decades, that's why. Now you can enjoy it," I told them.

I leased it to them at a modest price with no remodeling—they did the restoring. They found the jewel, and I, an appreciative tenant.

The street door leading to the second and third floors was about twelve feet high and five feet wide. It was thick and massive, with a coat of drab gray paint. I was ready to spend a thousand dollars to create an aesthetic entrance. I called in an architectural designer and asked his opinion. He closed his eyes in thought for awhile.

"George," he said when he came out of his reverie, "I've got the perfect answer. Leave the door exactly where it is. There's not another door as high and wide and massive in Milwaukee. Just remove the paint and antique it. Make it look old with new paint."

I took his advice and antiqued the door for $50. It's still there after 25 years.

The third floor walk-up presented another lesson in merchandising old charm. It consisted of an 80-foot x 100-foot clear-span ballroom, with a 22-foot-high ceiling. I was told by the 75-year-old broker who sold me the building that, in his youth at the turn of the century, he had frequented this stately dance hall in search of romance. Since there was no elevator in the building, leasing this space was quite a challenge. My twelve-year-old daughter, who was taking dancing lessons at the time, led me to the answer.

When I called for her one day at the dancing studio, I noticed how dingy and cramped the quarters were. Here, I thought, was the solution to my quest for a ballroom tenant. Before I left with my daughter, I made an appointment with the dance instructor to show her the third floor of the Bresler Building. She was captivated by it. I leased it to her and she put her students to work painting walls, varnishing woodwork, and sanding the beautiful oak floor. They made the studio gleam. Using pieces of antique furniture, knickknacks, and artsy doodads, she and her students created a terpsichorean atmosphere that was superior to any in the Midwest.

I leased the other half of the first floor to a carpet company, and the remaining second-floor space to an exclusive beauty salon. My total remodeling expenditure was only $25,000, spent mostly on plumbing and heating to renew the building's usefulness. The "as is" sold itself because I was able to locate tenants who appreciated the original architectural design—the Old World distinctiveness.

By preserving the old and adding the new only where necessary, I had breathed economic life into a dying building. With a gross rental of $28,000 and a net of $18,000 a year, I sold the Bresler Building a year later for $180,000. I earned only $35,000, but I created a slight stir among the other building owners in the area. I woke up a few "Sleeping Beauties"—princesses from another era that needed only a kiss of the imagination to give them new life and new profits for investors.

Today, 25 years later, the Bresler Building looks better than when I sold it. Naturally, there have been tenant changes, but its original 100-year-old charm is still there, in the French Mediterranean exterior and in the oak woodwork and century-old skylight on the first floor, where the Noble Art Company has moved in when the Bresler Galleries moved out. The second floor, with little change, is now used by a public media company, and the third floor by another dance group.

It's exactly the same and as beautiful as it was 100 years ago. Some buildings, like awakened princesses, live happily ever after.

BECAUSE I DIDN'T KNOW HOW TO RECYCLE FOUL AIR, I MUFFED A BIG DEAL—24 YEARS AGO

Because I failed to become involved in the full spectrum of recycling—from the sublime of the Bresler Building to the stench of the Greenebaum Tannery—I let my squeamish nostrils lose a million dollars for me. The Bresler experience exposed me to artistic beauty; the Greenebaum Tannery, to the stink of foul air. A recycler should be many-faceted, because opportunities often lie in the crudest and foulest of places.

A retired tanner offered to sell his vacant 500,000-square-foot plant, involving a chain of 17 connected buildings, for $1.5 million. Prospects looked at it but didn't know what to do with it. A year later, the price came down to $1 million, but there was still no interest. Wanting to get rid of it once and for all, the tanner offered it for $500,000, with only $100,000 in cash as a down payment. I decided to look at it for that price. One dollar a square foot, including land: it sounded incredible, especially since the acres of buildings had railroad siding and excellent truck-loading facilities.

As the broker began leading me through the building, my nostrils began to burn and my head swam from an unbearable odor that permeated every breath I took. I suffered uncomplainingly through the hour it took to inspect the buildings, and I'm sure the broker stayed with me only because he had to.

When I stepped outside, I gratefully gulped in the fresh air and said to my companion, "John, this isn't for me."

I didn't realize it at the time, but I was saying good-bye to over a million dollars.

Why did I dismiss this bargain so quickly? The foul air was the main reason; the labyrinthine maze of interconnected buildings was another. The immensity of potential repair and maintenance was still another. But I didn't think these obstacles through carefully, and that's why I muffed another profit opportunity of my recycling career—the first was the Mitchell-Mackie Building described earlier.

A businessman with less sensitive nostrils but more guts and imagination bought the buildings. He hired a chemist (I never thought of that) who disinfected the air so it smelled as pleasant as a department store perfume counter. In one year's time, he had leased the entire 500,000 square feet of the buildings for storage, to some thirty different tenants, at 40 cents a square foot. His gross income was about $200,000 a year.

With the buildings leased, he had no difficulty obtaining a $500,000 mortgage so that he had no money of his own in the deal. After debt service and fixed expenses, he cleared $100,000 a year.

The interest rate at that time was 5 percent. It would have taken $2 million invested at the going rate, to earn $100,000. It would have taken the lifetime earnings of perhaps five medical specialists, added to the earnings of five top lawyers, to accumulate $2 million after taxes. Our gutsy businessman accumulated its equivalent in only one year.

The irony of this spectacular reuse project was that the broker who sold the buildings leased almost all the space for the purchaser. The broker's leasing commission was a pittance, compared to what his client earned in the deal. But, we must remember, there are many brokers but few imaginative risk-takers. In a free society, we need both, and what's wonderful about it is that we're free to choose between being a functionary or a risk-taking entrepreneur.

In the fall of 1981, the elderly owner of the Greenebaum Tannery came to me for advice on how to dispose of his holdings. He was by now a millionaire, living on a yacht with his wife in a plush Florida yacht club.

"I'm retired now, and although I can manage the building from Florida through my manager in Milwaukee, I neither need, nor care to monkey around with my real estate any longer. I'd like to sell it, What do you think I can get?"

The rental of his buildings were now averaging 75 cents a square foot, and while half of them were still used for storage, the other half was now upgraded for offices and light manufacturing. The total income was about $400,000 a year, and the net, after all the increased fixed expenses but before debt service, was about $200,000 a year. With those figures as background, I now had to place a value on his buildings at a time when the prime interest rate was 20 percent. Keep in mind that I was facing an undereducated but street-smart man, who was aggressively competent in commercial matters but not intelligent in real estate economic theory.

"This will shock you, Eddie," I said, "but I don't think you're going to get more than $1 million for your building."

"You're full of ______, George," he spouted, "and I'll show you why. Twenty-five years ago when my rent was $200,000 and my cash flow $100,000, I could have gotten $2 million for my building. Now, when real estate values are sky high, you tell me they're worth only half of what I could've gotten 25 years ago? You don't make sense."

"Listen, Eddie," I said calmly, "you asked for an opinion and I'm giving it to you straight and gratis because I've known you for many years. I've respected your ability to take a bunch of smelly buildings that no one wanted, and which I passed up, and have them make a millionaire out of you." When I saw his burly face break out into a smile, I added a bit of levity—"You came out smelling like a rose."

"O.k., George, excuse my rudeness. But let's get to the point. Give me your reasons for the $1 million figure. I respect your opinion. That's why I called you. But your answer got me mad."

"Listen and learn," I said confidently. "You've heard of money market funds, haven't you, where you can get as high as 18 percent return on your money? Well, your $200,000 cash flow isn't much more than 20 percent return on $1 million. That's when you're fully rented, as you are now. But it can drop to $150,000 in the next few months. Why should anyone take all the headaches of managing, maintaining, and constantly rerenting buildings to have a return that's only a point or two more than what he can have, trouble-free, by investing in money market funds? What you're not aware of is, that in spite of high inflation , the high interest rate is what has cut the value of your buildings in half. Twenty-five years ago, 5 percent was a good rate of return, and your $100,000 cash flow was worth $2 million. Now, your $200,000 cash flow is worth $1 million, because the interest rate is almost 20 percent. Do you understand now why no one will pay more than $1 million for your buildings?"

He squirmed his bulky frame in his chair, and pointing his huge paw in my face, said: "You just wait. I'll show you how I'll get $2 million. And when I do, I'll call you, and you be sure to put in your book that I was right and you were wrong, and that you didn't know what you were talking about!"

It's 1982 now, and so far, he hasn't called! I don't expect to hear from him, as long as the prime rate hovers between 15 and 20 percent.

11

MY MORE RECENT RECYCLING PROJECTS REVISITED—HOW I COPED WITH NEW PROBLEMS IN MORE AMBITIOUS VENTURES

For 16 years, I'd been recycling in the minor leagues; earning and learning, progressing from apprentice to journeyman, from journeyman (if you'll excuse my immodesty) to master. If success and mastership are synonymous, then I guess I can claim to be a master.

I took longer to reach the master stage because I was groping alone. There were no books like the one you're reading now. But after a dozen small-time recyclings, I felt I had enough experience to step into the big time where the risks and rewards are greater. But, again, I want to caution you that the major leagues are for those who have the three prerequisites in great abundance: boldness, imagination, and persuasiveness.

MY FIRST BIG-TIME RECYCLING VENTURE: CONVERTING A WAREHOUSE INTO A MODERN MEDICAL OFFICE BUILDING—22 YEARS AGO

The foul smell of the Greenebaum Tannery taught me a fresh lesson in recycling: don't be stymied by new obstacles. That lesson took root when I was offered a 100,000-square-foot dust-laden warehouse that had become woefully misplaced because the neighborhood had changed into a residential apartment district. The location was no longer suitable for warehousing, and the reisdents were uncomfortable with this building in their midst.

The owner tried to sell the six-story structure for $500,000. There were many lookers, but no takers. The price dropped to $400,000, then $300,000, and still no one found an answer for converting the warehouse to a higher use.

I was teaching a course in Creative Real Estate at the University of Wisconsin in Milwaukee at the time, and used the building as an example of a problem that defied solution. One student suggested that it could be converted into a nurses' dormitory, since it was close to two large hospitals. Another proposed that it be converted into apartments to blend in with the neighborhood. Still another thought the building ought to be razed and replaced with a brand new luxury apartment building because the site was only a block from Lake Michigan and therefore, merited the highest development.

Then one student hit the jackpot with an excellent idea. Why not convert the warehouse into a modern medical office building catering to doctors from the two nearby hospitals. As soon as he said it, it rang a bell in my mind. It was a case of the student teaching the teacher. The more I thought about the idea, the more convinced I became that he was right. I bought the building for $205,000.

Converting a warehouse into a medical office building presents many more problems than building a new one. In planning a new project, one does not inherit the limitations of an existing structure. But this was only the beginning of my problems. The more formidable ones were ascertaining the cost of remodeling, mortgaging the building without knowing the costs in advance, setting up a rental schedule and methods of promotion, creating parking and, perhaps the most important of all, giving it the clean, attractive appearance that a modern medical office building should have.

The problem of ascertaining recycling costs was almost insurmountable. There were only a half-dozen windows in the entire building. The inside was a labyrinth of dimly-lit passageways dotted with steel doors, behind which were stored furniture, memorabilia, and sentimental, if not valuable, possessions of many well-known Milwaukee families. There were few heating and plumbing lines, and only sparse electric wiring in the building. The exterior was of white glazed tile that was badly cracked and discolored on the first two floors, yet for some reason, in pretty good condition on the upper floors. Since I had no idea whether I was going to fill the entire building with physicians or a combination of doctors and other commercial tenants, there was no way of determining the costs in advance. I decided on a bold plan of action that required face-to-face negotiation with my key contractors, on the basis of time and material, with an agreed upon a margin of profit. This is dangerous at best. I don't recommend it, but I had no choice. I couldn't think of any other way.

Financing a conversion without knowing the cost in advance cannot be arranged with an ordinary mortgagee: he or she has to be extraordinary. After being turned down by a half dozen lenders, I was fortunate enough to be introduced to Jim Gibson, a mortgage representative of The John Hancock Insurance Company whose Milwaukee mortgage correspondent was The Richter-Schroeder Company, Inc. I told Mr. Gibson that I had no tenants and that I could only guesstimate the cost of remodeling at about $1.1 million. However, I pointed out to him, I had the finest location for a medical office building, and there were no other commercial sites that could be zoned in the near future to compete against me.

I said to him, "If you're looking for a mortgage wrapped in blue ribbon, safe and cut and dried, this is not it. However, if you're willing to dream with me, risk with me, and back me on a real estate adventure that will not only secure a prudent mortgage, but could revitalize a neighborhood, then we will both be doing the extraordinary. In an adventure such as this, I need an imaginative mortgage man like I hope you are, and you need an entrepreneur like me. Together we can do the unusual."

After three hours of exhilarating negotiation, which often bordered on the inspirational, he agreed to make an $850,000 loan. But because the mortgage was a bit more risky than usual, he upped the interest rate to 6¼ percent. I didn't object, he was entitled to it. It was not run-of-the-mill.

In retrospect, the thought of expecting doctors to look at an old warehouse, and sign a lease on the basis of a word picture of what their offices would look like, staggers me now. But it didn't scare me then.My optimistic enthusiasm melted all doubts. I had a tremendous talking point: I was only one block from one hospital and eight blocks from another. Over 500 doctors were within walking distance of my building! This was my key argument in presenting the evidence to substantiate the $850,000 mortgage.

A former chief of staff of St. Mary's Hospital, along with a group of four other surgeons, cautiously explored the possibility of moving their clinic, located three miles away from the hospital, to my building. As I had anticipated, they were enchanted with being one block from their base of operation. They were hesitant about leasing space they hadn't seen. I pointed out that I had never seen any of them operate either, but if the occasion arose, I would be willing to have any of them operate on me. Why not some mutual confidence? This argument apparently had results. After more negotiations, they signed a lease.

This was the beginning of an avalanche. Doctors have a way of following each other, especially those with good reputations. I filled about half the building with medical men, and the other half with commercial and professional tenants. When top-flight lawyers and insurance companies offered to lease space in my building, I decided to take them instead of risking failure by waiting to fill the entire building with medical tenants. I leased part of the ground floor to a *Big Boy* restaurant, with a $600-a-month minimum against 5 percent of the gross, and after the first year of operation, I was receiving close to $20,000 a year rent from the restaurant. It was a pleasant financial surprise—a bonanza for me and a boon to my tenants who were delighted with its food, convenience, and pleasant atmosphere.

Creating ample parking was important, so I solved it in this way. Next to the warehouse, and included in the real estate I had purchased, was a one-story service garage of approximately 13,000 square feet. I removed the roof and added three tiers of parking. It provided about 130 parking spaces: enough for the all-day parking needs of the tenants in the building, in addition to the transient parking of the patients and clients who came to see them.

Function without aesthetics is like a body without a soul. Removing the warehouse look and creating a handsome structure without spending too much money was an economic, as well as an architectural, challenge. We solved it this way: the building was triangular-shaped. One of its angles nosed into the corner of Prospect and North Avenues. We snipped off a piece of this angle on the first floor, converted it into a lovely Japanese garden, and made it a part of the lobby. Since the white tiles on the first two floors were broken and discolored, I had them covered with new, white-painted brick, and picture-framed the brick with a black, ten-inch iron border. The exterior of the upper floors was of brick and tile, and in good condition. I had it painted white to match the two lower floors. The result was a dazzling white structure that looked brand new (my propensity for sandblasting didn't fit in this case).

Within 18 months after remodeling started, I had the building 100 percent occupied. The rent roll was $240,000 a year. The net before principal and interest payments was $120,000 a year, and the cash flow after mortgage amortization and interest was $50,000 a year. The building was appraised at $1.5 million. My cost was $1.3. It was a good deal, not a spectacular one.

The impact of this conversion, however, was spectacular. It sparked a neighborhood renewal program. Three new buildings were built in its wake, and others began to pretty up and remodel. The warehouse eyesore that had marred the residental tone of Prospect Avenue became a mark of beauty. The Big Ben clock, which was housed in a ten-foot high dome atop the warehouse and whose hands had not moved during the last 20 years, was repaired, painted white, and lit up so that people could read the time for blocks around. The doctors were the most appreciative tenants in the building, because their offices were now only a few minutes away from their hospital. Many of them seldom used their cars; they walked to the hospital and, being close to the lake and park, it was a pleasant walk.

New wealth had been created through private urban renewal, which made sense for the entrepreneur; created a safe, $850,000 loan for an insurance company; increased the tax-base for the city; and gave work to dozens of men for more than a year.

The warehouse conversion was by far the biggest, most complicated, and most interesting recycling project I had attempted up to 1960. It prepared me for a much bigger one to follow.

However, to wind up the medical building story, it would be profitable for the reader to know how I fared financially. During my 20 years of ownership, I averaged about $15,000 a year cash flow and about $30,000 a year amortization on my $850,000 mortgage. The reason my cash flow dropped from $50,000, when the occupancy was 100 percent, was because about ten years ago, St. Mary's Hospital built its own office building a block away, and most of the doctors moved to the hospital where they practiced.

In 1979, I sold the building for $1.25 million, with a $250,000 cash down payment and the balance of $1 million on a land contract which, in effect, was a wraparound mortgage behind my $250,000 that I still owed John Hancock. In order to give the buyer a $30,000 cushion of cash flow for his $250,000 cash investment, I had to structure the wraparound $1 million mortgage with monthly payments of only $6,300 to include interest and principal, interest at 6 percent until the entire amount was amortized, which was about 30 years. Why such a low interest rate when the going rate at the time was 10 percent? Because if I charged the buyer even 8 percent, he would only have a $10,000 cash flow for his $250,000 cash investment, and he would not have purchased the building. Had I been stubborn and asked for an all-cash deal, I could have gotten only about $850,000 instead of the $1.25 million for my property. It illustrates the point I made to the owner of the Greenebaum Tannery, that high interest rates depress the price of investment property when you depend on third-party financing.

However, the medical building still turned out to be a profitable recycling project. By 1983, I will have cleared the John Hancock mortgage, and then, for the next 25 years, I or my estate will enjoy a free and clear annuity of about $75,000 a year.

And to bring the story up to date, I've been informed by the present owner that his cash flow has been increased from $30,000 to $75,000 a year. The building is of such solid concrete and steel construction that I'm not exaggerating when I predict that it will enjoy a profitable investment life well into the 21st Century.

WHY I PAID $1.7 MILLION FOR A HALF-EMPTY APARTMENT HOTEL THAT WAS LOSING $100,000 A YEAR—15 YEARS AGO

As explained elsewhere, a hunch is a quick, prudent comprehension of a situation that defies ordinary reasoning. That's what happened when I "foolishly" bought the Knickerbocker, a dying apartment hotel for $1.7 million when it was losing $100,000 a year. A hunch spurred my decision.

The hotel is in an attractive residential location, and yet conveniently located a few blocks from downtown. It has charm and flavor, with half of the hotel rooms for permanent guests and the other half for transients. However,the hotel was a bit off the beaten track for transient hotel trade. A "jumping" restaurant and discothèque were on the premises, but these two operations only jeopardized the tenancy of the permanent guests. The hotel was neither fish nor fowl—neither permanent residential nor transient hotel. The restaurant and the discothèque were also operating in the red.

Why, then, did I pay $1.7 million for a building that was losing money? Because beyond its apparent disadvantages, I saw a magnificent fireproof structure, located one block from Lake Michigan, a property that would cost $5 million to reproduce. I couldn't resist the challenge to put it to its highest and best use.

But you must be careful when you become intrigued with meeting challenges, because sometimes they can inundate you. I was inundated with $300,000 of expenses during my first two years of operation, in addition to my fixed operating costs. This $300,000 had to be spent to stave off the tentacles of creeping obsolescence. The electrical, heating, and plumbing systems had to be overhauled; many of the apartments needed painting, carpeting and new furniture; the creaky elevators had to be replaced by new ones; and dozens of miscellaneous, mismanaged items had to be attended to.

I closed down the discothèque and restaurant, and leased it to a gourmet café operator for $15,000 a year. I discontinued the transient hotel trade, and concentrated on getting permanent guests to move back into the building.

After three years of operation, with the help of a $1.5 million mortgage and $500,000 of my own money, I still was losing $50,000 a year. Some challenges can indeed try one's soul and pocketbook.

Why couldn't I make a go of a building that had so many amenities—architectural uniqueness, ideal location, 200 charming apartments, and good management? I did some research. I found that Milwaukee's four other apartment hotels, of about the same size, vintage, and location, were doing worse than I was. I managed to get their operating statements, since each one was for sale.

In each case, the causes for the poor financial showing were the same. Higher operating costs compared to new buildings, lower rents, and higher vacancy rates. I was caught in the same vise.

I offered the building for sale, hoping that someone else had a hankering to test innovative ideas. About a dozen buyers looked at the operating statement and said no—except one.

"Yes," he said, "I'll buy your apartment hotel, if I can buy it with nothing down."

I must have looked surprised, because he said, with a twinkle in his eye: "That shouldn't startle you. I've read your *Leverage* book, in which you say, 'any damn fool can buy a building for a million dollars if he has a million dollars. The trick is to buy a million-dollar building with no money.' Well, I have no money, and I'd like to buy your building."

I smiled. "What you didn't read, apparently, is that if you don't have any money, you must have unusual ideas, and a track record showing that you've made some of them work. What's your idea and what's your track record?"

"I want to turn this building into communal living for the elderly. I managed such a building in Florida, and I think this idea could catch on in northern climates as well."

But you lose $5,000 a month the moment you take this building over," I said. "Where are you going to get the money to make up the loss? It will take you at least a year to turn this building around, even if your idea succeeds. Under these circumstances, aren't you asking too much to have me hand you a $2 million project with nothing down?"

Of course, his deal didn't work out, but he did give me an idea.

HOW COMMUNAL LIVING FOR MOBILE 80-YEAR-OLDS AND OVER STIRRED MY IMAGINATION AND SAVED MY PROJECT

If you are 80 years old and over, too mobile and healthy to live in a nursing home, but too insecure and weak to live all alone in an apartment, and if there is no place for you with your children, where should you live?

Every city has thousands of people like these. Many of them are at nursing homes against their will, and many others live alone, corroding in loneliness, often too weak to shop for food, let alone prepare and cook it.

Before we began looking for these people, we converted one of the luxury, 2,500-square-foot, three-bedroom apartments overlooking the lake into a charming, homelike little restaurant. We built a kitchen, hired a chef and a few waitresses, and we were ready to begin.

We formulated a price program. For an efficiency and three meals a day with minimal care (that is, if any of the elderly became sick, we would be responsible for calling their children or a doctor), the price was $350 a month; for a studio, $400 a month; for a one-bedroom, $450 a month; and for a two-bedroom, $500 a month.

We couldn't use the free public media because we had nothing to say and nothing to show. So we formulated an ad that featured pleasant, independent living, with 24-hour switchboard service, maid and linen service, three home-cooked meals, a recreation program, and a choice of private apartments.

We began to get one or two phone inquiries a week, and we responded by sending our brochure that described our program in detail.

Then we sent letters to every doctor in Milwaukee County, asking if they had any elderly patients who should not be in nursing homes, or who were too fragile to live alone and should be living with us where, with minimal care, they could prolong the independent management of their lives. We received only a few inquiries.

It took several months before we signed up our first member.

We took several one-minute spots on a local television station. The response was weak.

By the fifth month, we had only five members. To give some identity to the elderly who were living with us communally, we made them members of the Juneau Club. I was now losing more money than ever.

One morning while I was shaving, I hit on the idea that our newspaper ad should appear on the television page, since the elderly usually are avid TV-watchers. I called my advertising man and asked him to place the ad there. We received 15 calls. And from then on, every time our ad appeared on theTV page, our calls multiplied. Within six months, we had 20 members in the Juneau Club.

"Now," I said to myself, "I'm ready to put the public media to work." I had something to say.

I called the real estate editor of the Milwaukee Journal and gave him the story.

"Here is a way for mobile people over the age of 80 to prolong their independence," I told him. "It's a new idea that works."

The real estate editor did a magnificent story, with pictures of typical apartments and the restaurant full of club members at one of their meals. Within one month, as a result of this free story, we leased more apartments to Juneau Club members than we had leased in eight months at a cost of thousands of dollars.

We began getting inquiries from small towns within a 100-mile radius. I wrote a feature story about the Juneau Club, enclosed several pictures with it, and sent it to every small-town newspaper within that 100-mile radius. About ten of the twenty newspapers ran it. Our inquiries increased, as a result, and new members were added.

Then I hit on another idea. Why not have a documentary done by our public broadcasting television station? Sure enough, the station manager thought it was an excellent idea. The station taped the Juneau Club story: more inquiries and more members. Then our leading commercial television station ran a three-minute news feature on the Juneau Club, and our unique way of caring for the elderly became a household word in Milwaukee's metropolitan area. Then followed an interview with a radio reporter, and later a slick monthly magazine, catering exclusively to Milwaukee readers, did a feature on the Juneau Club.

What paid advertising couldn't do, the free public media did. They gave our idea visibility and success.

Graduate students in sociology and psychology became interested in our idea, and I gave several lectures on the new concept of caring for the elderly. Retired lawyers, musicians, teachers, businessmen, engineers, and school principals began to fill the Juneau Club ranks: people from the middle class and up.

Many of the active elderly came from nursing homes in which they stayed reluctantly, only because they were too feeble to fend for themselves with all the myriad duties of housekeeping. Others who lived alone in apartments or homes that were more chore to them than comfort came to live with us, and left the cleaning, shopping, and cooking behind.

The Juneau Club became permanent resort living for them—nutritious meals prepared by a fine chef, served three times a day by friendly waitresses; maid service; switchboard security; friendships if they cared to make them; entertainment several times a week; immediate reporting to their children or doctor when they took sick—all this indirect care took place in an uninstitutionalized atmosphere where they led independent lives, just like any of the other tenants in the building.

One day an official from Health, Education and Welfare came to look us over, to study what we were doing for the elderly. She was impressed. In parting, she offered this very wise advice:

"Don't make the mistake of institutionalizing your idea. That is, don't turn all your 200 apartments into a Juneau Club. If you do, you'll turn the Knickerbocker into and old people's home. Don't have more than 75 members. Let them be a part of, not the whole of apartment living. That's when you'll do them the most good."

I never forgot this advice. I understood what she meant when I saw the octogenarians ogling the mini-skirted permanent tenants who came through our lobby, making friends with the young couples who rented from us and chatting with people who were generally in the mainstream of active life. That interaction was good for the elderly and good for me. It stamped "Success" on my Juneau Club idea.

And this leads me into innovative idea No. 2: converting one-third of the apartment hotel into a "Home Away From Home."

HOME AWAY FROM HOME—A DYNAMIC IDEA THAT BOOSTED MY INCOME

You are an executive trainee who is away from home and being prepared to assume a new position in a new city. You have to be away for three months. Perhaps you have your wife along, or even your children. You can't rent an apartment because the owner or manager wants you to sign a year's lease. You don't want to live in a hotel, because it's too expensive and too busy. Where shall you stay?

Or, you are a professor who has been invited to lecture for three months at an urban university. You'll have the same problem as the executive trainee.

In Milwaukee, you'll have no problem. You can stay at the Knickerbocker Apartment Hotel, which has set aside about 100 units for "Home Away From Home" tenants. It does not demand a year's lease, nor does it ask you to pay the regular high rates. The average daily rental of an average hotel in our city *15 years ago* was about $18, or $540 a month. At our "Home Away From Home," the monthly rate for a furnished efficiency was $225; a studio, $275; a one-bedroom apartment, $325; and a two-bedroom, two-bath luxury apartment, $450. These monthly rentals reduced to daily rates amount to $7, $9, $11, and $15, respectively. We were giving them larger quarters, kitchens, a quiet atmosphere, a homey charm for less than half of what they'd have to pay for much smaller hotel rooms.

It's a pioneering real estate idea that has caught on because it meets the needs of a mobile society, and takes into account the popularity of exchanging lecturing professors. Not only that, but our "Home Away From Home" was used locally by people whose homes or apartments were destroyed by fires, by those who needed a temporary "home" between buying and selling houses, and by new families moving into town and looking for a home. A month didn't pass without at least one irate husband or wife who, after a spat with the spouse, would come to our hotel to "cool off" for a month or two.

However, our main monthly users were industrial trainees from out of town, visiting professors, people who live in the south and came to Milwaukee for the summer, theater people, and families from foreign countries who had reason to stay in our city for several months.

Our "Home Away From Home" idea succeeded because there is as definite a need for monthly transiency as there is for daily transiency, only it's on a smaller scale. That such a need exists is borne out by the fact that 60 of the large corporations in our city use the Knickerbocker "Home Away From Home" facilities on a regular basis.

Yet it wasn't an easy idea to sell because we didn't operate as a hotel and the housing personnel of large corporations didn't like to experiment with placing their out-of-town guests. That we finally were able to prevail is an indication that this unusual market can be cracked in any city in America.

The "Home Away From Home" required different promotional techniques from the Juneau Club. First, we were unable to rely on the free public media. Both the financial and real estate editors of The Milwaukee Journal turned me down when I submitted an article on how the "Home Away From Home" idea was meeting a new need in our society. I don't blame them—it didn't have the poignant human interest of the Juneau Club.

However, the *Milwaukee Sentinel* did run a feature article on how the "Home Away From Home" idea was meeting a unique hotel need, and I quickly followed it up by placing ads in its financial pages.

The inquiries from the ads (which were very expensive) didn't produce the results we hoped for. The article did not stir up any interest either. Here was an innovative, money-making idea, but I was having difficulty putting it across.

Sometimes we don't see the obvious. The housewife I had hired to tell the Juneau Club story to retirement clubs, and who had done such an excellent job, was the answer. I called her in and said:

"I want you to print the same copy we ran in the newspapers on cards and send them to about 500 personnel directors of all the companies in our metropolitan area that employ more than 100 people. Then I'd like you to follow up the mailing by making a personal call to each one of them, telling the "Home Away From Home" story in your own style."

That's what did it: direct mail advertising, followed up by personal solicitation. What worked for the Juneau Club didn't work for "Home Away From Home." We had to devise something new, and it turned out to be the obvious—inexpensive and effective. The leading industrial and business firms are now using "Home Away From Home" regularly, and the number is growing. And why not? They were getting better accommodations at half the price.

Efficiencies, which used to bring $120 a month from permanent guests, were now renting to "Home Away From Home" users for $225 a month. That was only $7 a day, compared to $18 a day for a smaller room in a transient hotel.

This new idea was not only an economic boost for us, but a morale booster to the Juneau Club members as well. The building had an interesting mix: one-third Juneau Club, one-third "Home Away From Home", and one-third permanent guests. And our operating statement was just as interesting.

When I purchased the apartment hotel, the yearly gross rent was $350,000. My expenses, including the debt service on a $1.5 million mortgage, were $400,000. This amounted to a loss of $50,000 a year. By adding the Juneau Club and "Home Away From Home" into the income picture, my gross rent rose to $550,000 a year, and expenses to $475,000 a year, leaving a cash flow of $75,000. Without these two innovative ideas, there would have been no way of keeping the 200-apartment hotel in the black under the constant payment pressure of a $1.5 million debt service.

In 1978, I sold the Knickerbocker for $2 million. During the course of my ownership, I had amortized about $400,000 I had spent on improvements out of profits, and paid income taxes on $500,000 profit when I sold it. At the time of sale, the rent rose to $800,000 a year, and the present owner is now grossing $1 million a year, all due to the burgeoning revenue from two innovative ideas.

I have received several calls from people in various parts of the country who read about the Knickerbocker's success with "Home Away From Home" and the unique way of caring for people over 80. One reader called to tell me that he had implemented the Knickerbocker idea successfully on a smaller scale in his own town, and that he was planning to franchise it in other cities. He ended with, "You've changed my life. I'm a success now, thanks to you."

However, I must end the Knickerbocker story on a sad note. In spite of its tremendous success, the present owner sees in the Knickerbocker the potential for even greater success, through converting it to condominiums. When he announced his intention to sell the apartments, the elderly, backed by their sons, daughters, and grandchildren, raised strenuous moral and legal objections. The octogenarians had been content to spend the rest of their golden years at the Knickerbocker. Now where were they to go? Although the owner is a good man (I know him) acting within his legal rights, who promised the elderly that he would not ask them to move until the first 140 apartments were sold, nevertheless, 30 of the 60 elderly residents moved out. With the threat of having to leave, some became ill and others reluctantly moved to nursing homes.

Converting to condominiums is a two-edged sword: it creates more individual ownership, which is good; but it also disrupts tenants who can't afford ownership, or prefer to rent. In the final analysis, the good or bad of converting a rental project into condominiums rests on a moral rather than a legal decision. If profit is shoved too far ahead of people, it's morally wrong. That's why legislation is being considered in various parts of the country, on a selective basis, to inhibit the conversion of rental units into condominiums if it can be proven that the tenants' lives will be drastically affected.

In my opinion, the Knickerbocker's elderly would be more than drastically inconvenienced if they were forced to move. The present owner would have taken a giant step toward putting people ahead of profit if he had increased the Juneau Club membership from 60 to 85. The need to help octogenarians in Milwaukee is far greater than the need for more condominiums.

Enlightened capitalism should be just as concerned in meeting people's needs as it is in getting profits. In fact, in the long run, concentrating on meeting people's needs begets more profits than concentrating only on the bottom line. It's an idealistic theory that happens to be extremely practical.

A LOCAL YOKEL TAUGHT ME A LESSON—IT'S MORE HAZARDOUS TO RECYCLE IN A TOWN OTHER THAN YOUR OWN—TEN YEARS AGO

Yokel is not used in a deprecating sense here, but rather to convey the savvy of a local person in a small town. To give you a respite from my recycling successes, I'd like to relate a bit of levity from which I learned a sobering lesson.

I was invited to give a talk to the Sheboygan, Wisconsin Board of Realtors. The president introduced me as a successful rehabilitator, and then looked down at his notes to read what I had given him as the subject of my talk: "There's an Answer to Every Real Estate Problem." That speech cost me $25,000 and a dozen, fruitless, hundred-mile trips to Sheboygan and back, searching for tenants who weren't there. It was like looking for a black cat in a dark room.

This is what happened. After the talk, a middle-aged, folksy broker called me aside and said:

"Would you do me a favor and look at a building a few blocks from here? You said every building has an answer. I've got one that hasn't."

It was a direct challenge to the theory I had just propounded, and I readily accepted.

"Sure," I said, "show it to me."

It was a white brick four-story building, comprising about 35,000 square feet on the main street of Sheboygan's downtown, a block away from its largest department store, and two blocks from the largest bank. Montgomery Ward had used it, then vacated it many years ago.

It was a handsome building. The exterior of the second floor was indented with several colonnades to give it a pleasant

Southern appearance, and the immensely high-ceilinged first floor had a beautifully balustraded mezzanine. A wide-open stairway leading to the mezzanine gave the interior an air of elegance. The upper floors were ordinary, but in fair condition.

"What's your problem?" I asked after I examined the building.

"I can't sell it. As you see, it's a beautiful building, yet nobody wants to buy it," he replied.

"What are you asking?" I queried.

"$175,000," he answered.

"There's your problem," I said. "Get the price down and you'll have your answer."

"What will that be?" he asked.

I wanted to be sure my answer worked, even if I had to shock him. "Like $50,000," I said nonchalantly.

He didn't blink an eye. In his slow-talking, small-town manner, he asked shrewdly, "That would be an unheard of bargain, wouldn't it?"

"Yes, it would," I said forthrightly, "but it would be a quick answer to your problem."

"Would you be interested if I could get it for that low price?" he countered.

"I think I would," was my answer.

"Maybe you'll hear from me," he said, as he escorted me to my car.

Two weeks later he called.

"You've solved my problem. You bought yourself a big bargain! The owner will take $50,000."

I detected the "naive" broker's selling aggressiveness, but I took him up on it, nevertheless, because I really thought the Montgomery Ward building was a tremendous bargain at $50,000.

I bought it.

I set out to prove at the Sheboygan brokers that there's an answer to every building problem. I called several savings and loan associations to interest them in the first floor. They were too deeply rooted where they were; a better location didn't interest them; they were too comfortable to stir themselves loose. I tried clothing stores; jewelry shops, restaurants, and a dozen other categories. I heard the same response—no!

I found out, a month after I bought the building, that a new shopping center was being developed at the edge of town. That nailed my chances to the mast. The inspired optimism that I dazzled before the Sheboygan Board of Realtors had fizzled. It not only hurt my pocketbook, but my ego as well. I hired an agent part-time to spend several days a week soliciting every conceivable prospect, even printers and light manufacturing tenants. The zero results astonished me. After two years of failures and $25,000 of expenditures, I sold the building to the City of Sheboygan for $50,000. It had gotten a Federal grant to build a mall in order to save its downtown, and hoped to resell the building to a local recycler after the mall was in place.

Several years later, I drove to Sheboygan to visit my failure. It was now a huge success. The four-block mall was grandly landscaped, but I couldn't find the white Montgomery Ward Building. I was standing near a beautiful red brick building, through the wide windows of which I could see a fine restaurant and gift shop. Could this be the building that had given me so much resistance? I couldn't believe my eyes! It was! Upon closer examination, I discovered that the rich brick had always been there under the white paint. I also found out that the upper floors were now used as bank offices.

What I wasn't able to do, a recycler who was more familiar with Sheboygan and its people did, on a grand scale. Of course, the Federal grant that built the mall helped, but knowing who's who in the city was an additional plus that tipped the scales toward success.

The lesson of this incident is obvious. With few exceptions, don't try to become an expert in someone else's town. I can quote chapter and verse where experts from other cities lost millions in Milwaukee. My personal proof taught me a lesson that I hope will not be lost on you. Don't lose money in unfamiliar places.

WHEN RECYCLING BECOMES EMOTIONAL, WATCH OUT: A SAD FINANCIAL SAGA THAT ENDED IN A HAPPY NEIGHBORHOOD RESULT—FIVE YEARS AGO

When an automobile showroom, a used-car lot across the street, and a car storage building, all about a block away from the warehouse I had remodeled into a medical office building, came on the market, I was the natural prospect for them. But the broker asked an unnatural price—$800,000. Of course, I turned it down. A year later, when a dozen other prospective buyers also turned it down, the owner came to his senses. I bought the three parcels for $350,000. It was a steal, and yet not a steal, because the challenge of what to do with the vacant properties defied solution. That's why so many prospects were not interested. Frankly, I bought the properties without having a definite plan. If it's a bargain, it's not too dangerous for an experienced recycler, but it is too dangerous for a beginner, even if it is a bargain.

The automobile dealership consisted of a dingy showroom on the first floor and an oil-slicked repair shop in the basement, a total of 35,000 square feet. The building was a sturdy concrete structure facing Prospect Avenue, a densely populated street of apartment dwellers. The used car lot across the street was about 210 feet x 110 feet. The third building a block away was used for storing cars, and was about 20,000 square feet. Quite a lot for $350,000! What attracted me was that they were all a mere seven-iron golf shot away from the office in the Prospect Medical Building, which for me, shooting in the 90's, is about 125 yards.

To reduce my financial risk, I sold the automobile storage building for $125,000 to an adjoining owner. In January, I left for my winter vacation to the West Coast without any definite idea as to what to do with the other two properties. But after visiting many mini-malls in Santa Barbara, LaJolla, Carmel, and San Francisco during my holiday, I decided to convert the automobile dealership into a small shopping center, with the used-car lot across the street as parking space. The more I thought about the idea, the more I liked it. It would also be a first for Milwaukee—that was the intriguing fact that triggered my decision.

As I was preparing my mind to go ahead with it, two unrelated things happened to stop me. One was a call from a broker who represented a fast-food hamburger empire. He offered to lease my used car lot for $17,500 a year for 20 years. I could have sold that lease for $200,000, leaving me the main, 35,000-square-foot building at the minimal cost of $25,000. Soon after, a boat company showed an interest in leasing the dealership for boat storage at $20,000 a year.

While I was squirming with the decision whether to go ahead with my mini-mall or take a $20,000-a-year profit for no work and practically no investment, a community action group called me when it heard that I was dealing with a fast-food chain and a boat company. The president of the neighborhood upgrading association, who lived in a beautiful home overlooking Lake Michigan a few blocks away, said appealingly:

"You've done such a wonderful job converting the ugly warehouse into a beautiful medical building, why don't you do something unique with the auto garage, rather than downgrade the neighborhood with a fast-food operation and boat storage? We've heard about your mini-mall idea. That would be great."

She was right. Besides, to be honest, I thought the mini-mall idea, if done successfully, might earn more than the $20,000 a year my two offers, which didn't require risk or work, would bring. I happened to be reading something about Aristotle at the time, and came across one of his famous sayings: "Man is made for work." That did it: it was the final nudge. I decided to do the mini-mall.

That's where I got a doctoral degree in dealing with hidden defects, handling cost overruns, choosing tenants, and above all, learning a sobering lesson that with the excitement of pioneering comes unpredictability and hardship. I tried to lease stores without walls, a concept that worked in Santa Barbara, California, but it didn't fly in Milwaukee. I gave chances to young, inexperienced, undercapitalized tenants, and they boomeranged in two ways—toward me and them. My reward, however, was that a few made it and clawed their way into the business world.

When the financial and sociological dust settled on my Prospect Mall, as it is called, I had spent about $800,000, or better than $20 a square foot, to shoe-horn all the tenants in place. That brought the cost of the Prospect Mall to over $1 million, including the $225,000 cost of the auto agency and used car lot. I obtained a $750,000 mortgage from an insurance company, so that I had an investment of $275,000 in cash. My total rent was about $180,000 a year, and the cash flow, after fixed expenses and debt service, was about $40,000. That would not have been bad if all the tenants had paid their rent, but they didn't. About six of the twenty lessees were delinquent in the amount of $4,000 a month.

Dealing with delinquent tenants is unpleasant, and for me, being more interested in creating than managing, it was more than unpleasant—it was frustrating. What do you say to young men or women who are struggling to make ends meet and can't tie them together? They're not the least bit interested when you say, "If you don't pay your rent, I can't make my mortgage payment and pay for your heat and electricity." When one's drowning financially, one is too self-interested to listen to reason.

Prospect Mall became the centerpiece of revitalization in the neighborhood, but not a centerpiece of profitability in my investment portfolio. The neighborhood action group applauded me up and down Prospect Avenue. I was invited to give speeches to various civic clubs. But, in spite of the mall's problems, I continued to extoll the virtues of rehabilitation. Thousands of people "oh'd" and "ah'd" as they viewed the beautiful boutiques, the three restaurants, the two unusual mini-theaters, and the bright young faces of many of the first-time entrepreneurs who graciously greeted them. The physical success was visible, but the financial problems were not.

This time I did a lot for a neighborhood but little for myself. Of course, I would have gotten ahead financially by renting to the fast-food chain and the boat company, but the area would have gone downhill instead of up. I consoled myself with the thought that, "Granted, I didn't do well financially, but didn't I revitalize a neighborhood?"

I decided to sell the mall. A Chicago syndicator put together $250,000 worth of limited partners and assumed my $750,000 mortgage. I lost about $50,000 and two years of hard labor in my recycling venture, but besides reviving a dying neighborhood, I learned many valuable lessons for my next $3.5 million rehabilitation venture.

Now the area is alive and prospering. The medical office building is 95 percent occupied, and the new owners of the Prospect Mall have replaced some of the weaker tenants with stronger ones. It's gradually becoming a small, institutionalized neighborhood shopping center, meeting the needs of many people. The area would not have been the same without these major improvements. It would have become another eyesore, joining the many other unrehabilitated eyesores. Instead, taking a cue from the Prospect Mall and the Prospect Building, other buildings have begun to be spruced up and have joined the upgrading parade.

I consider the Prospect Mall a success in spite of my failure to make money. A pioneer must be prepared for setbacks. Besides, I've had too many successes to become cynical about a slight financial loss. Remaining fearless in failure builds character faster than constantly riding the crest of success.

CHALET AT THE RIVER—A ONE-YEAR RETROSPECT

I wrote Chapter 4 about the "Chalet At The River" during its completion, and wanted to narrate a detailed picture of the problems as they were happening.

Now, I'm writing in retrospect a year later. It's a huge success, 100 percent occupied, and with a waiting list.

The "Chalet At The River" is the talk of Milwaukee. Why? Because out of the grime of a blighted building, there has arisen a clean new environment, in which an interesting mix of people are finding downtown living an exciting adventure. They're matching my pioneering spirit with their own. They made my dream come true financially, sociologically, and functionally. What's more, it's a success model for others to follow.

In contrast to the Prospect Mall where I hit 50 percent—a financial failure but a neighborhood success—I hit 100 percent with the Chalet which was both a financial and a neighborhood success.

In round numbers, my fixed expenses and debt service are $500,000 a year, and the gross rental is $550,000. My $250,000 cash investment in the project should be averaging about a $50,000 cash flow—not a tremendous return, but that's just the tip of the iceberg of the profitable financial picture. In addition, I've gotten $100,000 in investment tax credits and, using the component depreciation method, I'll be able to show about a $175,000 depreciation loss against my ordinary income.

More important than my personal gain is the community success story. The Chalet not only provided moderately-priced commercial space for small businessmen and below-market-price apartments for elderly and young white collar workers, but it also revitalized a dead downtown area into a lively and interesting residential and commercial center. The Chalet was the catalyst for the renewal of six adjoining buildings, the start of three new restaurants and the beginning of about 50 small business enterprises. Altogether, $1 million of old properties have been upped, through rehabilitation, to a value of $5 million and it all happened within a short span of two years.

By now, you know how I feel about recycling. If you've labored through all my examples without being wearied, and if you've caught a spark of the inspirational spirit I tried to convey, then all my work to put this material together will not have been in vain. As others have spurred me on, so I hope you will be spurred on too. That's the joy of writing—to influence, to share, to give.

12

KEY PROBLEMS AND SOLUTIONS IN THE RECYCLING BUSINESS

The following, in essence, is a question and answer approach on how to reach the peaks and avoid the valleys in the recycling industry; it's an attempt to show how to soothe the agonies and enjoy the ecstasies of a new form of art and make big money. It's a rare combination. If the list of problems and solutions at times becomes repetitive, please bear with me, because my aim is to make sure that the key points of recycling remain indelibly inscribed in your minds.

Problem 1:

What mental gymnastics should you go through in recycling a *good* building in a *poor* neighborhood?

Solution:

It's a slippery problem that needs a firm grasp of the many factors involved. I've recently been tempted to buy a vacant, 100,000-square-foot, four-story, 20-year-old plush office building in a ramshackle neighborhood. Its space would easily rent for $10 a square foot if it were located downtown. Although it would have cost $8 million to reproduce, the multimillion dollar corporation that owned it asked only $1 million, and couldn't get it. Here's why several dozen prospects and I turned it down.

I estimated it would cost $250,000 a year to operate the building before debt service. Even if I offered the office space as low as $3 a square foot and couldn't rent it, the loss would be prohibitive. Yet, the magnificent building, with its 200 adjoining parking stalls, tantalized me. I called a half dozen social agencies whose rental budgets were low, in order to determine interest. It was lukewarm, but the broker's interest to sell it (pardon the cliché) was red-hot.

"George, you're the guy who could fill the building," he said. "Make an offer, I don't care how ridiculous. I think the owners will accept it. They want to get rid of it that badly."

When a broker talks that way, don't be ashamed to make a ridiculous offer. I did. I offered $350,000 with $50,000 down in cash and the balance to be paid at the rate of $25,000 a year, including interest and principal, at interest 6 percent, with a balloon payment at the end of 15 years. And, to protect myself, I advanced the closing date six months, during which time, if I didn't lease 50 percent of the building, I didn't have to go through with the purchase.

Sure it was a ridiculous offer, and everything was in my favor, but what if I couldn't rent the building? I, instead of the owner, would be losing close to $250,000 a year. Even if I had gotten the building for nothing it would have been a poor deal. That's why I inserted the 50 percent occupancy clause.

I wasn't surprised when it was turned down, but I would have been foolish not to protect myself against a possibly huge loss.

A good building in a bad location presents an anguishing dilemma. The pull and push between the two can be an agonizing experience. With lots of ingenuity and luck you could make a fortune, but you could also hang a financial noose around your neck. A novice should stay away from a good building in a poor location, and an experienced recycler should explore it with great caution.

Problem 2:

What thinking process should you go through if you can buy a *poor* building at a bargain price in an *excellent* location?

Solution:

This question poses different problems than that of a good building in a poor neighborhood. The focus is on the building. If it's mill-constructed, the recycling should be cosmetic rather than extensive. The old should be preserved everywhere to affect economy. The purchase price should vary in proportion to the estimated income and its use, determined by the type of city and the characteristics of the potential tenants.

Again, I'd like to illustrate from personal experience. In the fall of 1981, I was offered an excellently-located, four-story, 75,000-square-foot downtown building for $700,000 cash. I turned it down for two good reasons: the mortgage interest rate at the time was 17 percent, and the building was mill-constructed. Its floors were sagging, the plumbing was shot, the electric power inadequate, the elevators antiquated, and the heating was of the same vintage as the building—75 years old. It had been used as a furniture warehouse sales outlet.

But the location was supurb for stores and offices, and the building's architecture was extremely attractive, consisting of a series of two-story brick arches superimposed on a brick facade that fronted 150 feet on each street of its corner location. But the cost of converting its 75,000 square feet to even medium-priced stores and offices would easily have come to $1.5 million, based on my expenditures of $20 a square foot in both the Prospect Mall and "Chalet At The River." With interest close to 20 percent, such a huge investment in a mill building would have been sheer folly.

Here's how I addressed the problem, and if yours is similar, here's the way you ought to solve it. My game plan was threefold, involving the manner of recycling, leasing, and purchasing.

I decided that I would spend only $100,000 cosmetically—$10,000 for sandblasting, $15,000 to repair the two old elevators, $15,000 for adding electric power and a few hundred inexpensive florescent light fixtures, $15,000 to shore up the old plumbing, $15,000 for a few modern heating units, $10,000 for an interior paint spray, $10,000 for some partitions, and $10,000 miscellaneous. With these minimum changes, I would then go after discount houses who look for cheap space because Milwaukee buyers, by and large, are conservative, bargain-hunting customers. I estimated that I could lease the building at $3 a square foot to gross $200,000 a year.

That rounded out the recycling and leasing parts of my plan, but the purchasing part was the most important because it had to fit with the other two. The $700,000 cash asking price was a figment of the seller's imagination. Even if a 100 percent mortgage was obtainable, the interest payment on that amount would be

$120,000 a year, plus principal payments of perhaps $15,000, making the debt service $135,000 a year. That would not fit with my $200,000 a year gross rent projection, and my estimated fixed expenses of $80,000 a year. I would then have a negative cash flow of $15,000 a year for all my work. It was too risky a deal, even with the generous investment tax credits and 15-year depreciation allowance.

I therefore proposed to buy the building for $700,000, with payments of $60,000 a year to include interest and principal, and interest at 7 percent. On that basis, I could expect a $60,000 cash flow for my $100,000 cosmetic recycling investment, providing the first two steps of my game-plan worked. However, the seller refused my offer.

"George," he said, "I know how you feel about saving buildings, but I have an offer from a parking corporation to raze the building and lease the land for parking at $82,500 a year."

I had no choice but to pass up the deal. And if you find yourself in similar circumstances, I'd advise you to do the same.

Problem 3:

If you have a choice between recycling an excellent building in a poor location and a poor building in an excellent location, which should you choose?

Solution:

My preference would be the poor building in an excellent location. It stems from my theory that it's better to buy an old home in a good neighborhood than a new one in a poor neighborhood. A poor location drags values down; a good one pulls values up.

There's more money to be made in an excellent, bargain-priced building in a poor location only if the city or other private entrepreneurs will join you in your upgrading efforts. Then you gain both ways—you have a good building in a potentially good location.

There are many more options available for recycling neglected buildings in good locations than the reverse. Location, location, location is not a euphemistic theory; it's a hard, practical real estate fact. An office-user is more concerned with location than in the physical condition of his or her premises. A merchant, especially, would rather be in a first-rate location, occupying third-rate quarters, than in plush quarters in a third-rate location. Visibility, accessibility, and adjoining successful neighbors are the prime considerations.

If the many variables between the two choices are about evenly balanced, I would definitely lean in favor of a poor building in a good location than the other way around.

Problem 4:

Not so long ago, rehabilitators ripped out stained glass, old fireplaces, decorative plaster, aged wood beams, weatherbeaten clapboards, and other Old World amenities, and replaced them with modern materials. Is today's desire for the restoration of the old just a new fad, soon to fade away and depress values, or will the restorative ethic help preserve values far into the future?

Solution:

I would opt for the restoration of the old as an added value factor far into the future for two good reasons. First, in an age of scarcity, retaining the old saves material, which translates into much needed energy and economy. Second, preservation as an incremental aesthetic value will sink deeper into our collective consciousness and become a cultural plus as it has in Switzerland. As our civilization ages, so will our appreciation for aged objects.

Problem 5:

How do you determine whether a new use will fit a particular location?

Solution:

Introducing a new use in any location is risky, especially in a city where the inhabitants are traditionally grooved and slow to move out of their customary ways. For instance, a mini-shopping mall would be a chancy undertaking in a traditionally-oriented town. So would shops in apartments (Chapter 4). Or will "Home Away From Home," on a monthly transient basis (Chapter 11), catch on where it has never been tried before? Maybe. Or will recycling an old mansion near a large commercial hotel provide enough income from its overflow for a profitable mama-papa operation? Perhaps. These and other new uses introduced into towns that change slowly pose greater risks than merely recycling a building that matches ordinary uses, yet the answers would be all "go" in a rapidly changing tourist town.

To introduce something new requires new thinking, in addition to imaginative recycling. Obviously there's extra risk involved in pioneering. A demographic study of the neighborhood is risk-reducing, and your local newspaper can furnish it. A fix on the type of people in the area is a must. Freeway access, bus route proximity, and ample adjacent parking must be included in the feasibility equation. Finally, you have to use your "sixth sense" before you plunge into creating something new. If that extra-dimensional sense is sharp, you'll cut into success. If it's dull, all your accumulated statistics will not be enough. Remember, when you're plowing new ground, you have to dig deeper, and your intuition may be your only tool to get you there.

Problem 6:

How do you protect yourself from cost overruns?

Solution:

The first and foremost way to cushion overruns is to buy an old building at a bargain price. When you can reduce the price by $25,000 in a $100,000 project, or $250,000 in a $2.5 million project, that's the best place to save money for overruns. Of course, getting the proper financing will also lighten the inevitable burden of hidden costs.

Plumbing, heating, electrical, masonry, painting, and carpentry contractors are a smart lot—they can make you or break you. I've seen some who maneuver for exorbitant profits, while others are content with fair and legitimate ones. I've often had bids vary 100 percent for identical jobs. How do you protect yourself from these street-smart contractors? Two ways: one is to pick an honest, established contractor, whose workers are known for their high productivity. It's worth the effort to sift and winnow until you find one in each of the trades. When you do, they can help you to not only keep costs down, but also to show the architect how to short-cut certain operations. I've often found that honest contractors can offer more practical cost-cutting ideas than the architectural theorists.

The other money-saving method is to compare unit costs among the various contractors. Recently, I asked two plumbing contractors for an estimate for five washrooms involving about 50 toilet bowls, sinks, and urinals. One came in at $500 a fixture and the other at $1,000 a fixture. I was edified but not amazed. I've experienced those discrepancies before.

Whenever possible, whether you're contracting for paint, electricity, or drywall, don't be satisfied with a rounded number for the total job. That's where you get caught. Know how many square feet of painting area, the number of electrical outlets, and the number of square feet of drywall involved when you're getting bids. Then you can compare and negotiate the lowest price per unit cost.

There's still another way not to be fooled by an eager-beaver contractor. Get an estimate from the contractor as to how many man hours a certain job will require and measure them against the price.

About 20 years ago, when the rate per hour for a carpenter was about $4, I was looking for a small contractor to fix some windows in an old building. There was no way to get a unit price because each window was a different state of disrepair. I got a bid for $1,000. I then asked the contractor how long it would take him to do the job.

"Oh," he said, "me and my helper work fast. We'll have it done in two days."

"Then there's something wrong with your bid. It's all labor and I'm not going to pay $500 a day for two men. It's way out of line."

"Then get someone else," he snapped.

"I will," I assured him, and I did.

Another way to control overruns before buying a building is to get a compilation of general estimates from honorable contractors (and there are many), so that you have a general guideline of cost before you commit yourself to a project.

If you had questioned contractors carefully and arrived at a figure, add another 10 percent and use it as your final recycling cost guide.

Prepare well. Use every caution and precaution you can think of. When you've done that, plunge in boldly, wholeheartedly, and optimistically. Your psychological attitude is as important as all your preparation for the project's functional execution.

Problem 7:

When should you sign a mortgage personally, and when corporately?

Solution:

To say that this is a difficult question is not much help. Let me offer a few observations and then *you* decide.

The new 1981 tax bill offers enticing tax goodies in the form of investment tax credits and accelerated depreciation for the rehabilitation of old buildings. The inducements are more advantageous in a proprietorship than in a corporation, because of the additional tax when earnings are transfered from the corporation to its owner. By signing the mortgage personally, the double tax is avoided.

Also, it's easier to obtain a loan signed personally than one signed by a corporation, especially if it's a "dry" corporation formed to own a particular property. The lender is always skeptical of such a move, and will often demand a personal signature anyway to support the corporate liability.

Of course, the ideal situation is to buy a building at a bargain price, obtain the best financing available, rehabilitate at the lowest cost, and have such a high degree of confidence in the success of the project that you have no fear of signing personally, thus gaining all the tax advantages that flow from it.

Here are the dangers of signing personally. What if you've been unable to line up everything to fit the ideal situation? What if the economy takes a downward turn and lowers the occupancy to cause a negative cash flow? And what if you'd like to cut your losses by relinquishing ownership to the mortgagee?

If you have nothing, the lender can get nothing. But if you have other assets, he'll go after those to recoup his losses. However, if you had not signed personally, you'd be safe. You'd only lose your equity in the property. The more you have, the more careful you have to be about signing personally.

However, you can have your cake and eat it too if you can persuade the mortgagee to give you an exculpatory clause; that is, you limit your liability to the equity in the project. Or, if you can't get that, then settle for guaranteeing the upper 20 percent of the mortgage. It's a sound trade-off for getting the benefits of the investment tax credit and depreciation shelter personally, rather than going through the more tax-expensive corporate route.

If the lender is adamant about getting your personal signature, then you have to weigh the project's rewards against the risks. Then, after spending a few sleepless nights, make up your mind whether you want to risk assets beyond your equity. I know several developers who passed up deals and lost millions by adopting a policy of never signing personally, and several others who made millions because they accepted the risk of signing personally.

I hedged. When I built the first 200,000-square-foot, centrally-air-conditioned office building in our city in 1958, I formed a corporation to sign the $3 million mortgage. When I built the first 94-unit project for the elderly in our city in 1960, I signed the $500,000 mortgage personally. My reason for each was that I felt the office building was riskier than the housing project.

I hope these insights will help you make the final decision. It's not an easy one.

Problem 8:

If you're earning $300,000 a year, how can you shelter it and still contribute to society more than what the government loses in taxes?

Solution:

The answer is that the government does not lose and society gains when recyclers shelter their income, providing they effect two worthy results: they help the elderly, and save buildings. Let me explain.

A friend of mine built several large apartment buildings 25 years ago. When the mortgages were paid off, his ordinary income subject to taxes was $300,000 a year. He wasn't interested in airplanes, oil wells, or any other scheme to shelter his income. He was a builder who loved to create as much as he loved to avoid taxes. A stock market bonanza that could have accomplished the same result would not have interested him in the least. He was a lifter, a doer.

He converted an old, 170-room hotel in Miami, Florida into 102 apartments for the elderly under Section 8, in which the government pays the difference in rent to the recycler between the going market rate and what the elderly can pay out of their meager incomes. Together with a partner who had a $200,000-a-year income, he funded a $3 million mortgage, via a 9 percent city bond issue, and because they limited the rentals to the indigent elderly, they were allowed by the I.R.S. to depreciate the project in five years or show an approximate loss of $600,000 a year. The income-loaded partnership also recycled a decrepit apartment hotel in Palm Beach into 72 units, and another in Miami Beach into 140 units, using the same funding methods and getting the same lucrative depreciation bonanzas. When the depreciation ran out of one project, they quickly buttressed it with another.

On the surface, it would appear that the fly in these deals, for you and me, was that the government used our tax money to subsidize the elderly, and indirectly subsidized my wealthy friends through tax avoidance. True, the first subsidy is a loss, but not the second. The government will get a big portion of the tax savings back when the partners sell the buildings, or when the time comes to settle their estates. We, the government, will let them have fun for awhile, but we'll get them in the end.

A word about the first subsidy—the loss. Is it really a loss when we collectively pitch in with our tax money to get indigent elderly out of high-rent, substandard housing that cuts into their food money? Why not provide them with small, functional apartments, at low rents, so that they have a bit more money to spend on food? Without Section 8, hundreds of thousands of apartments for the elderly would not have been built. It was part of the safety net of the Nixon and Carter administrations, and it's unfortunate that the Reagan administration eliminated it.

When we add up the advantages flowing out of the recycling efforts of these wealthy men, we have to come out with several pluses: shoring up neglected buildings, cleaning up run-down neighborhoods, helping needy people, and creating work for idle hands.

While the 1981 tax law has not retained Section 8, it nevertheless provides new tax bonanzas that should be irresistable to wealthy individuals. Robin Hood robbed the rich to give to the poor. The new law has been described by the political Left as the opposite—robbing the poor to give to the rich. However, a penetrating look into the real estate part of the law will find strong support for the same societal advantages that flowed from the efforts of the wealthy Florida recyclers.

The new tax law opens up great opportunities for those who have money but want to be silent partners, and for those without money who can make it by partnering with those who have. The only flaw, in my estimation, is the elimination of Section 8 that helps the elderly.

It's true that the rich will get richer, not a particularly great societal contribution, but the effect of putting their money to work in reviving buildings and communities will, more than not, offset what many might consider the unfairness of gold lining the pockets of the rich. If you still think that it's not fair, perhaps this philosophical insight might convince you.

Why not encourage the wealthy to put themselves and their money to work to increase the wealth of our nation? Let them work themselves into a frenzy (which most of them consider fun); let their efforts percolate down into work for the idle and new life for dying buildings. As long as we legislatively guide the eager-beaver lifters into legitimate channels, and see to it that they perform with integrity, we all gain.

Problem 9:

How do you uncover hidden defects at the beginning of a recycling project so that you are not unpleasantly surprised at the finish?

Solution:

Hidden defects are the nemeses of the recycling business. No matter how closely you look, you're bound to overlook some of them. The reason for this is that you're dealing with the unseen and, therefore, difficult to detect. Here are a few tips on how to find these defects and reduce the risk of being surprised by cost overruns.

Before you buy, spend time and money with a knowledgeable, all-around engineer to test the footings, floor load, soil condition, old or new cracks, roof, elevators, plumbing, heating, electric, sprinklers, window frames, availability of wheel chair entrance, exits, etc. Then check the city code with the building inspector to see what's required, based on up-to-date code rules.

Let me give you an idea of some of the prices incurred in bringing a building up to functional use. Of course, they will vary some in different parts of the country. A new roof costs $3 a square foot, or $45,000, for a 100′ x 150′ building. A four-step elevator, with a speed of 125 feet a minute, carrying a 2,500-pound load, costs approximately $35,000 if it's hydraulic, and about

$50,000 if it's electric. If the floor load is weak for tenants needs, increasing it with steel beams or steel columns, or both, could be anywhere from $10,000 to $20,000 for a 15,000-square-foot floor. Building an interior fireproof exit, including cutting through the floor, closing it with partitions, and building a stairway, is about $5,000 per floor, not counting lighting, heating, and painting. Removing old partitions, getting rid of debris, and a general cleaning of an old building is expensive. I spent $40,000 for such a cleaning on the "Chalet At The River."

If the footings are of wood and the water level is too low so that dry rot has set in, then watch out. It's difficult to calculate the cost of such a shoring up operation except to warn you that it's apt to be prohibitive, and it's best to stay away from such a building. If the footings are of concrete but are sinking because of marshy land, that too could prove a hornet's nest of spiraling costs. It's best to pass up such underground defects before they sink you financially.

Plumbing, heating, and air conditioning are standard items and can be determined fairly accurately, depending on how sparse or plush you want to make them. There's nothing hidden about them. But check the amount of electrical power in the building. When I replaced 150 ice boxes in the Knickerbocker Apartment Hotel (Chapter 11), I was surprised with a $25,000 bill for an increased power line to deliver electricity for the new refrigerators. I had the same costly experience when I recycled the furniture warehouse into 109 apartments: the increased power demand for 109 tenants necessitated an additional power line costing $30,000.

To sprinkler a building costs about a dollar a square foot. Replacing rotted frame windows may cost from $200 to $400 apiece. Providing wheel-chair access may cost from $10,000 to $25,000, depending on the steepness and length of the rise from the sidewalk to the main entrance. I spent $10,000 in the Prospect Mall for electric chair lifts to provide transportation down stairways leading from the first floor to stores at the lower level, and up to shops on the mezzanine. The code required it.

However, the serious defects lie hidden below the building. That's where you can get financially buried if you don't get expert advice.

Another area that needs more than careful attention is ascertaining that floors are properly supported. That defect is extremely rare, but I was nearly ensnared by it once. While I was toying with the prospect of upgrading a certain 50,000-square-foot office building, my attention was drawn to a newspaper article in which the building inspector ordered the owner to vacate the building in three months because the floors were dangerously close to collapsing. Upon investigation, I found that, when some of the interior partitions were removed during previous remodeling, the overall floor systems lost much of their support. They were so serious that the value of the building dropped overnight, from a $750,000 to $250,000, just about the value of the land. A friend of mine in the construction business bought the building for $250,000, and spent $300,000 to shore up the floors from the bottom up to make them safe for occupancy.

Such a hidden defect is a rarity, but if you're thorough in your search for defects, you'll avoid the rare, the not so rare, and the obvious ones.

Problem 10:

Does it pay to cope with government's smothering regulations to gain better financial terms or tax perquisites?

Solution:

Definitely yes! However, there are those who are so politically conservative and cynical that they'll have nothing to do with projects that require government regulations. They are short-sighted. They forget that governments are people, public people helping private people. Bureaucrats are like people in the private sector—some are rigid and some are resilient.

Getting a landmark designation, for instance, is a bureaucratic obstacle course. A local historical committee has to approve it before it can be presented to a city committee, which in turn has to be approved by the state, and then by a Federal agency before the designation is finally approved or rejected. This may be a tedious process, but the results are worthwhile: for the city because it preserves historical buildings, for you because there's an additional investment tax credit of $50,000 on a $1 million rehabilitation.

If you have a worthwhile recycling project, you can fund it through city or state revenue bonding which, because of its tax-free status, could reduce the interest rate by as much as four to five percentage points, thus making an unfeasible project feasible. Sure, the government agencies make you toe the mark, but the financial rewards are worth the extra effort.

A periodic check with H.U.D. to see what kinds of financial aids are available in elderly housing, nursing homes, or housing for indigent families is an excellent way to acquaint yourself with their latest programs. Too few people are aware of the treasure trove of financial help available at H.U.D. It pays to put up with its regulations because the benefits far outweight the red tape.

Problem 11:

If you spot a bargain and don't have time to check its recycling feasibility, do you buy and plan later, or pass it up?

Solution:

The ideal solution would be to get an option on the property, but unless you can develop a special relationship with the owners, that is not easy to obtain, and for a very good reason. Why should the owners lock themselves into a price when they can keep it open for a higher one that might come along?

So, what do you do when you become enamored with a property, but have a short time to decide? I say buy it if it's a tremendous bargain, then take your time to analyze its recycling potential. If you find unsolvable hidden defects, the cost of rehabilitation too high, or the new use unworkable, then sell the bargain at a profit if possible, and at a slight loss if necessary.

But I'm assuming that you have good enough judgment to see the building's potential even from a cursory examination or, better still, from walking through it with an engineer. I hope that after reading this book and backed by its new insights, you'll see at a glance whether to risk and plan later, or not to risk at all because you'll recognize the dangers immediately.

One word of caution, and this is important: do not risk buying a $1 million building when your pocketbook is in the $100,000 class, or when you've not had any recycling experience. In other words, no matter how great the bargain, if the size of the building is out of your financial range or experience, by all means pass it up. Risk the small bargains before you jump into the big ones. That's just plain common sense, but I've seen too many people plunge into financial waters that was over their heads when they didn't know how to swim.

Problem 12:

Should you try something new in a staid town?

Solution:

It's risky, but try it—providing you value creativity as much as making money. But use prudence. Don't let your creative restlessness carry you into the syndrome of doing something just to be different or "just for the hell of it." That's not creativity—that's foolishness.

Precede your action with a great deal of thought. Don't grandstand and fail. There's no fulfillment in it. It will only diminish the potential success of your next project. Lenders shy away from nonsensical projects, nonsensically conceived by nonsensical people. Being creatively different—successfully—is what brings true fulfillment and financial rewards.

For instance, if you have your mind fixed on a mama-papa motel, don't do it in a staid small town away from a main highway. Or don't recycle an old building into a mini-mall just because your sleepy town doesn't have one and your only reason is to wake it up. You've got to have a better reason than that. The same goes for "Shops in Apartments" described in Chapter 4. And don't try for a factory outlet if your town is not near a large city from which to draw bargain-hunting customers.

But, if your town is astride a highway, or if it's within 20 miles of a population center, then try either a mama-papa motel or factory outlet. Or, if a small building you have in mind for a mama-papa motel is next to the largest hotel in a large city, that too is worth a try for a small intimate inn. And, if an architecturally attractive building is in a populated area where there are few shops, and would therefore lend itself to a mini-shopping center, then go to it, and good luck to you.

If you have trouble financing your dream because the lender lacks your imagination, tell him or her to read this book. Perhaps it'll edify him or her enough to see things your way. If you've been inspired, perhaps some of it will rub off. If you get the "bug," there's a better chance he or she will catch it too.

Problem 13:

When you have a choice to recycle a building into residential, commercial, or office space, which should you choose?

Solution:

The safest and costliest is residential. There are more partitions, more plumbing and heating, and stricter code regulations in producing residential shelter than in the other two. That's why it's more expensive. But it's less risky because it's easier to lease and maintain a high occupancy. And, because the demand for apartments is more constant, it's easier to finance.

Renting office space requires more expertise, and even with it, the results are uncertain. I've seen doctors and lawyers buy buildings for partial use with the idea of leasing the rest to other tenants in order to get depreciation and free rent for their own offices out of their cash flow. It rarely works that way because professionals (especially doctors), are "pigeons" for sharp contractors, and because of their lack of time and expertise, the high vacancy factor usually causes their small projects to have negative cash flows. The pediatrician who took care of my children didn't follow my advice 20 years ago and got into a 12,000-square-foot medical building when he only needed 1,000 square feet for his own offices, and eventually lost $100,000 in the venture.

Recycling into stores is even more hazardous than rehabilitating into offices. The remodeling for them is less costly than for office space or apartments, but obtaining financing for shops is very difficult and for good reasons. It takes a great deal of know-how to find, evaluate, and negotiate with merchants. They're usually tied up on long leases, so that even if they like your space, their leases may expire two or three years out of your time frame. Also, there's great uncertainty in knowing how tenants will do in a new location. The percentage of failures is extremely high. I've read in several publications that among restaurants, eight out of ten fail after two years.

My advice is that, unless you have some unusual circumstances that favor one of the three categories, your recycling choice should be apartments, offices, and stores, in that order.

Problem 14:

When should you keep your annuity as a result of your recycling efforts, and when should you sell it?

Solution:

As a general rule, you should build an investment portfolio while you're young, and sell it as you're growing older, beginning at 60. Aside from that general rule, you should keep the projects you enjoy managing, and sell those that give you trouble. Also, you may have to sell one that you enjoy owning for the greater joy of creating when you need money to express your creativity. I've had to do it several times.

I've owned some properties for as long as 20 years. Management can be fun when you develop a host-guest relationship. That's management at its finest. If you're the type that likes to take care of people's needs, then you should own your project for as long as possible. But when management degenerates into harsh commercialism, when it becomes a battleground between you and renters, management is not for you. Then recycle, sell, and move on to another project.

While I enjoy ownership management and the profits that flow from it, I find greater fulfillment in creating projects, especially ones that have never been tried before.

In making the important decision whether to keep or sell a recycled project, keep my suggestions in mind. However, in the final analysis, the decision has to be a subjective one, depending on the many variables of your personality.

THE AGONIES AND ECSTASIES OF RECYCLING OLD BUILDINGS TO NEW USES

The Agonies

Yes, there are agonies—battling antagonists on many fronts, appeasing the unreasonable code enforcers, smothering in regulations, and coping with shrewd contractors, ice-water-veined financiers, and capricious tenants—all these and more can make recycling a miserable business. Things can go wrong on a dozen fronts: strikes that delay construction while interest costs pile up, vandalism during remodeling, hidden defects in spite of your closest scrutiny, unexpected cost overruns, feeble tenant response to your leasing promotions.

Situations can arise in which your life savings are on the line, your silent partner's money is hanging in the balance, or your business reputation is swinging by a thread that can snap if things turn against you. Worry wakes you at night and doubt doubles you up by day. Risk demands a price and as courage diminishes, the price rises.

The artist only risks his time. You risk your time and money. The artist only involves himself, you involve yourself and others. If the artist fails, there's only a small ripple: his. If you fail, the ripples spread from you, to the lender, to your partners and throughout an entire neighborhood.

A failure closes many doors on your future. Even if the fault is not yours, the blame will be yours. Those who believed in you will become skeptical; those who were neutral will become negative; and those who were negative will crow "I knew it."

While creating aesthetic shelter out of a dilapidated structure is not nearly as difficult as chiseling a beautiful statue out of a slab of marble as Michelangelo did, we're not geniuses like he was, and it's not surprising to be intimidated by musty, cavernous buildings. It's easy to rationalize ourselves into fright when taking on the responsibility of converting junk to beauty and solving the crucial financial problem of taking in more money than goes out.

No wonder, while many old buildings are worth saving, only a few realistic dreamers are brave enough to save them.

The Ecstasies

If you had a choice between earning $10 million playing the stock market, or working hard to earn $1 million recycling old buildings, which should you choose? If you selected the easy way and larger amount, I'd say your consciousness has not been raised enough to experience the ecstasy of creation. If gambling, getting something for nothing, if manipulating yourself into a big inheritance, or making money in some easy manner is your main object, then the joy of creation and the glow of contribution will not be yours. You'll be settling for material things instead of things of the spirit, consuming instead of creating. You'd be sentencing yourself to inferior living, even though you may be wallowing in unearned money.

The end of successful recycling can be like the opening of a beautiful rose, but before you pluck it, watch out for the sharp thorns. Or, to change the metaphor, if you're exhilarated by the exertion of climbing a high mountain, be ready for slides and falls. It's part of the challenge.

Rehabilitating buildings is a new art form and you should throw yourself into its work with the spirit of the artist and the enthusiasm of the businessman. Blending the old and new with an eye on the bottom line requires a balancing act that links prudence with art into an aesthetic composition.

Businessmen vibrate on a different frequency than artists, but when the two blend, they produce a new harmony that neither could compose alone. The business nature is ennobled by the artistic, and the artistic is disciplined by the business. It's a wedding of creation and function.

Renewing our land, forests, waters, and air has become a veritable revolution of survival. And because we're entering an era of scarcity, recycling used material has become part of that revolutionary spirit. Renewing buildings fits into this new thinking more crucially than building new ones.

Environmentalists will applaud you, job seekers will be grateful, community leaders will praise you, and tenants will sing your accomplishments when you provide functional shelter at moderate prices.

Now that you're armed with new insights, why not march boldly with the army of revolutionists, recycling your way to a bright, new, creative, and profitable future.

Index

A

Accelerated depreciation, 83, 171
Accessibility, 23
Advantages, economic, 18
Advertising, 28, 68-72
Analysis, objective, 157-160
Analyzing, 99
Angel, 89-90
Annuity, 94-97, 103-104, 224-225
Antiques, 18
Apartment hotel, 193-202
Apartments:
  commissary, 24
  downtown area, 139-140
  8 into 16 units, 163-164
  elderly, 124-125, 140, 195-198
  40- unit into 18-family, 101-103
  gross rent, 79
  loft, 30, 118
  luxury, 117
  old rooming house, 162-163
  $150,000-a-year annuity, 94-97
  parking, 24
  shop-apartments, 52-78 (*see also* Shop-Apartments)
  size, 79
Appraiser, 20
Appraising, 162
Architect, 20, 58
Architecture, 29
Army base, 130-131
Austerity, 18, 19
Auto garage, 25-26

B

Balustrades, 29
Banker, mortgage, 20
Bank letters of credit, 64
Bargain, 18, 210-212, 222
Barter plan, 86-87
Beams, 30, 59, 61
Boutiques, 55 (*see also* Shop-apartments)
Bresler Building, 181-184
Brick configurations, 29
Brochure, 65-66
Broker, 20, 21
Bronze trim, 29
Buildings:
  agonies of recycling, 225-226
  bargain, 222
  city planning, 34-35
  codes, 30, 219
  column spacing, 32
  concrete, 30, 36
  cosmetic vs. total rehabilitation, 35-36
  costs of recycling, 36-39
  cracks, 31-32
  craftsmanship, 29-30
  ecstasies of recycling, 226-227
  electric power, 33
  elevator shafts, 33
  exits, 32
  expeditor, 39
  exterior, 29
  financing, 38
  fire damage, 35
  fireproofing of floors, 30

Buildings *(cont'd.)*
- floor configuration, 32
- floor load, 30
- footings, 31
- good, in poor neighborhood, 209-210
- hidden defects, 219-221
- interior, 29-30
- investment tax credit, 39
- legal permissions, 38
- location, 34
- mill, 30, 35-36
- older, 29
- option, 222
- parking, 35
- poor, in excellent location, 210-212, 212-213
- pro forma statement, 37-38
- rectangular, 32
- recycling choice, 223
- roof, 33
- selling or managing, 39-40
- size, 79
- soil, 31
- sprinklers, 34
- square, 32
- water lateral, 33
- water level, 31
- windows, 32-33
- wood-constructed, 30
- wood piling, 31
- zoning, 36

Bureaucrats, 74-76, 221
Businesses, matching, 23
Bus line, 34
Buying, 21, 42-43

C

Cancellation offer, 173
Canneries of Monterey, 122-123
Cannery, San Francisco, 111
Capitalism, 128
Carriage house, 132-133
Case studies, outstanding, 109-127 (*see also* Unusual projects)
Cash flow, 56
Ceilings, high, 30
Chalet At The River, 52-78, 207-208 (*see also* Shop-apartments)
Chart House Restaurant, 127
City:
- apartment project, 139-140
- hotel, 141, 142
- matching rehabilitation, 139-160
- office space, 141, 142
- stores, 140-141
- tourist town, 142-148 (*see also* Tourist town)
- type people, 139-142, 152-157 (*see also* Tenants)

City planning, 34-35
City revenue bonds, 90-91, 221-222
Civic affairs, 168
Coca Cola, Office, 127
Collateral, 64
Column spacing, 32
Commercial rehabilitation, 76
Communal living, elderly, 195-198, 200, 201-202
Community, 168
Community cultural center, 130-131
Community Development Block Grants, 136
Comparative market value, 162
Concrete building:
- bargain price, 36
- codes, 30
- durability, 30
- fire protection, 30
- good location, 36
- longevity, 30
- preferred, 30
- total rehabilitation, 36
- unique, nostaligic touches, 36

Conditional sale contract, 83-84
Condominiums:
- advantages, 85
- advertising, 84
- apartments, larger, 84
- architectural plans, 84
- attorney, 85
- attorney's fees, 85
- Chicago, 117-119
- contribution to society, 85
- conversion, 201
- don't have to disturb tenants, 85
- enlightened capitalism, 85
- feature newspaper articles, 84
- interim two-year financing, 84
- land contract, 84
- legal problems, 39
- lender of mortgages, 85
- lower cost, 85
- planning and selling, 85
- potential profit, 85
- prevailing interest rates, 85

Condominiums *(cont'd.)*
price, 84
private mortgage insurance, 85
selling costs, 85
sophisticated financing, 84
varied in size, 84
Conservation, 19
Contract furnishings, 22
Contractors, 214-215
Conversion, 23
Copper domes, 29
Corporations, 129
Cosmetic remodeling, 28, 35-36, 97-98, 165
Cost of reproduction less depreciation, 162
Cost overruns, 214
Costs, 36-39, 58, 79
Cracks, 31-32
Craftsmanship, 29
Creativity, 52-78 (*see also* Shop-apartments)
Crown Life Insurance Company, 26
Cultural center, 130-131
Custom House Block, 127
Cutler-Hammer, Inc., 174-175

D

Damage, fire, 35
Dancer-Fitzgerald-Sample, 126
Debt service, 56
Defects, 64, 219-221
DelMonte Food Cannery, 111
Depreciation, accelerated, 83, 171
Direct mail advertising, 68, 200
Domes, copper, 29

E

Economic advantages, 18
Economics, 18
Education, 137
Efficiencies, 198, 200
El Convento, 108
Elderly, apartments, 124-125, 140, 195-198, 200, 201-202
Electrician, 94-97
Electric power, 33
Elevator shafts, 33
Emotion, 204
Energy, 18, 38, 49
Entrepreneurs, 137
Equity:
half to lender, 88-89
offer seller equity position, 82
participation, 89
seller's subordination, 80-82
syndicate need for capital, 87-88
Exculpatory clause, 216
Exits, 33
Expediter, 39
Exterior, craftsmanship, 29

F

Factory outlets, 22, 23, 223
Facts, 157
Fanueil Hall, 126
Feather Factory, 127
Federal funds, 136
Fees:
janitorial, 38
management, 38
Ferendiono-Grafton-Pancoast, 126
Figurines, sculptured, 29
Financial incentives, 136
Financial overview, 37-39
Financing:
"angel," 89-90
apartments, 79
barter plan, 86-87
buy on land contract, 83-84
convert to condominiums, 84-85
cost of rehabilitation, 79
guideline and model, 79-80
half your equity to lender, 88-89
hidden costs, 214
H.U.D., 38, 91-93
millionaires, 90
offer seller equity position, 82
offices, 79
people earning over $100,000, 90
revenue bond, 90-91
Rotarians, 90
size of building, 79
stores, 79, 80
subordinate seller's equity, 80-82
syndicate, 87-88
Fire damage, 35
Fireplaces, 29
Fireproofing, floors, 30
Floor load, 30
Floors:
configuration, 32

Floors *(cont'd.)*
  fireproofing, 30
  Florentine tile, 29
  hardwood, 30
Foundations, 129
Freeway, 23, 34
Fulton House, 117
Funds:
  Federal, 136
  soliciting, 129
Funeral home, 103-104
Furnishings, contract, 22

G

Garage, 127
Garage, space above, 161-162
Gay Nineties, 17
General Merchandise, 168
General Revenue Sharing, 136
General Services Administration, 134
Ghirardelli Square, 109-110
Gigantism, 19
Gleason Corporation, 173-175
Government:
  benefits from recycling, 133
  bureaucrats not imaginative, 135
  can help recycler-developer, 135-136
  can save by recycling, 133-134
  city-controlled Federal funds, 136
  economy, 133
  era of austerity, 133
  example of waste, 134
  involvement in recycling, 135
  large segment of office market, 133
  legislative mechanism, 133
  long-term leases, 136
  middleman, 135
  mortgage insurance programs, 136
  New York City's J-51 Program, 136
  preserving architecture, 133
  public improvements, 135-136
  reduce or share risk, 136
  smothering regulations, 221-222
  tax increment financing, 136
Grand Central Hotel, 113
Greenebaum Tannery, 184-187
Greenwich Village, 122

H

Hardware, 30
Hilton International, 108
Historical buildings, 22
Holiday Inn, 108
Home Away From Home, 198-202
Horizontal revitalization, 49-51
Hotel rehabilitations:
  America and Europe, 108
  debt service, 108
  El Convento, 108
  Hilton International, 108
  Holiday Inn, 108
  Howard Johnson, 108
  Hyatt Regency, 108
  independent operators, 108
  large hotel chains, 108
  "new" hotels, 108
  Pfister, 105-106, 107, 108
  Schroeder, 106-108
  Sonesta Hotel, 108
  Stanford Court Hotel, 108
Howard Johnson, 108
H.U.D., 57-58, 60-64, 91-93, 222
Hunch, 157-160
Hyatt Regency Hotel, 107-108

I

Ice House, 127
Incentives, financial, 136
Income approach, 162
Income tax shelter, 217-219
Indecision, 99
Individuality, 161
Innovation, 161
Interest-during-construction fees, 58
Interest rate, reduce, 76-78, 171
Interior, craftsmanship, 29-30
Intuition, 157, 158
Investment:
  buying, 42-43
  leasing, 45
  recycling, 45-47
  selling, 43-45, 47-49
Investment tax credit, 39, 83, 101, 171
Investor, inactive silent, 89

J

Janitorial fees, 38
John Hancock Insurance Company, 25
Journal Square, 177
Judgment, 157

K

Knickerbocker, 193-202

L

Land contract, 83-84
Landmark designations, 221
Larimer Square, 127
Latent defects, 64
Leases, 22, 136
Leasing, 45, 64-67, 166-170
Legal permissions, 38
Lenders, 20, 38, 88-89
Liability, 172
Light fixtures, 30
Limited partnership liability, 172
Loan officer, 25
Local people, 43
Location, 22, 23, 34, 181, 209-213
Loft building, 23, 30
Loft look, 70
Long-term leases, 136

M

Mail advertising, 28, 68, 200
Mall, 25-26, 115-116, 223
Mama-papa motels, 22, 23
Management, creative, 73-74
Management fees, 38
Manager, 20
Managing, 39-40
Manpower International Inc., 114-115
Mansion, 23
Manufacturing space, 172-175
Manufacturing tenants, 27, 28
Marc Plaza, 107-108
Material shortages, 49
Maynard Building, 113
Media, 196, 197
Medical center, 24-25
Medical office building, 188-193
Merchandise mart, 23
Merchandising, 176, 181-184
Mill building:
  code, 30
  cosmetic recycling, 210
  cosmetic vs. total rehabilitation, 35-36
  fire damage, 35
Millionaires, 90
Mitchell-Mackie loss, 171-172
Montessori School, 128-130
Mortgage signing, 216-217
Mortgage banker, 20
Mortgage insurance programs, 136
Motels, 22, 23
Movie theater, 95-97

N

National Register of Historic Places, 118
Neighborhood:
  demographic study, 214
  excellent, 210-213
  poor, 209-210
Newark Community Center of Arts, 132-133
Newspaper ads, 28, 68, 69-72
New York City's J-51 Program, 136
1981 Tax Bill, 76-78, 101
99-year lease, 166
Nostalgia, 18, 19
Nursing homes, 22

O

Objective study analysis, 157
Obstacles, 18
Occidental Park, 113
Offices:
  gross rent, 78
  net rentable space, 79
  renting requires expertise, 224
  warehouse rehabilitation, 27-28, 114-115, 188-193
Old City Hall, 126, 136
Old Town, 127
Option, 222
Oriental motif, 96
Outlets, factory, 22, 23, 223
Owner, 20-23, 178, 180

P

Parking, 23, 35
Partitions, absence, 59, 61
Past, turning to, 18
Pereless Building, 164, 165, 166
Performing Arts Center, 131-132
Permissions, 38
Personal liability, 172
Pfister, 105-106, 107, 108

Piling, 31
Pioneer Square, 112-114, 135
Plaster, ornamental, 29
Points to lender, 58
Power, electric, 33
Prices, 22
Printing House Row, 118
Private revenue bonds, 91
Pro forma statement, 25, 37-38
Projects:
  early ones revisited, 161-187
  building saved, 175-178
  8 apartments into 16, 163-164
  foul air, 184-187
  kind of owner, 178, 180
  manufacturing space, 172-175
  merchandising, 181-184
  Mitchell-Mackie loss, 171-172
  office building, 164-166
  rooming house, 162-163
  space above garage, 161-162
  storage building, 166-171
  techniques of yesterday, 161-187
  unusual (*see* Unusual projects)
Prospects, finding, 168
Public improvements, 135

Q

Quaker Square, 125-126
Questions and answers, 209-227

R

Radio advertising, 68
Real estate, 52
Real estate taxes, 58
Recession, 170
Rectangular building, 32
Recycling Buildings, 127
Recycling projects, unusual, 109-127 (*see also* Unusual projects)
Red Cross, 128
Regulations, government, 221-222
Rehabilitation center, 103-104
Rehabilitations, unusual, 109-127 (*see also* Unusual projects)
Rent, 25, 38
Rental market, 56
Renting building out, 22
Rent performance formula, 170
Repairs, 38
Repetition, 161
Reputation, 88-89
Resale, 22, 136
Residential building, 224
Restoration, 37
Restored look, 59
Retired couple, 23
Reuse, 136
Revenue bond financing, 90-91, 221-222
Revolving loan funds, 136
Rezoning, 36
Risk-taking, 167, 185, 225
Roof, 33
Rooming house, 105, 162-163
Rotarians, 90
Roth, William M., 109
Rouse Company, 126

S

Sales expert, 67-69
Salvation Army, 128
Sandblasting, 60, 176
Saturday Review Industries, 127
Savings and loan association, 129
Scholarship, 137
Schroeder, 106-108
Schumacher, E.F., 19
Sears, Roebuck and Company, 117
Security system, 74
Seller:
  equity position for building, 82
  land contract, 83-84
  subordination of equity, 80-82
Selling, 39-40, 43-45, 47-49, 97-98
7½ percent plant, 91-93
Shelter:
  functional, 20
  income tax, 217
Shop-apartments:
  accountants, 73
  "amateur" sales expert, 67-69
  amount of debt service, 56
  apartments not partitioned, 59, 61
  approvals, 60
  architect, 58-60
  artists, 65, 66, 72
  atrium configuration, 61
  attorneys, 73
  bank letters of credit, 64
  beams, 59, 61

Shop-apartments *(cont'd.)*
- beauty shop owners, 73
- brochure, 65-66
- bureaucrats, 74-76
- burglar and fire alarm system, 74
- cash flow, 56
- classified ads, 68
- collateral, 64
- completion of rehabilitation, 64
- compromise, 73
- cost of remodelling, 56, 58-60
- cutting costs, 58-60
- direct mail advertising, 68
- electrical piping, 60
- embellished the old, 59
- equities, 64
- expediting, 58
- fire-protection plan, 63
- footings, 60-61
- free valet parking, 74
- guard, 74
- handicrafters, 65, 66
- health spa/clinic, 72
- heat, 58
- highest and best use, 54-55
- hobbyists, 65
- H.U.D. financing, 57-58, 60-64
- insure against operating losses, 64
- interest-during construction fees, 58
- interior decorators, 73
- latent defects, 64
- leasing, 64-67
- location, 53
- loft look, 70
- lower level and first floor, 56
- management, 73-74
- massage and cosmetology, 72
- negative aspects of building, 53
- newspaper features, 69-72
- nostalgia, 55
- 1981 Tax Bill, 76-78
- one-year retrospect, 207-208
- operating expenses, 56
- plumbing, 60
- points to lender, 58
- positive aspects of building, 53
- potential gross rent, 56
- preliminary analysis, 56-57
- preliminary closing, 60
- processing application, 60
- promotion, 58
- quilts and aprons, 72
- radio ads, 68

Shop-apartments *(cont'd.)*
- row concrete columns, 59
- real estate taxes, 58
- rental market, 56
- rentals reasonable, 56
- residential floors, 73
- restaurants, unusual shops, 56
- restored look, 59
- retired people, 65, 66
- sandblasting, 60
- security system, 74
- services offered, 73
- shop owners, 73
- smoke detectors, 74
- "soft" costs, 58
- sprinklers, 74
- television stations, 72
- tenant mix, 72-73
- treasury bills, 64
- twelve-foot-high ceilings, 59, 61
- two-models, 67
- untried market, 64
- unusual people, 65
- vitamin shop, 72
- window space, 62-63
- working capital, 64
- wrong type of town, 223

Shopping center, 26, 125-126, 223
Showrooms, 22, 23
Signature, mortgage, 216-217
Small Is Beautiful, 19
Small-town:
- antique shops, 149
- art galleries, 149
- clean, aesthetic, pleasant, 149
- community-mindedness, 149
- condominium projects, 149
- factory outlets, 149-150
- fully retired individuals, 149
- future growth, 148
- government, 149
- industrial workers, 149
- labor force, 148
- leaders, 148
- main highway, 149
- mama-papa motel, 149, 151
- mini-malls, 149
- motels, 149
- nursing home, 149
- profitable recycling, 149
- real estate values, 149
- recreational centers, 148
- resistance, 150-151

Small-town *(cont'd.)*
restaurants, 149
semi-retired people, 149
stagnant or growing, 148
trend, 148
vacation homes, 149
well-to-do people, 149
white-collar workers, 149
Smith, Hinchman and Grylls, 127
"Soft" costs, 58
SoHo, 121-122
Soil, testing, 31
Solicitation, 200
Soliciting funds, 129
Sonesta Hotel, 108
Space modules, 32
Specialization, 98
Spensor's Corner, 120-121
Sprinklers, 34
Square building, 32
Stained glass, 29
Stanford Court Hotel, 108
State revenue bonds, 90-91, 221-222
Steinmeyer Building, 175-178
Storage building, 166-171
Storage tenants, 27
Stores:
gross rent, 80
hazardous recycling, 224
net rentable area, 79
refitting, 140-141
without walls, 119-120
Subordination, seller's equity, 80-82
Switzerland, 19
Syndication, 87-88, 101

T

Tandem 221-D4 H.U.D. insured mortgage plan, 91-93
Tannery, 184-187
Tax assessor, 38
Tax Bill, 76-78, 101, 171
Tax increment financing, 136
Tax shelter, 217-219
Technology, 19
Television stations, 72
Tenants:
art and picture framing, 153
attitudes, 142
Bratburger Restaurant, 155-156
card store, 152-153
Tenants *(cont'd.)*
couples or singles, 140
downtown workers, 140
elderly wealthy suburbanites, 140
fish restaurant, 155-156
good merchants, 140
low-paying, 176
making custom jewelry, 153
marginal inexperienced dreamers, 152-154
mix, 72-73
office space, 28, 141-142
size up, 152-157
storage, 27
stores, 140-141
"therapy," 154-155
tobacco shop, 156-157
twin movie theater, 152
type in your town, 139-142
unreasonable, 155-157
wealthy bargain hunters, 152
white-collar office workers, 140
Terra cotta, 29
Theater, movie, 95-97, 116-117
Thompson, Elisabeth Kendall, 127
Throw-away syndrome, 19
Tile, floor, 29
Title, 83
Tourist town:
apartments or offices, 143
botanical garden, 143
Carmel, California, 144
Chinese restaurant, 144
dazzling decoration, 143
derelict look, 145
galleria of shops, 147
high prices, 147
high rent, 147
imagination, 143
international mart, 143
Lausanne, Switzerland, 144-145
merchants, 142, 143
Montego Bay, 146
more flamboyance, 142
Palm Springs, California, 144
Quebec, 145
real estate value, 144
Rodeo Road, 145-146
shops, 143
store space is king, 144
St. Thomas, 143-144
unique items, 143
unusual merchandise, 147

Tourist town *(cont'd.)*
- upper-floor shops, 144
- Venice, 144
- Victoria Island, 143

Town, recycle in own, 202-204 (*see also* Small-towns; Tourist towns)
Transportation Building, 118
Treasury bills, 64
Trim:
- bronze, 29
- window, 29

Trolley Square, 123-124

U

Uncertainty, 98
Underpinning slippage, 32
United Way, 128
Unusual projects:
- apartments for elderly, 124-125
- bookbindery, 118
- canneries of Monterey, 122-123
- Cannery, 111
- Chart House Restaurant, 127
- Custom House Block, 127
- Dancer-Fitzgerald-Sample, 126
- Fanueil Hall, 126
- Feather Factory, 127
- Ferendiono-Grafton-Pancoast, 126
- former college, 118
- furniture showroom, 118
- garage, 127
- Ghiradelli Square, 109-110
- Grand Central on Park, 113
- Ice House, 127
- Larimer Square, 127
- mail-order warehouse, 117
- mall, 115-116
- Manpower International Inc., 114-115
- Maynard Building, 113
- Occidental Park, 113
- Office of Coca Cola, 127
- Old City Hall, 126
- Old Town, 127

Unusual projects *(cont'd.)*
- Pioneer Square, 112-114
- Printing House Row, 118
- Quaker Square, 125-126
- refrigerated warehouse, 117
- rubber refinery, 118
- Saturday Review Industries, 127
- Smith, Hinchman and Grylls, 127
- SoHo, 121-122
- Spensor's Corner, 120-121
- splitting old theater, 116-117
- stores without walls, 119-120
- Transportation Building, 118
- Trolley Square, 123-124

Urban Renewal agency, 136
Use of building, 22-24, 54-55, 168, 213-214

V

Vacant buildings, 27
Value of property, 162
Vaudeville house, 131-132
Vertical revitalization, 49-51
Victorian Park, 110, 111
Voluntary work, 128

W

Warehousing, 22, 24-25, 28, 114-115, 172-175, 188-193
Warranty deed, 83
Waterfront Renewal Project, 136
Water lateral, 33
Welch Building, 178-181
Windows, 32-33
Window trim, 29
Winter, Elmer, 114-115
Wood-constructed buildings, 30

Z

Zoning, 36